You Are Here. . .

You are in attendance at a Corona Class conducted by Saint Francis in the Inner Retreat of Jesus the Christ.

This brother, affectionately called "Kuthumi," addresses a large body gathered from every nation who have come to sit at the feet of the Lord, to hear *him* preach *his* Divine Doctrine—uncomplicated by centuries of misinterpretation.

Seekers, teachers, ministers, rabbis, priests of holy orders East and West, lovers of souls, brethren of Buddhist monasteries, worshipers of Kali—all are attending his Word. The great and the humble come to hear of the true ecumenism born out of the Spirit of Unity, all-pervasive, of the Sun of Righteousness.

Lo, He comes with healing in his wings—healing for the schism in the whole Body of God on earth!

Yes here, at last—raised to that higher consciousness where the Law of Love is the standard-bearer—all understand the point of Origin: consummate self-knowledge in the heart of the little child . . .

"All who would follow in my footsteps must understand that unless they are able to contact the great Source of life and continually renew their strength, their mission will not be carried forth in the manner desired by God."

Jesus

Kuthumi speaks:

"My Friends Who Have Espoused the Spiritual Life...

"Eventually, all who ponder the truths of the visible and invisible cosmos come to a conscious desire to study the works of God's hands in greater detail.

"Now, some are quite naturally drawn to the study of Light and Truth from early childhood, and many of you in this class are among these. Some of you began along orthodox lines and perceived at one point, as we all have, the futility of being bound by roots of schism, a closed doctrine, or an uninspired ecclesiastical hierarchy.

"Your hearts became convinced of the oneness of all Life and you began to seek the unity behind the diversity of religious thought. Your search for Truth took you far afield from your point of origin and you began the journey toward a greater understanding of God's laws. Some of you were buffeted about and, finding no solace or peace in the pursuit of material goals, turned toward the spiritual life as toward one last hope.

"Whatever your beginnings or the bumpy road between then and now, it really matters not. The important fact is that you are here..."

The Lost Teachings of Jesus are being shouted from the housetops!

Let the disciples of the Lord who have sat at his feet join him and his beloved Francis to deliver to his own these precious dictations that enable the soul to make contact with the great truths of her immortal being in God.

Let their 48 Corona Class Lessons lead you step by step up the mount of transfiguration as you learn with Peter, James and John the mystery of the Lord's transfiguration—and your own.

Then take up the Lord's mantle whereby he empowers you to preach his Lost Teachings to the world.

Yes, the teachings are meant to be taught, God-taught, by each one who has drunk from the cup of the Saviour. Hearts reach out to you who know the true meaning of his life and mission. They call to you to teach them the way of personal Christhood—the path of Love that freely gives to all the living Bread which is come down to us from heaven today.

The supreme joy of reading Jesus' own words (*after* one has studied at his Inner Retreat), of finding his Teachings dictated to the Messengers Mark and Elizabeth Prophet—and of entering the heart of Saint Francis—is beyond many a soul's hope for comfort and enlightenment in this life.

Yet here it is—the most profound, the most essential knowledge about yourself, so needed by seekers for Christ's healing Truth, made simple and practical for everyone—even a child can understand it!

Let Jesus and Kuthumi open your understanding of the Divine Doctrine and show you how to face and conquer life with the Spirit of Christ's victory, even as you show others how to prepare for the Lord's coming—bodily into their temple—with the Holy Spirit and his saints.

Corona Class Lessons—
written especially for you

who will not rest until you shout the Everlasting Gospel from the housetops and teach men the Way, all the way home to God—with Jesus "my Saviour."

"Psst...Come, we must not be late," your angel escort whispers. "Saint Francis is speaking of his conversion to Christ through Mother Poverty and the Nature kingdom and of how the Love of God which burned in his heart was the key to his oneness with all life.

"Come, let us fly to the House of the Lord beyond the mountains of the Holy Land where many are gathered to hear the Corona Class Lessons taught by Jesus and Kuthumi.

It's a spiritual retreat...

for those who would teach men the Way."

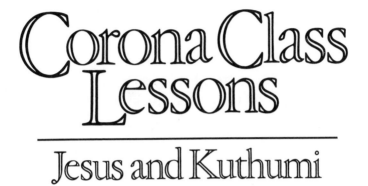

Corona Class Lessons

Jesus and Kuthumi

...for those who would teach men the Way

Dictated
to the Messengers
Mark and Elizabeth Prophet

SUMMIT UNIVERSITY ✺ PRESS®

To the true shepherds
who will feed my sheep

JESUS

Corona Class Lessons
. . .for those who would teach men the Way

Copyright © 1986 Summit University Press
All rights reserved.

Library of Congress Catalog Card Number: 83-51445
International Standard Book Number: 0-916766-65-9

This book is set in 11 point Bookman Light with 2.5 points lead.
Printed in the United States of America
First Printing: December 1986

For information on the magnificent art of Nicholas Roerich,
write Nicholas Roerich Museum, 319 W. 107th St., NY 10025.

Cover: *Saint Francis of Assisi,* by Nicholas Roerich

SUMMIT UNIVERSITY 🌙 PRESS®

Corona Class Lessons

Contents

viii   *Contents*

At the same time came the disciples unto Jesus, saying, Who is the greatest in the kingdom of heaven?

And Jesus called a little child unto him, and set him in the midst of them,

And said, Verily I say unto you, Except ye be converted, and become as little children, ye shall not enter into the kingdom of heaven.

Whosoever therefore shall humble himself as this little child, the same is greatest in the kingdom of heaven.

And whoso shall receive one such little child in my name receiveth me.

But whoso shall offend one of these little ones which believe in me, it were better for him that a millstone were hanged about his neck, and that he were drowned in the depth of the sea.

Woe unto the world because of offences! for it must needs be that offences come; but woe to that man by whom the offence cometh! . . .

Take heed that ye despise not one of these little ones; for I say unto you, That in heaven their angels do always behold the face of my Father which is in heaven . . .

Even so it is not the will of your Father which is in heaven, that one of these little ones should perish.

Matthew

Correspondence

cor·re·spon·dence \ ¦kȯrə¦spändən(t)s,
¦kär- \ *n* -s [ME, fr. MF or ML; MF
correspondence, correspondance, fr.
ML *correspondentia,* fr. *correspondent-,
correspondens* + L *-ia*] **1 a :** the
state or condition of agreement of things
or of one thing with another **:** relation of con-
gruity **:** resemblance or similarity
of detail ⟨Joyce elaborates a point-to-point
~ between the spiritual movements
of a little Dublin city-dweller and the mythical
wanderings of Ulysses —Francis
Fergusson⟩ **b :** an instance or point
of agreement, similarity, or analogy ⟨many
~s between the two plays⟩ **c** *math*
: definite association of certain members
of one aggregate with each member
of a second and of certain members of the
second with each member of the
first **2 a** *archaic* **:** relations between
persons or groups **:** social or business relations
or communication **b :** the communication
between persons by an exchange of letters ⟨a long
~ between the two friends⟩; *also*
: any communication by letter ⟨application
should be made by ~ or in person
at our offices⟩ **c :** the letters exchanged
by correspondents ⟨publication of
the Holmes-Laski ~⟩ **d :** the news, information,
or opinion contributed by a correspondent
to a newspaper or periodical
e : study or instruction carried on
by written communication between student
and a correspondence school

Corona Class Lesson 1

Brotherhood

"Feed My Sheep!"

To My Friends
   Who Have Espoused the Spiritual Life—
   There is so much in life you seem to just take for granted; and you are not alone in this, for in a sense all mankind, to a greater or lesser degree, may be found in this state of unawareness, few being altogether free from it.

   With almost childlike simplicity, those who in other respects are wise about many things seem to accept much of God's visible creation without considering the magnificent design behind the physical form/appearance. Eventually, all who ponder the truths of the visible and invisible cosmos come to a conscious desire to study the works of God's hands in greater detail.

   Now, some are quite naturally drawn to the study of Light and Truth from early childhood, and many of you in this class are among these. Some of you began along orthodox lines and perceived at one point, as we all have, the futility of being bound by roots of schism, a closed doctrine, or an uninspired ecclesiastical hierarchy.

Your hearts became convinced of the oneness of all Life and you began to seek the unity behind the diversity of religious thought. Your search for Truth took you far afield from your point of origin and you began the journey toward a greater understanding of God's laws. Some of you were buffeted about and, finding no solace or peace in the pursuit of material goals, turned toward the spiritual life as toward one last hope.

Whatever your beginnings or the bumpy road between then and now, it really matters not. The important fact is that you are here in harmony with the ascended ones. With blessed Saint Germain, you can declare, "I am here!" This is of paramount importance. For in so doing, you acknowledge the unity of the I AM Presence. And your desire to serve in expanding the Light and in spreading the message of the Father's kingdom among all people is made plain.

Now let me assure you that the Father's arms are open to all, to receive every seeker and to assist each aspiring one in the process of raising himself into the arms of his own God Presence—the only divine reality and haven of safety above the storms and trials of mundane life.

To the present day, the help extended by the Ascended Masters to the people of earth continues to be of immeasurable value; yet it is not apparent to most men. Because we are graduates of life's schoolroom, well acquainted with its problems and their solution, and because the needs of earth are so very great, God uses many of us, your ascended brothers and sisters, as his hands and feet—his very heart extended as wisdom personified. Through our ascension we have attained a blessed oneness with Him. This we long to bestow upon each one of you as your own God Presence directs.

Remember: God, the Mighty I AM Presence, does know the day and the hour of your ascension in the Light. This knowledge the Presence retains in its own safekeeping. You may be closer to your victory than you think, for the sign is not always outwardly given or made known to others.

Beloved Jesus and I as World Teachers have undertaken this Corona Class by correspondence with an end in view—the multiplying of our own hands and feet. Is this not true correspondence in many ways?

You see, through faith you become our hands, our feet, our presence on earth. You *correspond* to us by outpicturing our consciousness before mankind. Do you see? Your own hearts become chalices into which we pour the fragrances of our spiritual graces, thereby enriching everyone with receptive mind and spirit so fortunate as to come in contact with you. Thus, seeing you, these can begin to believe that God dwells in human form. Oh, I do hope you see this! For it is the secret of the love that has always existed between Master and disciple. The accomplished goal of the Corona Class will therefore reveal *what (and whose)* divine radiance encompasses the faithful.

So many of earth's children, intrigued as they are by their study of God's laws, assume that by a magical or semi-magical process they will automatically be transformed into ascended beings or walking adepts. On this moot point many hirelings have gone forth to make a living by dispensing the gospel of a mere human brand of freedom — often not feeding the sheep of Christ the necessary spiritual food. [1] However, in all fairness, let it be said that through sincerity and honor in the hearts of the students, much good has been accomplished despite the hypocrisy of these hired shepherds. And certainly you would agree that some service is often better than none at all.

Of course, each one is judged according to his own works; [2] and if he does well, good shall come. [3] The Law cannot be broken. Nevertheless, let it be made plain that we prefer the anointed teachers whose dedication has brought them to the feet of their own Holy Christ Self with hearts full of love and devotion and the humility to dispense our teaching with Ascended Master purposes held in mind.

Not for all the world would we take from anyone his blessed hope or uproot him unnecessarily, even from a false teacher, unless we could benefit him thereby; neither would we wish that any false hope should lull him into a slumber of false security where much valuable time and energy could be lost pursuing nonexistent goals. Hence, our keen sense of discrimination, which we are willing to transfer to you, should be sought.

We want nothing from you except an unselfed love, which you can give right now if you will. Think about this! We long to see you enjoy the selfsame beautiful freedom which we have.

When I was embodied as Francis of Assisi, I came to realize through studying the birds and animals that my power of concentration, saturated as it was with the love of God and his love in man, would draw me into an understanding of the God-intelligence acting in Nature which earlier I had so studiously ignored. Oftentimes more concerned with pleasure-seeking than religious fervor, I had not formerly been aware of the great love of God and the joy which that love could bring, far exceeding any outer source. Then, too, my prior contemplation of the realm of Nature had led me to think of heaven as a place apart from earth.

Imagine, if you can, the joy in my soul when I found that the lovely trees were endowed with spiritual beings, angelic overseers of great stature and beauty whose power guided the development of molecular form, pattern, luster of leaf, and inherent healing properties. I felt the radiant energy (life-force) reaching out from these silent sentinels capturing the heart—as did one majestic tree deva who inspired Joyce Kilmer to write his heartfelt poem "Trees."[4] I also found to my amazement that the tiny furry creatures of the forest had a life-intelligence all their own, reflective of the Creator; and I saw how the life in them responded to the Life in me.

Oh, heaven was not apart from me! For I perceived all things visible to be but the hem of the garment of heaven. Touching just the physical hem, I was made whole![5] What would happen when I touched the whole robe? I longed to know.

Thus, in order to reach this transcendent goal, which I firmly believed was attainable—for I knew in my heart that God had ordained it— I set my mind to the path of spiritual illumination. Day by day, my mind was made holier still through contact with the spiritual realms. My one-pointed dedication to the Path and my contemplation of the holiness of all Life—and of the holiness of the God who had created all things to his delight, including man—were the keys to my assimilation of that holiness, which clearly seemed to permeate myself and everything around me.

Dear hearts, there is something foreign to reality in the idea of God being separate and apart from his creation. No mere doctrinal pantheism is the affirmation of God as the All-in-all, but a truth that cannot be refuted.

For, while it is true that the creation lies *in* God, it is also true that he is *in* his creation; but it is evident that his love, wisdom, and power cannot be *contained* therein. (". . . Behold, the heaven and heaven of heavens cannot contain thee; how much less this house that I have builded?" said Solomon of old.[6]) Moreover, the fact that the God Presence, the individualized I AM, does far exceed the personal creation of the individual (and the macrocosmic creation as well) is proof of the dominion with which God has so lovingly endowed your Real Self, made in his image and likeness.[7]

As my soul expanded in the transfusing light which God poured into me, I was exalted time and again by his glory expressed through the Nature kingdom. The seemingly dumb creatures of field and forest came into unity with me through God's love, and then at last I, too, could speak their language, calling them "brother." How much more should all children of the Light love one another and have reverence for the smallest part of Life (God)!

Out of all these transcendental experiences, my soul was stirred with a great yearning to communicate to others the boundless wisdom vouchsafed to me by God. At this point in my spiritual awakening, I found that a literal wall of human resistance—denser and higher by far than any medieval castle—had gone up between me and my friends and the townspeople of Assisi. Most men I sought to reach could not understand my life, my aims, or my God-chosen ways—which to me were so self-evident, so plain to see, so logical! I became to them a *poverello* (one who voluntarily embraces Mother Poverty). It was then that I was abruptly cut off from family, friends, and funds.

Fortunately, among my friends were some so sincere and devout as to continue to pray for me. And God (whose ways are not always understood by men[8]) winked at me in answering their prayers *his* way—by taking me deeper into his own heart and embrace even while they assiduously called for my return to the beaten orthodox path! Thus, I did not suffer disillusionment by the loss of my friends, nor did I return to the vanities of the material world. But, drawing ever closer to God to become a divine poverello, I drew around me by kinship of spirit those of like mind and wisdom and from them fashioned my holy order of brothers Franciscan.

I have drawn briefly from my earthly experiences so that you will not be excessively concerned about those who seem disinterested or who may lack humility when you try to expound to them from your pure hearts the knowledge of God's laws. Remember that the Father tried long to reach you to give you all his love, and in due season took you from among the multitudes to draw you closer to his own heart and to his brotherhood of Light.

Spend your energy, then, as we did, in interior correction and self-instruction, paying special attention to our current precepts as manna for your souls—until, like a great organ of expansive timbre and pitch, you stand as the perfect instrument through which the Divine One

may play those exquisite harmonies of healing light and comforting tone, revealing to all,
through a more perfect example, the efficacy of
heaven's grace.

As you lift up the Presence of God "I AM" in
yourself, the Presence will draw all men to its
greater Light.[9] Bear in mind, as beloved Morya
has said, that we are a forthright brotherhood;
and do not become weary in well-doing![10]

Jesus, who wept over Jerusalem,[11] has long
poured his love to the tired, the hungry, the
poor, and the bound—yearning, as I do, but to
refresh, feed, enrich, and free in the dignity of
the Holy Spirit all souls who love Light. (We
would equally free those who, because they do
not know the Light, do not love the Light.)

And unto those men who love darkness
rather than light because their deeds are evil,[12]
we would bring Light and the love of Light and
an example of righteousness—through you,
each and every one who would teach unenlight-
ened men the way.

Such is the ideal of the Great White Brotherhood. Such is the path of just men made perfect
through the living image of Christ.[13]

To this calling the Spirit of the Brotherhood
leads you, that by expanding your light you may
answer the call of Christ to "Feed my sheep!"[14]

The salutation of the ascended Jesus Christ
be with you, together with my own.

Your cosmic teacher,

Kuthumi

Corona Class Lesson 2

You

"Whom Say Ye That I Am?"

Beloved Students Who Would Teach
         the True Communion of Saints—
    The opening letter from blessed Kuthumi,
my brother, has so beautifully described to you
some of the sweetness of his own awakening
to the power of God during his Franciscan embodiment.
    In his instruction, he wisely advocated the
giving of the teachings of Light's perfection to
every sincere seeker but stressed the need for
every teacher to maintain his harmony, even if
some men should choose to reject the teachings
after hearing them.[1] He advised a closer walk
with each one's own I AM Presence (the Father)
and Holy Christ Self (the Son) as the antidote for
every problem. Let us see why this is the best
part of divine wisdom.
    You will perhaps recall that I spoke unto my
disciples, saying, "Whom say *ye* that I am?"[2]

Well, beloved hearts, you could ask the same question of your associates today. And what do you think the answer would be, or what would you have it be?

Would you want them to describe you as just so much energy, so much accumulation of weight, of such an age or color of skin, with certain characteristics, mannerisms, and personal idiosyncrasies? Or would you prefer their description to include all the beauty, the ageless perfection and thrilling ever-new, ever-expanding dimensions of your own I AM Presence and its invincible power of Love's victory?

The choice is clear, as you can plainly see; for Wisdom always chooses the better part wherein the eternal truth of what you are, the eternal hope of what you are to be, and the Father's eternal love of your soul's purest intent are in perfect harmony. This, our immaculate concept held for each one of you, is our everlasting instruction—eternal, changeless, yet full of glories untold, of melodies unsung, of reaches and expanses uncharted, unprobed even by the ascended.

So deep is immortal Love that, lost in its depths, one finds solace supreme. Yet the joy of the eternal mystery remains even when all is made plain, for such is the nature of God's heart—the center of ineffable wisdom, the altar of eternal peace. As recipients of such a love, how can the cup of our zeal refrain from overflowing in the wish to call all Life to share the blessings and unity of our octave—the kingdom of heaven!

What, then, is the best way for a teacher of the kingdom of heaven to reach people—especially where the zeal of that teacher is very great, reaching out arms of love to embrace the whole world?* As I proceed to answer this question, there is one concept I should like first to convey to each of you; for it concerns who and what you really are:

Within every atom and system of worlds there is a central focus of great light. In the solar systems the magnitude of this light is easily perceived; but in a relative sense, when you are dealing with microscopic parts of the whole, it may seem but a spark of imagination to most of you, so small is this central focus. Yet to us it is still a flame from the Great Central Sun, no matter how tiny it may seem to be.

Such is the divine spark within you—the threefold flame of Life burning on the altar of your heart. Though a mere sixteenth of an inch in height, it is the sun center and source of Life to your physical body.

Now, all that is coalesced in form around this center should be instrumental in the fulfillment of your divine plan according to the original seed idea held in the heart of the tiny flame. This plan of your life's perfection is intended to expand through the world of form in concentric rings of living, God-joyous, God-radiant light

---

*My outreach has been so beautifully outpictured in the magnificent statue *Christ the Redeemer*, which provides a wonderful focus in Rio de Janeiro for my love to the people of South America.

and color; for the energies of the threefold flame, born of the eternal radiance,* sustain the entire physical creation!

By contrast, the human misqualification of the power of the divine spark manifests as gross condensations of selfishness, accumulations of discord and earthly qualities that actually solidify around the flame as mental density, feelings of resentment, and physical disease.

The buildup of discord in the body and the subconscious mind can be seen by the clairvoyant as shadowy clouds gathered round the central flame of being, blocking the penetration of the Light, whose healing, vivifying rays would naturally and swiftly disperse the grayness and heaviness of accumulated fear and doubt from the troubled hearts of humanity.

This clearance will take place when human stubbornness—the altogether human reluctance to accept change ("putting off the old man and putting on the new"[3]) and the willful ignoring of the inner voice of the Real Self—ceases to muddy the pure stream of God's energy as it flows forth unceasingly from his Spirit to the souls of his own.

Every one of us (the Ascended Masters) was compelled to leave behind this human consciousness and world view long before our ascension. We have given to the flame of God—to this precious focus of his intelligence which he has placed in us and in you—the authority for our individual worlds. Yes, beloved, we give

*Born of the Shekinah glory of the I AM Presence. (See lesson 19, note 8.)

allegiance to the flame of God in *our* life; and you can give allegiance to the flame of God in *your* life, if you will determine to do so with all your heart!

What, then, is the course of worldly living engaged in by the masses of so-called society but weavings upon a temporal loom? Year after year, the shuttle of time weaves strands composed of living light misqualified by human thought and feeling. These retain all the old habits and momentums of the race which never have and never will bring men their God-freedom or even personal peace.

Dear ones, so strong have been the dyes of human thought and feeling and so coated has the cloth become with astral dust that no matter how horrendous the completed tapestry, because of the hardened matrix people have continued to weave discordant patterns (even studying the lives of the infamous) in imitation of all that mocks and is contrary to heaven, out-picturing all that is anti-Christ (contrary to, or 'anti', the Real Self) and must therefore come to naught.

The Holy Christ Self can never permit one's improperly executed art to be displayed in the universal gallery of divine art—and therefore, by cosmic law and mercy, has no choice but to consign such weavings of the lesser self to the flames of mercy and forgiveness, where their forms *dis*-integrate and their atoms return to the heart of the Great Central Sun for purification (repolarization).

Now, it is sometimes difficult for unascended beings to understand how certain theologians when face to face with the transparent simplicity of Life as it stands almost self-evident have complicated the Father's teachings and laws so as to create great fear in men's hearts. Yet it is so, regardless of how good have been their intentions.

God is often pictured as being the dispenser of *human* vengeance, desiring appeasement or sacrifice for the many sins of mankind, in the absence of which he should forever consign men to a most grim future from which there would be no escape (although it is written, "Vengeance [i.e., *divine* justice] is mine; I will repay, saith the LORD"[4]). Yet the scriptures these theologians are subjecting to their private interpretation eternally declare the mercy of God to be from everlasting unto everlasting.[5]

O my beloved, my Galilean life was not sacrificial but *sacramental.* It was a freewill offering to God which you, too, shall one day make (and some of you have already begun the process) in the course of your journey back to God's heart.

Blessed Hilarion, when embodied as the apostle Paul, clearly understood the matter of man's works—both his positive and negative karma—for he saw them being judged in the trial by fire when he declared:

"Every man's work [karma] shall be made manifest: for the day [the 'Daystar,'[6] the blazing Sun of the I AM Presence] shall declare it because it shall be revealed by [spiritual] fire;

and the fire shall try every man's work of what sort it is. If any man's work abide which he hath built thereupon, he shall receive a reward. If any man's work shall be burned, he shall suffer loss; but he himself shall be saved; yet so as by [sacred] fire."[7]

Only unprofitable patterns of karma, poorly woven garments of misqualified energy (such as thistles of human hatred and vengeful thought-forms), and the clay whose molding lacks the Christic beauty to please the Eternal Potter are rejected.

The blessed atoms that temporarily and lovingly sacrifice their life to compose and hold together (sometimes for aeons) such misshapen humanly created densities in man and Nature are not to blame for the mistakes and clumsy experiments of the learners in God's great school—where Life, as God, has destined waves (particles) of energy to obey the commands of his children who are engaged in the grand experiment of free will.

Even though it appears to be otherwise, if the students of earth's schoolroom knew of the divine plan or were convinced with the conviction of God-certainty of Life's nobler purpose, they would not continue to bring any creation to the door of the temple of Life that was not a perfect work of art. Furthermore, we would help them to produce such perfect works—as we will you—if they would but ask our help.[8]

When I cried, "Father, forgive them, for they know not what they do!"[9] I spoke not alone for the then-present multitude, but for the whole planetary evolution unto the present day.

How can the human self, fashioned so often in images of imperfection and bowed down by its own self-created discords and densities (i.e., karma), be expected either to yield to or to respond to appeals of perfection? Did I not say, "Do men gather grapes of thorns, or figs of thistles"? [10]

Seldom, therefore, do appeals to the outer man produce the winning response, except where that man, as weaver of the garment of his soul, has wisely incorporated much devotion and love into his nature; for then he will respond spontaneously, naturally, and quickly to the truth that "I AM the Light of the world." [11]

Address your appeals, therefore, to the Holy Christ Self of men, except when individuals express a natural willingness to learn. Only then give them our words and our teachings which are cups that carry light and salvation to all.

The wisest on earth have much to learn. I myself took all the beginning initiations in the temple, [12] although from the inception of my Galilean embodiment it was known by the sages that I would be considered wiser than the doctors and the wise men of that day. I continually taught that he that would be great must be the servant of all. [13] As has been said, a great leader places himself above his followers only when it is a question of bearing responsibility.

When you call with all the intensity of your

being for your own perfection in the Light, believing beloved Victory when he tells you that your own victory is possible today—there and then you make it possible!

Communion with us must be on our level, do you see? We cannot have communion with the changing outer self, which from day to day runs hot and cold, much of the time being luke-warm. [14] We appeal to and reach your soul through your Holy Christ Self. And, believe me, that is how we are reaching you right now.

For this hallowed gift of personhood through the Son of God (represented by your Holy Christ Self, who is the 'Sun of Righteousness' shining in his strength in the very temple of your being [15]) descended from your own I AM Presence to act as your mediator in raising you to the fulfillment of your divine destiny. Your Holy Christ Self has the power to reach not only your outer mind and self but also the mind and psyche of *any* human on earth—as well as *all* of them! They cannot argue against it or resist its action, for their life-streams also flow through the one Christ who is the Lord of all.

Therefore, lift up the Christ Self in all souls and teach them the true communion of saints, that they may realize that the God Presence of each one is one with every other manifestation of the I AM Presence—worlds without end.

Teach them the simple faith in the eternal Presence whose everlasting arms enfold them through their Holy Christ Self—resurrecting their thoughts, their minds, their worlds, their affairs, even their physical forms out of a prison house of stone (solidified human doubt and fear) into a world where we do not say, "I think, I believe, I want, I have," but declare with the Father: "I know, for I AM!"

How I long to receive you into that Holy Communion of your own I AM Presence, which you ought to keep daily in remembrance of me[16]—I who am one with (the "I AM" in me who is one with) your own Holy Christ Self. Then the chaff (bad karma) of your nature will be separated from the wheat (good words and works) because you desire it even as do I. For the "fan is in his hand, and he will throughly purge [purify] his [threshing] floor [your consciousness]."[17]

Through all the eternal cycles, the seed, or divine idea, of the soul is planted with the express hope of its multiplication and harvest, that by the refinement of heat (sacred fire) it may become a sacramental loaf even as I did, declaring for all: I AM the bread which came down from heaven. . . . Take, eat, this is my Body of eternally purified substance, molded willingly, consciously in the Father's image.[18]

This Life which you call your own, flowing in your veins, is in truth the consecrated wine of the Father which he has sacrificed (sanctified) *for you* by placing the essence of his own Presence within it. The Father requires no suffering or loss save the surrender of that which is unreal, but gives to you his love and that temporal dominion over his Life which is your portion.

This is his divine plan, conceived that you

may of your own choice learn to drink the cup wisely and thus by free will enter into your eternal dominion and oneness with him. For, by your leave, he, acting in you as in us, will sanctify you with the gift of his love and eternal friendship in the Life everlasting.

All students who are willing to drink of my cup (because they would be teachers of men)[19] will assuredly call for the full implementation of the Law of Love which we the Ascended Masters offer. Thus, by our transforming power shall they verily drink that Communion which makes of every communicant the selfsame manifestation of the Son of God that I AM.

To this table I welcome you evermore, brother or sister of Light. Again I say, Come, drink of the water of eternal Life freely![20]

I AM the Wayshower for you,
one with your own Holy Christ Self—

Jesus the Christ

Corona Class Lesson 3

Holy Christ Self

"For God So Loved the World. . . "

Beloved Who Offer Your Life
 Willingly to God—
Your own beloved I AM Presence is the fulfillment of every precious promise which the Father has ever made to his offspring throughout the ages.

When beloved John (who has oft been quoted by clergy and laity, but seldom fully comprehended) wrote, "For God so loved the world that he gave his only begotten Son, that whosoever believeth in him should not perish but have everlasting Life,"[1] he set forth one of the most potent promises ever given.

But, dear hearts, did God love the discord? Did he endow the discordant manifestation with the gift of everlasting Life? I think not, for it is plainly stated that the gift must be believed in and accepted in good faith in order to be effective; surely this anticipated belief must be more than a blind faith.[2] Surely this faith requires works as well,[3] particularly the inner service of opening the door of your heart and training your mind to be receptive to the promptings of the Holy Spirit, who will guide you into all Truth.[4]

You know, blessed ones, perfection is not nearly so far away as some would lead you to believe; for it dwells right in your God Presence, the I AM THAT I AM, often abiding just a few feet above your physical head—especially near when you draw nigh unto it.[5]

Blessed Mary, when she was with child, declared in the wonderful wording of the Magnificat the power and presence of the Great I AM with her: "My soul doth magnify the LORD, and my spirit hath rejoiced in God my Saviour. . . . For he that is mighty hath done to me great things; and holy is his name. . . . He hath shewed strength with his arm; he hath scattered the proud in the imagination of their hearts. He hath put down the mighty from their seats and exalted them of low degree!"[6]

Her song of praise unto the divine incarnation is a mantra of the Spirit of Motherhood that ought to be recited daily by expectant mothers (see Luke 1:46-55). Its repetition gathers unto itself and all who enter its song the devotion of the World Mother as well as the nearness of the I AM Presence of each member of the family— even the Divinity of the incoming soul!

How wonderful is the power of the Presence of God as it works through the spoken Word answering both prayer and praise, often contrary to human concepts and opinions, to bring about the highest good for you and the most divinely practical solutions to every single problem. Many times only a few steps remain unto one's perfection, and then God can and does quickly bring up the valleys (raise the consciousness) to the mountain heights of perfection,[7] at the same time leveling those mountains of human egoism which so often shut off the individual's view so as to hinder his spiritual progress for centuries.

The blessed Holy Christ Self is the Light, or *Christos*,* whose flow of love, wisdom, and power combined is the conductor of Life's energy from the Spirit (the I AM Presence) to the body, soul, and mind. As such, the Holy Christ Self is the illuminator of the heart of every man, woman, and child.

The key to true wisdom need not be complicated, for it lies very simply in understanding what God has wrought. Individuality is a precious gift of God which makes you *you!*

Whenever you feel alone, realize that your connection with God is identical to that of everyone else. As Saint Germain has told you, the chart of your I AM Presence is your 'eye picture' of your connection with the God of your being. Your divine rights throughout the creation are identical with those of Jesus the Christ and every other ascended being, once you accept and enter into your rightful place in the ordered plan of cosmos.

---

*The word *Christ* is derived from the Greek *Christos*, meaning "anointed," from *chriein*, "to anoint."

Unfortunately, men's misunderstanding through the centuries has envisioned a Creator who would require appeasement and sacrifice to atone for violations of his Law. The abortion of the correct understanding of this Law came when men first violated the great commandment "Thou shalt not *take* life!"[8] whereas the true understanding of the acceptable offering to God has ever been found in the command "Thou shalt *give* life!"

And so, God gave Jesus life, he gave you life as he gave all his children life that they might use the gift in love and grace and become thereby recipients of greater and greater power and glory, eventually entering into the full dominion of their own I AM Presence.

Jesus offered his life willingly to God (through his I AM Presence), and at the river Jordan the Father accepted his offer made out of the purity of his lifestream, declaring for all to hear at his baptism from John, "Thou art my beloved Son. In thee I AM well pleased." (In thee the I AM Presence dwells, well pleased.)[9]

Now, the Universal Christ has existed from everlasting unto everlasting. It was this great truth that Jesus affirmed when he said, "Before Abraham was, I AM."[10] The Master Jesus was a singular incarnation of that Christ. He received his personal initiation of acceptance at Jordan, being anointed of his Presence for his soul's mission in the performance of the Word in his Galilean embodiment. This selfsame opportunity lies before every lifestream.

In your love of God and devotion to his will, you, too, can receive the blessing of the Father, personified in your beloved I AM Presence, to perform the word and work of Christ in this life. Day by day, through practical and needful service to Life, you can put on the Christ Mind [11] and become one with your Holy Christ Self until one day, you, too, will hear the words of the Father spoken of you: "This is my beloved Son in whom I AM well pleased."

Jesus has often said to me, "One of the greatest weaknesses of so-called Christianity lies in the fact that they have deified me as a god to worship or bow down to and to make wishful prayers to; yet my mission and message they often neglect, knowing not that their own Initiator waits with arms of love to bestow upon them all that I ever received from God."

Beloved ones, none are unique, but all are given a unique opportunity to attain a supreme unity with God. In the parable of the prodigal son, men may learn much concerning the present state of world affairs. [12]

Recently we assisted a mother and her daughter who were bound in an interesting karmic tie whereby the mother served for years in ministering to the daughter who was paralyzed and mute from the effects of poliomyelitis. One day the mother found herself removed from the octave of earth (through the change called death), whereupon she intensely petitioned God for help for her daughter, who remained for approximately six days without food or attention, helpless and despairing, feeling certain that her blessed mother had passed on.

We secured a special dispensation from the Karmic Board through beloved Kuan Yin, the Goddess of Mercy, whereby the daughter (who after many days was found alone) also made the transition, being cut free from a condition of despondency to be reunited with her dear mother, thus affording them freedom from their binding physical karma. Their life plan for the future now presents all the aspects of hope which the opportunity for reincarnation allows.

You would perhaps be surprised, if you could see the aura as clearly as we do (and you will when you can hold an immaculate concept as we do) at how many people resent many aspects of their lives and wish they were different.

Some inwardly castigate the Deity and blame God for the state of personal or world affairs. They feel that because he has the power to correct conditions, he ought to use it. They no longer recall that sometime, somewhere, at inner levels they asked for the authority to govern their own affairs and then chose voluntarily to listen to voices other than the voice of the Presence of God. This is why God does not seek men; for the Law which they chose to ignore is not violated even by the Deity, who impartially dispenses the comfortable stability of its eternal constancy everywhere. [13]

In returning to the Father's house (as the prodigal son did after spending his portion), men must decree for a restoration of the divine authority of God and the Ascended Masters in their own world, mind, and affairs—even being willing to be a servant (chela) before full Sonship is regained—as the most practical method on earth whereby anyone can return Home. Believe me, dear ones, it pays to hold our hand and nestle very close to your Presence!

Trusting in human opinions, you will not go very far in the right direction. One of the claws of human creation is opinion, which is about as inconsistent as humanity can be. Usually when advice is sought and then not heeded, individuals become upset. Now, we are not so. If you choose to ignore our advice, we will not be upset, but you may find that you will be!

One particular matter I would call to mind in connection with establishing greater communion with our octave is the feeling of self-condemnation people sometimes have when they become enclosed by a seeming wall of human creation and discord. Because of the old law of sin and retribution ("an eye for an eye and a tooth for a tooth" [14]) which was set aside many years ago, they don't feel good enough to pray, decree, study the teachings of the Ascended Masters, or perform charitable deeds which would direct them to us. Therefore, they place their attention on human matters for fear of desecrating us by placing their attention on us.

Now, isn't this a paradox? We are directed by God to assist mankind, we are the freeing authority for this earth, and our way (which is Christ's way) is the only way they can ever escape human thralldom (for everyone who wants to escape must do it through the way of the ascension, which the Master Jesus demonstrated); yet the sinister idea is put out not to desecrate us! And what's worse, they accept it!

Beloved ones, we ourselves made many mistakes prior to our own ascension; but we must have your sustained attention in order to hold contact with your soul long enough to channel a sufficient quantity of assistance into your world to set you free.

Do not fail, therefore, when the heavens seem leaden, to keep on with your prayers and decrees—and when in urgent need of help, call to beloved Victory. He loves to respond. And, while we hope none of you will ever be in prison, I think he would even enjoy responding to you there. Ours is also a momentum of victory, you see, for we all share his love.

What God loves in you is precious. Discord is not of his creation, it is of yours—and if you insist on clinging to it, you will never be free.

We are the freedom for this earth, but the only way we can help you win *your* freedom is for *you* to invite us to do so. The stronger and more persistent the invitation, the greater the response we can give; for by cosmic law the wave of your energy must at least be equaled by our response: And the call compels the answer!

Have you ever considered just how practical our instruction is? Why, it is the most practical gift on earth! Yet it can be stated so simply that even a child can understand it. And this is truly wonderful for the perceptive who do see it.

For example, why do you think many of you are involved in mundane tasks—washing dishes, scrubbing floors, managing finances, gardening, marketing, helping people or ministering to the sick? Because it is an appropriate discipline, tried and proven, for your self-mastery of Life's energies which you might instead channel, ignorantly or otherwise, into the taking of heaven by force. [15]

The true path of discipleship is the path of self-discipline through the Holy Christ Self. On this path you assist us, teaching and demonstrating the Way made plain as you assault the earthly bastions with your love, overcoming all things by the power of your God-given victory and, equally important, by the grace of assisting others to find the blessed way of hope.

How many lepers do you think Jesus cleansed in his day, or how many spiritual lepers since his feet trod the shores of Galilee? Some of our chelas are like the little Dutch boy who kept his finger in the dike until help came, thus staying the riptides of the sea. These perform thankless tasks, all for the building of a divine momentum that will endure forty days in the human wilderness [16] and then, when lifted up (exalted), will refuse the sinister temptations of the wilderness or the wish for human recognition, showing forth that strength which Jesus knew full well at its apex in Gethsemane when his disciples slept. [17]

You, too, must know that the meaning of *disciple* is "one who is self-disciplined," and you must still your restless energies for the supreme purpose of activating them aright. The full powers of your Presence will be given into your hand only when you are free from both the will to harm and the power to harm. Would God indeed defame heaven by entrusting its government to those who cannot even get along on earth? That is why initiation (the testing of the soul) is provided, and that is why few find the way. [18]

To wear your seamless robe of white light, [19] you must daily open your heart and mind to the communion of heaven. This must be valued above earthly matters. People will not willingly be denied food. Let them refuse to be denied spiritual food!

This is practical, unvarnished Truth, beloved ones. Let them wear robes of Christlike discipline with the same honor that we feel. Let not the children of human creation or human mockery affect your love for God, the Mighty I AM Presence! The hosts of the LORD actually outnumber the children of mammon as the stars of the heaven and as the sand upon the sea shore innumerable! [20] This is universally true.

Remember, too, that the Presence is interested in everything that you do. If you lose a needle or lose your car keys, call to your I AM Presence to show you where they are. Learn to ever rely on the Presence, making the Father your confidant—and don't always tell people about your inner life; for they may laugh at you and tell others, thus amplifying your problem. In every way reorient your thinking back to your God Source and the realm of the Ascended Masters, and you will soon see the light begin to shine on your way.

Cosmic miracles will happen, have no doubt of that! For some it will come quickly, for others it may require a little longer, but come it will as it did to us. One day you who came from heaven which is your Home, trailing clouds of glory, as the poet said,[21] will return to your glorious God-estate which awaits you. This happens not by chance but by Law, by determination, and by offering oneself to God.

Know that every day, right while millions live in discord, we continue to have and enjoy harmony and Christ-communion in an atmosphere where the veil is removed and we see clearly the face of our God Presence and live.[22]

As Above, so below—so may it be!

Keep that flame blazing daily on your heart's altar, that many may also be lighted and inspired by your life. It is as much a part of God as I AM!

Kuthumi

Corona Class Lesson 4

The Father

"Before Abraham Was, I AM"

My Beloved Who Have Called,
    I Bid You Come into My World Apart—
    I AM the Resurrection and the Life[1]—the faultless, matchless Presence who gives the sweetness of Life to every lifestream whether experienced, known, recognized, enjoyed, or accepted by him or not.

    I know so well that the divine intention (that Good which God intends for every lifestream) goes almost wholly unnoticed by the majority of mankind insofar as the true outpicturing of Life's perfection is concerned. Consider how many great scientists, educators, industrialists, or financiers life produces; yet, by comparison, how few of those we call saints or ascended beings.

    The natural plans of God intend the ascension to be the sole destiny of every man. Certainly this marvelous goal is of true worth and everlasting gain to each lifestream so honored by its fulfillment. For is not an ascended God-illumined, God-free being above the greatest scientist human life could produce? Did I not say that of unascended men John the Baptist was greatest, yet the least in the kingdom of heaven was greater than he?[2]

Know also that the Father has an essence, or spiritual fragrance, with which he envelops persons, places, conditions, and objects (focuses) in a hallowed circle of his love whenever he is called upon with sincerity and reverence. Yes, each time you invoke the light of your heavenly Father with intense faith and love poured out to your I AM Presence, the Father's response is clothed with his essence. This essence is very real and its tangibility is sensed in wondrous ways by those advancing along the spiritual path. This path leads to the unfoldment of man's Christlike nature which I AM and which even now I embody.

Naturally, the Father is more than his essence or emanation—although someday you will find out that the essence of the Father, in all its great purity, is likewise so much more than just a series of pleasing sounds or letters of the alphabet intelligently arranged. The Father of many manifestations is also the "Wheel of the Law," that ever-revolving, magnificent wheel of world dharma turning in its appointed rounds of the eternal cycles of Life.

Hours fly hand in hand with the centuries, and the effects of human error and its corresponding human bondage still prevent many from realizing the ineffable sweetness, joy, and love of the Father, the Mighty I AM Presence, which I know so well.

Turning now to the perennial parade of spring manifesting differently in the two hemispheres (according to natural law) and to the present universal feast of the resurrection which occupies the attention of all Christendom, I AM beholding the day when, by the pressure of your own demands upon Life, many will be obliged to acknowledge our presence among men as a tangible, ever-present reality that has spanned the centuries to this very day.

I still walk among the old familiar surroundings even while I observe with you, dear hearts, new and different scenes on the world stage. Truly the drama of the ages is being outplayed. But I know that my true chelas will consider its climax near when, before their very eyes, I step through rainbow rays whose sunlit reality yet separates us, though by ever-thinning curtains of light's substance. Our octaves are so close!

When in my luminous Presence I step through the veil into your octave, it will be to say to you as I do today: "Peace, be still!" and "My peace I give unto you."[3]

As I draw back the substance of light which forms the veil[4] (curtain) dividing our realm from yours, you will know that the rose, whose petals are so wondrously soft as to exceed the finest velvet, symbolizes the gentle but symmetrically beautiful caress of God's love. The Father would give to every man, woman, and child the embrace of his nearness, his encouragement, his Law of Love, and even his very Life every hour.

The fragrance of his heart is therefore an aromatic balm whose sweet savor is often sensed by you when your God Presence is rendering a very special service in your behalf. As with a fragrant perfume, your atmosphere is thereby blessed. His light and mighty love flow into your world like a vital current from your I AM Presence or the starry electrode of an Ascended Master's heart.

Now, among all the practical accomplishments of the material world which you could ever perform, there is one toward which I would direct your earnest attention. Therefore I am come today in answer to your call—to call you, in turn, to come into my realm of practical spiritual experience. For I would acquaint you with the science and soul advancement of all eternity.

Come into my world apart. Leave for a little while the temptations of the wilderness—that is, the outer world illusions. Leave behind the record and memory of strife and religious or secular intolerance. Still the restless energies which assail the peaceful heart and know, for a time at least, the meaning of true communion with the God-progress of your own heart's light.

You see, ye call me brother, and so I am. Ye hope for a resurgent resurrection flame to confer upon you, when needed, eternal hope and immortal Life like unto my own. Ye hope for the call of your own God Presence to come up higher, yet ye tarry frequently in the memory of some of the elements of human decay.

Like Lot's wife, who turned into a pillar of salt (her consciousness crystallized by her own recalcitrance) when she looked back at the burning Sodom and Gomorrah[5] (which symbolize the discordant elements of life in the process of transmutation by the sacred fire), you have pondered and dwelt upon, revolving over and over in the memory, the human elements of discord from which you have asked, or should have asked, to be delivered.

Beloved ones, from Eden the voice of the LORD God who walked in the garden among the spiritual fragrances of your own God Presence has been heard by all but heeded only by the few: "...Of every tree of the garden thou mayest freely eat, but of the tree of the knowledge of good and evil, thou shalt not eat of it. For in the day that thou eatest thereof thou shalt surely die."[6]

The day when many shall turn to God is at hand![7] It is at the very door! No one can ever deceive the Law; and the Father, known by any other name than Love, is just as sweet. Keep my commandments to love one another even as I have loved you; otherwise, how can ye be mine or the image which I AM?[8]

Think back beyond the memory of human error or mortal discord to the pure Edenic state where "before Abraham was, I AM."[9] The life plan of the Father is like the most beautiful rose in existence, whose unfolding petals (the form) yield to Life's direction and become cups of fragrance offering golden liquid light which can enshrine in each lifestream all the joy and glory of the Masters' unfolding plan of the ages for that one.

Life is God, Life is I AM, and it was intended to be beautiful, eternal, powerful, and happy. This can be so only through your outpicturing of all that is the power (will of God), the kingdom (wisdom of God), and the glory (love of God). *There is no other way.* The seven days of the week are manifestations, as are individuals, of the magnificent seven planetary color rays, the radiance (ray-d-ance, or 'ray-dance') of the Father's light.

Every year during this holy season, I am drawn nearer and nearer to every human heart with as many blessings as the cosmic law allows. Truly, I AM with you always!

Do not fail to watch with me, disciples of this hour, [10] for Life ever tests each aspirant, and I AM so willing to assist all who ask!

May the highest sense of the beauty and perfection of the Presence enfold your hearts and lives this season and forever.

I AM your ascended

Jesus the Christ

Reciprocity

"And I, If I Be Lifted Up . . ."

Beloved Hearts Who Give All
        and Receive the All of God—
    In the hour when the Father acknowledged
the glorification of his name—I AM THAT I AM [1]
—within me, I declared for all time and eternity:
"And I, if I be lifted up from the earth, will draw
all men unto me." [2] And today I declare it again,
that you might derive the higher confirmation of
my Word in your life, for the import must not
be lost.
    This, then, is the true meaning of this scien-
tific statement of the Godhead dwelling bodily [3]
in every one of his servant sons and glorifying
his name within them, even as he has glorified
them by the gift of the Mighty I AM Presence: As
the I AM Presence is lifted up within me and I am
lifted up with it, so do I draw all men unto the
selfsame God Source of each one's life.
    You see, beloved, the 'I AM' Name and
the 'I AM' Presence *are* the glory—one and the

same—of the Son of man. Now ponder the reciprocity of the Father and the Son!

Two thousand years ago I said, "It is finished!"[4] Aeons before, the Father said, "It is Good!"[5] and rested from the labors of his creation. Completion, then, is the end of an era, an age, a plan, or a phase. It is the fulfillment of the endeavors of God or man where constancy and effort have adhered to Principle or Purpose now self-realized.

Completion signals the hour of the glorification of the Son of man—when the light of God is intensified both in man and in his manifest work. The glorification is the sealing and the raising up of man's offering of himself upon the altar of God—signifying that the Father is well pleased in his Son's outpicturing of Himself.

Now, let us see how the Law of Love and the Law of Life—which are the best part of divine wisdom—provide an understanding of the necessary give-and-take on the Path which only true love and real life can afford.

Dear ones, almost all love is given in expectation of reciprocity, and divine love is no exception. Today many people deceive themselves into believing that so-called impersonal love is unselfish (altruistic) and wants nothing in return. Some even believe it is wrong to have any wants or desires or preferences. This is not true if the wants or the desires or the preferences are necessary and beneficial, for then they are but God's own yearning for the expansion of his gifts to you which he communicates through you.

Those who feed on spiritual manna will understand through my parable of the talents[6] God's statement of the I AM Presence concerning the man who had buried his talent in the earth. This unfortunate servant (chela) supposed that the law of God was unjust and haphazard, or indiscriminate, in the conferment of reward. Believing his lord (guru) to be "an hard man," reaping where he had not sown and gathering where he had not strawed, he acted accordingly.

Hiding the talent entrusted to him and keeping it intact, he stultified the gain and hindered both his spiritual and his material progress. Thus he remained in a shadowed and painful state of resentment, burdened by his own sense of struggle and smarting injustice toward his lord—all this because of his misuse and misunderstanding of God's laws.

You see, God does expect to receive from you good fruit after its kind.[7] He has planted good within you. Beloved Kuthumi and I have also planted good seed through these Pearls of Wisdom and we, too, expect good fruit to manifest through your application of the laws of God and your continuing spiritual progress. As you review our teachings and forge ahead with all the Ascended Masters, we expect to see those "signs following"[8] in your demonstration of physical and spiritual self-mastery.

May your multiplication of the talents of your Holy Christ Self be abundant, filling you with the Ascended Masters' full understanding of the scriptures, free from human distortions.

Now, this reciprocity of the Father and Son,

Master and disciple, is witnessed in the push/pull, 'yin and yang', of the laws of Love and Life. Nevertheless, the unprofitable servant reflects the deceit born of greed and the inordinate desire to clutch and cling to the things of Spirit and Matter, stopping the flow of giving and receiving—of self-emptying and self-infilling. This he does through his ignorance of the law of the abundant Life which declares: I AM come that men might have Life—the fullness of God through the Mighty I AM Presence—and that they might have it—Him and the fruits of His Tree of Life—more abundantly. [9]

Those who bargain with Love (God) for a penny [10] can expect no more, no less. Those who, like the widow with her two mites, [11] can open their hearts to give all of themselves cannot fail to receive the all of Love (God)—and ought to expect to do so.

For, in order to receive from Life (God), who so often uses the human guise (illumined men become his hands and feet, his Presence, his love, cloaked yet in human form), men must give without reserve (to the divine beggar in disguise) that which Love has first given to them!—from glory unto glory. [12]

I live today as surely as you do and I AM your friend for all eternity. You are never forsaken. Be not afraid. Be of good cheer, it is I who comfort you now—the One, the same I AM—who have overcome the world. [13]

And that I AM is the Resurrection and the Life of all your Good. Therefore your good works and your good words shall live forevermore in the causal body of God. So lift up the Presence of the Father and the Son, by deeds exalt His name, and He will glorify (raise up and intensify) the I AM within you, drawing all men unto Himself through your blessed manifestation of His image! Do you see?

Blessings in the glorification
of the Son of man,

Jesus the Christ

Crown

"Ye Shall Receive a Crown of Glory . . ."

Blessed Students of Wisdom's University—
   The darkening shadows of Good Friday symbolize humanity's crucifixion of their own God Self and the subsequent entombment of their pure Christ nature, following their feeble attempts to put aside or ignore the voice of the Law (Logos). This they do to the complete silencing of the Word in the agony of the crucifixion, thereby ignorantly, albeit willfully, destroying the Christ potential—the Light and Life of their own world!
   The resurrection of the soul sealed in the heart of the Christ Self is the only resolution of

this dilemma. Not only does the resurrection prove the eternal truth of the I AM promises, which confirm the covenant of eternal Life, but it also demonstrates the soul's inevitable encounter with Christ and the logical conclusion of her attempt to escape the treadmill of rebirth.

As in the case of Saul, the blinding of the mortal eyes that would not see mandates the choice either to come up higher or to continue to kick against the pricks of thy innate Christhood. [14] With or without the soul, that Christ by reason of its immortal nature will rise again! Thus, there is a choice to be made and an answer which must be forthcoming to the Christ who calls.

When the fiat of Life—the voice of the Christ who raised the widow's son at Nain, [15] Jairus' daughter, [16] and Lazarus [17]—is heard in the sacred temple of one's own heart, its unmistakable leading, its infinite peace, and its promises of immortality pervade one's life. This the disciple must decide to make his own. To this he must surrender until the shadows and storms of struggles past are of no consequence on Easter morning.

When at last the soul has ceased to crucify its own True Self, conquering instead the carnal mind and all enmity with the LORD, [18] the I AM THAT I AM, it is forevermore bound by cords of love to the cross of Self-giving/Self-receiving Love. The soul enters into the joy of the Presence. This is victory: all that matters, all that really counts is risen!

To turn men to the way of peace and the way of wisdom is, then, the united goal of every ministering servant, every preacher of righteousness, no matter what exoteric or esoteric school he calls his alma mater.

As the corona appears around the sun, revealing its flaming diadem as mighty light rays in divine action, so may each one of you bearing our light also be its crown. Light is king and Love is queen, but the scepter of Wisdom is used by both.

While in a larger sense the Corona Class has only begun, our next lesson will conclude this first phase. When you are ready, we will summon you again without fanfare for the trek to a higher understanding. Ours is Wisdom's university, a refresher course freely given by the Ascended Masters of Light and Love.

Privileged as you are to be the corona of the Sun of Wisdom, think carefully how best you can represent all that we are, bearing no defamation in conduct but ever honoring the risen Christ within you.

Freely ye have received, freely give to Light the preeminence which Light always deserves to receive.

My blessing for your victory this Easter,

Kuthumi

Jesus' Victorious Crown

O Master Jesus, Love's sweet King—
Within my heart to thee I sing!
The Mighty I AM Presence fair
Proclaims Love's victory everywhere.
The crown of thorns which once thou wore
Remove from mankind evermore.

The thorn is but thy love aborted
To take a shape and form distorted.
The rose's fairer face we see
As God intended life to be.
His love now blazes round thy head
To trace in outline symbol fair
Not thorn, but crowning rose instead.

Love itself transmutes all woe—
Changes come and changes go—
But none can mar the plan divine
Nor take from me God's gift sublime.
I AM the victor now with thee,
I feel the spur of Life in me
And know that raised I, too, shall be,
By God's own hand thy Face to see.

I AM thy child as are all men—
O come thou, Lord, to earth again!
That all breathe reverence in thy name
To feel the balm that frees from pain,
The thorns of life all broken then,
Our life moves upward to the sun—
Where coronation rays we wear:*
We hear thy voice now say—"Well done!"

---

*Corona-tion denotes the action of the Light-emanation of the corona,
or halo, of the Teacher now transferred to the disciple as a crown of life.

Corona Class Lesson 6

Constancy

"Faith without Works Is Dead"

My Dear Brothers and Sisters
 of the Cosmic Light—
In concluding the first set of the Corona Class Lessons, I would speak to you who aspire to be corona rays around the sun of divine wisdom about inconstancy—hardly a quality of the sun!

Constant requests reach the Darjeeling Council from students and others telling us from their hearts of a love lost (a fleeting ecstasy which has not returned or which is sensed only seldom), of an affection which seems to have played itself out, and how they deplore the inconstant side of their nature.

Now, beloved ones, that is just what it is: the *inconstant* side of their nature—the human side, where God's magnificent light flows through the imperfect human prism, revealing its sometimes mottled distortions.

We answer these requests with the word to the wise that the perfecting of the instruments of their four lower bodies would permit, as it has for us, an unimpeded flow of God-purity and eternal happiness into their worlds—magnified by the prism of the Christ Mind. This is why every earnest student seeking the source of purity's fount must make correction on those lower bodies—vessels of thought and feeling, action and recorded memory.

You will recall that the early Christian teachings declare that salvation is a gift of God, "not of works, lest any man should boast."[1] Yet the statements of James are also clear: "Faith [believing in the promise of the divine gift] without works is dead."[2]

When the four lower bodies of man—physical, etheric (i.e., memory), mental, and emotional—are brought into a state of harmony by determined effort and sheer constancy of will, the divine service of the mercies and graces of God can flow naturally into one's world to break up patterns of human domination—old habits of thought and feeling which so frustrate the flowering spiritual aspirations of God-seekers.

This clearance will alleviate a great deal of distress in the world of the unascended chela, giving him a lot less to handle, notwithstanding that opposition which he may encounter from those who feel the need to challenge him, as they did beloved Jesus and other teachers of righteousness in the past.

The magnificent physical sun is surrounded by powerful emanations of solar energy, streaming rays of light's victory which warm and revivify Nature. Now, those who are able to comprehend the mystery of solar bodies and of the spiritual Sun behind the sun understand that this center of the solar system is the home of beloved Helios and Vesta, twin flames who are the God-parents of this planetary chain. Their spiritual fire, as well as the display of physical power, manifests as the constant corona and perpetual outpouring of light, calling each Easter season for the resurrection of all Life on earth.

In a larger sense, this is the high calling of the Corona Class: to call the Children of the Sun to the resurrection in God's name, I AM, teaching them how to tap the spiritual light and radiance of their own God Presence and threefold flame as well as the beautiful flowers of their own divine memory, their divine identity, and their soul (solar) union with all that truly lives.

How sad, dear hearts, that some do not know that we, the Ascended Masters, are more alive, more charged and infilled with the life-energy of the Great Central Sun than any unascended being. We truly live in the fullness of that Life which is undiluted God, for we have transmuted our entire human creation. Therefore our capacity to receive and retain Light's limitless energy is greater in the ascended state than yours is in the less-accelerated earthly state.

What's more, until your four lower bodies are aligned and attuned with the inner blueprint, healed of all schism within their members, and the tears in their 'skins' carefully mended, you are still functioning with leaky vessels, not able to hold the available energy, therefore unable to store energy for a concentrated release of power. Then, too, you do not have as many coils (of spiritual fire) wound round the pole of being as we do.

These are only some of the reasons why in the unascended state the life/consciousness/energy you experience is not the same as ours. Thus your ability to sustain the momentum of the Great Central Sun Magnet is also not as expanded as our own.

Moreover, our capacity to communicate eternal Life is also greater than your own, and you feel the vibration of our transfer of love and illumination by the extraordinary power available to us. In our presence you experience the heightened sense of our reality, as well as your own, through our ability to sustain in you our energy level as you place your attention on the spoken and written word of our release.

Your attention is the lever that connects your circuit to ours. So long as your attention is harmoniously sustained, you enjoy the closed circuit of oneness in Ascended Master love which we maintain twenty-four hours a day for and with our chelas.

This will enable you to understand why one dear chela told our Messenger, "These words of Jesus and Kuthumi spoken today make me feel the presence of the beloved Master even more than reading the holy scriptures of the past. I feel the Master is speaking directly to me!"

This is true, dear hearts—we are! Did not Jesus himself foretell this, saying, "If you believe in the Christ in me, placing therefore your attention on me, you will do greater works even than I did because I go to my Father"?[3]

The Master opens the scriptures:[4] "As my light/energy/consciousness is accelerated today through my oneness with the Father in heaven, I am able to transmit to you through your loving tie to me greater power than when I was in the unascended state. Inasmuch as you also have access to the Holy Christ Self, as I did two thousand years ago, our combined effort can and shall produce through you greater works than were possible in the previous Piscean dispensation."

Try to realize therefore the close, direct contact you have with us through our words. In God's love and name, realize, know, and understand that no one in this endeavor is concerned with aught else than bringing our words and radiance to all mankind for their upliftment and resurgent glory to the joy of the eternal Cause.

This is, in a larger sense, Wisdom's cosmic university for all Life upon this planet—for all those willing to be molded into that perfect prism (which all men are at inner levels) for the projection of divine light rays through that eternally pure pattern of the Creator's original intent and plan.

It matters not that you have made mistakes in the past. This is quite common on earth today. What really counts is that you are willing to become the purity of your own Godly nature. As you sustain this God nature, being "good-natured" with the constancy of a saint, meeting every trial and temptation with equanimity of heart, the love and pristine wholeness of your own I AM life-currents descending through your crystal cord will pass through the matrix of your Godly nature, thus multiplying the hands and feet of each Master (Chohan) of the Seven Rays of cosmic light.

Each lifestream vibrates principally with one of the seven color rays—the blue, yellow, pink (rose), white, green, purple (ruby) and gold, or violet—expanding the qualities of the Godhead respectively as (1) the will of God, (2) the wisdom of God, (3) the love of God, (4) the purity of God, (5) the truth of God, (6) the devotion (service) of God, and (7) the freedom (alchemy/transmutation/forgiveness) of God. By spiritual attainment, some people do embody several of the rays or even the full complement.

I am concerned with the number of individuals who do want to intensify their love for God, who deplore their lack of progress on the Path, and who are not smug with a false sense of security regarding their spiritual life. It is a good sign if they do not sink into this sense but realize that wherever they are, God wants to raise them up.

In that magnificent song "The Lost Chord"[5] we find expressed the feeling shared by many that some splendid ecstasy they once knew has passed them by or been lost. This is not so. It is *they* who have passed *it* by, choosing instead to externalize manifestations other than the divine graces; and in so doing, they may have in fact lost the formula for God-happiness.

Now, therefore, they must become even more diligent, breaking down Jericho-like walls they have built which have become self-made, self-entombing sepulchres. They must replace human trivia with good works in the Master's name, and backbiting with constructive conversation in his honor. These will provide them with true spiritual treasure[6]—pearls of great price![7]

Then their attunement with us, which may come and go like an ethereal melody so easily drowned in human discord, will become stronger by far than any exterior forces because they will have verily contacted their own God Self, the I AM Presence, and those of us who are World Teachers. This is how you know when your victory is at the door—when unbroken constancy of attunement shows the pure life-wave of the Father in permanent manifestation.

Faint heart never won fair victory.[8] Remember, the Life (God-force) in you is omnipotent. Only Life can declare, "I AM." Only *that* Life in beloved Mother Mary could crown her the handmaid* of the LORD.[9] Only *that* Life in Jesus could move from Bethlehem to Golgotha through countless Gethsemanes to the eternal victory of the resurrection and ascension in the Light. That Life is your victory if you will accept it!

God is the eternal Father of all that is good. This is the message of a victorious Easter which ought to remain with you long after the season is past as a perennial inspiration from God for all the years to come. So it was intended. God in you declares, "I AM"—and this Life can never cease to be! This is your hope and eternal substance. This is your faith become a tangible reality.

As a miner stakes his claim, you must plead for the power of the coronary light to flow from the heart of God into your world, making you a postulant for admission to the higher initiations of the Great White Brotherhood. May they be victoriously passed! May you go that way, even as we have. It is not enough to stake a claim to divine graces and gifts; such claims must be developed diligently, as a miner goes after his ore.

I know of and have observed down through the Christian centuries countless saints of holy orders—including those in Christian, Tibetan,

*female attendant, or servant, feminine chela; soul, bride

and even so-called heathen monasteries—who became disciples of Love's wisdom. Many of these labored with the weight of enormous karma, under abbots and superiors who could have been much more kind. Scarcely a word of approval did they hear in a lifetime until the Master's blessed voice said, "Well done." Yet, they were constant.

You who enjoy the freedom of the outer world and belong not to holy orders—what opportunity is yours to overcome temptation and to be really strong for right and God! How you should welcome the opportunity, as have many disciples in the past who never made recorded history, remaining unknown, unhonored, and unsung.

Nada, our beloved sister (Chohan of the Sixth Ray and member of the Karmic Board), was one of these until her ascension. In a number of embodiments, she chose to push others forward, while remaining the wellspring of divine invocation to call forth virtue in her family members and friends—which they scarce realized was transferred to them through her pure and loving heart. And in the meditation of her spirit upon the ancient maxim of the ascending ones, "He must increase but I must decrease," [10] she won—she won forevermore!

Speaking of divine mysteries and holy wisdom, it is difficult for mankind to realize that greater wisdom by far than was possessed by Einstein is present in a sunbeam. Many ask for great expansion of their light and wisdom beyond the offering we are currently giving or have given.

The meaning of "a little child shall lead them"[11] and "except ye become as a little child, ye shall in no wise [with no wisdom] enter in"[12] completely escapes them. They ask to sit at the Master's feet, although they have passed by the wisdom he has already given them and they continue today to live in human shadow. They quarrel at trifles when Life (as God) cries out to end discord, and crisis looms ominously all over the planet. Yet the solution is simple!

As children, some of them sang sweetly, "Jesus wants me for a sunbeam to shine for him each day."[13] They knew more the meaning then than now, for their immature gleanings remain unappropriated, unused, unapplied, and sometimes completely forgotten.

I shall now trace in light, with my own consciousness blending as one with the Ascended Master Jesus Christ's own light, an affirmation, or decree, for you:

> I AM a created ray from the very heart of God. I AM shining each day with the lifting, living light of resurrection's eternal flame, awakening my divine memory to the infinite wisdom in a sunbeam, a ray-o-light within me, within all God's children!
>
> I glory in Light's apparent simplicity, knowing that therein lies locked the mightiest power, most profound wisdom,

and greatest love of eternity. My own I AM Presence ever unlocks for me this wisdom-balanced power in daily manifestation of all the ascended Jesus Christ love, beauty, grace, and perfection now made manifest.

In childlike humility, I sit at the feet of the gracious Ascended Masters until, sweetly crowned by them, I AM ever the sunbeam-ray which shines for them each day!

Pax in te! Sicut parvulus in gremio matris suae, ita in me est anima mea. Pax vobiscum!

Peace be within you! As a little child on the lap of its mother, so is my soul within me. Peace be with you!

Kuthumi Lal Singh

In the name of the ascended Jesus Christ, to the glory of the Cosmic All-Christ!

Purpose

¹pur·pose \ 'pərpəs, 'pə̄p-, 'pəip- \ *n, pl*
purposes \ -pəsə̇s, *in rapid speech sometimes*
-psə̇z \ [ME *porpos, purpos,* fr. OF, fr. *porposer* to
purpose] **1 a :** something that one sets before
himself as an object to be attained : an end or
aim to be kept in view in any plan, measure,
exertion, or operation : DESIGN ⟨it was our ~ to
get home before the storm⟩ ⟨his ~ was above
reproach⟩ **b :** RESOLUTION, DETERMINATION ⟨infirm
of ~ —Shak.⟩ **2 :** an object, effect, or result
aimed at, intended, or attained ⟨energy applied
to little ~⟩ **3 :** a subject under discussion or
an action in course of execution **4** *obs* **a** (1) :
PROPOSAL, PROPOSITION (2) **purposes** *pl* : a game
like conundrums or riddles **b :** DISCOURSE, TALK,
CONVERSATION **c :** PURPORT, INTENT, MEANING
5 : an old Scots dance in which the couples
talked together in an affectedly secretive manner
syn see INTENTION — **in purpose** *adv* **1 :**
in one's mind as a purpose **2 :** on purpose—**of
purpose** *or* **of set purpose :** on purpose — **on
purpose** *adv* **1 :** by deliberate intent and not by
accident : INTENTIONALLY, DESIGNEDLY **2 :**
in order to attain an end ⟨did it *on purpose* to
fool his friends⟩ — **to the purpose :** to the
point ⟨little. . .said that is at all *to the purpose*
—Clive Bell⟩
²purpose \ " \ *vb* -ED/-ING/-S [ME *purposen,* fr.
MF *purposer, porposer,* fr. OF, modif. (influenced
by *poser* to put, place) of L *proponere* to put forward, propose — more at PROPOSE] *vt* **1 :** to
propose as an aim to oneself : determine upon :
resolve to do or bring about ⟨did nothing
~ against the state —Shak.⟩ ⟨*purposing* to write
an account of the tragedy⟩ **2** *obs* **:** to set forth :
PROPOUND **3** *obs* **:** DESIGN, DESTINE ~ *vi* **1 :** to
have a purpose **2** *obs* **:** to proceed to a destina-
tion : to be bound for some place **3** *obs* **:**
DISCOURSE, TALK **syn** see INTEND

Corona Class Lesson 7

Perfection

"Let Not Your Heart Be Troubled . . ."

To My Blessed Who Love and Worship—
   The present worldwide turbulence is in fact a general hypnotic condition, widespread by reason of advanced means of travel and communication. In the archives of history are to be found proportionately as many examples of tyranny as there are in the present day.
   Let not your heart be troubled.[1] The peace which I AM and which I yet give to my disciples is the direct opposite of the disturbed state. If individuals are to more quickly escape from the pull of every unhappy situation—personal, domestic, or so-called foreign—they must universally recognize the root causes underlying their unhappiness and then try to uproot these causes with our assistance and intercession.
   I would point out that occasionally individuals without this understanding are found to be living in such a harmonious way solely from the inner Light of their own lifestreams as to

naturally counteract the effects of mass unhappiness. Such as these are like self-luminous sunshine; they contribute much to mankind wherever they are and add to the general sense of worldwide well-being.

For the average person who is easily disturbed or basically controlled by his feelings, who is yet desirous of being a real student of Truth capable of understanding first principles, we recommend that he first endeavor to come to a realization of the truth of his own being. This will enable him to better understand the essential differences between people, at the same time perceiving the great common heritage which all have universally received from the Creator.

To this end, beloved Kuthumi and I in our role as World Teachers wish to make known the present purposes of the Brotherhood concerning mankind and those particular goals which every teacher or would-be teacher of spiritual truth ought to emphasize and exemplify to the best of his ability each day.

The familiar idiom "having an ax to grind" is reminiscent of the statement I made long ago in Judaea that every tree that does not bring forth good fruit is cut down and cast into the fire.[2] We of the Great White Brotherhood who have "clean escaped"[3] from the wiles of the world and its control do not have personal axes to grind—neither from a political, a religious, nor a commercial vantage. Rather, we seek to outpicture in vibration those holy truths which from time immemorial have had the power to set men free. [4]

Now, if in the process of setting men free, the cosmic law in its great wisdom and discriminating intelligence sees the need to hew down the fruitless tree, then mankind should understand it as God's will for perfection in manifestation which always terminates in time and space all qualities which do not merit permanence. This will to perfection is always balanced against man's so-called free will, which brought the onus of imperfection into temporal manifestation in the first place.

Countless individuals visiting the religious shrines of the world, such as Lourdes, Fátima, and others (many of which were established by my blessed mother, Mary, for the hope and healing of men's hearts), have realized for the first time the awesome futility of life without God. The great influx of the magnetic attraction of the Divine has thrilled their souls with such an outpouring of light, such a sense of nearness to the Presence, as to flush out of the electronic structure of their flesh all the inharmonious patterns they had previously established through the misuse of free will. This has produced what mankind call a miracle but which I declare again to be simply the reestablishment of the Father's love—which never should have been usurped by human discord in the first place!

Today, when the lingering desire for recognition is fed and amplified by the human race but seldom understood (even by the psychologists who seem unable to justify their theories based on half-truths[5]), it becomes increasingly important that the distinction accorded one part of Life or the temporary extinction of another part of Life be likewise comprehended.

The Ascended Masters hold in common a sense of humility in recognizing themselves as omnipresent facets of the Godhead dedicated as One to the service of the All. As such they are always obedient to the cosmic intelligence of the Mighty I AM Presence in the Great Central Sun, yet humble and compassionate enough to respond to the heart calls of the most discordant or intemperate human on earth.

Every ascended being is likewise solicitous of every other ascended being, expressing kindness with Ascended Master gentility, which is quite unaffected and very natural to our estate. I tell you truly—in place of saying, "Oh, we're only human, you know!" you ought to declare more often: "Oh, we're really divine, you know!" and furthermore that you are likewise capable of expressing your own natural estate, which is the same as our own.

The mere wearing of flesh bodies does not change your Spirit! As the ancient Bhagavad-Gita declares, "Never the Spirit was born; the Spirit shall cease to be never; . . . Death [mortality] hath not touched it at all, dead [extinct] though the house of it seems."[6] Not, then, as bodies having appetites or unappeasable longings should men regard themselves, but rather as sparks of the Infinite, longing for reunion with the glory of the cosmic fires of Home.

Well do we know that our shores may seem very distant to mankind, formed and informed as they are in the mold of the human consciousness. But I am equally certain that the initial adventure of becoming embodied and losing the freedom of the Edenic world was likewise a cause of much inner longing for the return to Elysian comforts in the power and the glory of the kingdom.

Cathedrals have been built by countless hands and by the efforts of many hearts united in ordered service who never sought to carve their names on any stone and who were satisfied with the memorial: "To the glory of God who is the All of us and more—all that we ever shall be and more!"

So much achievement today is sought for the forthcoming recognition. To do and to do with infinite care and skill is to worship in the doing. The first principle of achievement, then, as pertains to the individual path of self-mastery lies in active love and worship.

Wouldst thou create, endow, or ennoble life? Love and worship while you spin, weave, paint, sculpt, build, teach, heal, write, serve, play, and sing! Love and worship as you enjoy family relationships and heart ties with one another. Endow your life with love and worship as you expand the teachings of The Summit Lighthouse or other constructive endeavors; for then you shall be fitted to be temple master-builders,[7] and I am certain the Temple of Life's Victory will be more speedily externalized.[8]

Becoming immersed in love and worship,

you shall do as I have done and be as I AM—
the Light of the world. [9] Your individual 'light-
houses', patterned after the Summit, the highest
of every man, shall make you beacon lights
everywhere you move. [10]

Loving and worshiping in the bonds of
peace, you shall increase your skill and care
without tension. You build, then, not for name
and fame but to externalize God. I am certain
that none of you will take from the foregoing an
excuse for callous indifference, withholding
your praise of others. Praise amplifies and
expands. Thus, while seeking no praise for
yourself, continue to give it to others whenever
and wherever it is deserved.

Thus, by law shall the love you send out
return to you free from karma (and freeing you
from karma). As a cosmic flame, ever welcome,
ever Christ's consciousness in the universal
spirit of one accord, this love gives all recognition
to God, the Mighty I AM Presence.

By allowing the Presence to take full dominion in your life, you will experience an expansion
of Christ consciousness equal to (and I hope
greater than) that which manifested in me during my thirty-three years (and more) of focusing
the sacred fire in the temple of my then-unas-
cended body.

Everlasting peace be unto you,

Jesus the Christ

Sainthood

". . . How Sayest Thou, Show Us the Father?"

To Joyful Hearts
    Who Extol the Love That Is God—
    Various lifestreams I have known and with whom I have served in numerous embodiments have suffered much from the malady of overconcern. Among these blessed but most unfortunate individuals were some who were determined to be sober of face to the point of stiffness—so much so that nothing ever seemed to make them laugh. It was as though they were afraid that if they should even smile, it might crack the mirror of the universe!
    I recall one blessed sister of a holy order with whom I once served. She had been born and spent her girlhood in a home of great wealth and therefore had the feeling that she had given up a great deal to serve the Lord. She tried very hard to conceal this from the other sisters, so much so that toward the close of her embodiment she spent most of her free time in prayer,

interceding for her own soul that it would cease to be puffed up. [1]

Experiencing alternate periods of depression and ecstasy, she would feel encouraged even by a little sign of progress, only to be plagued by the haunting specter of more of the same self-importance whenever a new sister arrived. Surely she must not show this new sister her own greatness—and therefore behind the mask of great austerity and a sober face, she concealed the depth of her personal suffering and her struggle to be virtuous and humble.

Toward the close of her embodiment, she became extremely distressed when a vivacious young novice arrived. Her smiling face and delightful sense of humor stemmed from an attitude of not taking herself too seriously. Therefore, she did her best to see the good in every situation—even to the point of finding humor in some of the holy rituals. This, of a truth, stemmed from no lack of devotion but from her blithe young spirit desiring to bring cheer to others in the midst of the sometimes somber atmosphere of monastic life.

The older sister, whose name was Veronica, was abashed to discover that the younger sister's nature seemed to grate on her very soul, bringing to her at a moment when she had thought that victory was in sight, alas, the greatest trial of her life! So discordant did she become and so distressed, that her attention, inverting upon herself, attracted to her person a fatal illness and she soon passed on.

When her case was reviewed in the spiritual realm, the Karmic Board decided on the basis of her good intentions to give her extensive training at inner levels in order to reduce the probability that such wasteful and introverted self-attention should divert her soul's pure service to the Light (her heart's true desire) in her next embodiment. She actually spent more than twenty-seven years at inner levels in the retreats of the Great White Brotherhood reviewing the psychological aspects of her own case, taking training from the Ascended Masters so as to prevent a recurrence in her next life of excessive self-consciousness.

All this took place before she was summoned by the Lords of Life, according to the necessity of her karma, to enter once again the gates of birth. The happy ending to my story, beloved, and one that holds a promise of hope to all, is that she became a real saint in her very next embodiment!

So does heaven ceaselessly bring its blessings the Ascended Masters' way to every part of Life, even when that part seems to fall short of the mark. [2] Truly, heaven has many remedies!

Now, countless millions of well-meaning individuals seem to lack the common sense that distinguishes the saint from those who never quite measure up to the desired standards of their inward aspirations. Most of this is caused by paying too much attention to the outer personality and not placing enough upon the great discriminating Cosmic Christ Intelligence of their own being, their Holy Christ Self—also known as the Higher Mental Body, the Higher Consciousness, and the Mediator between God and man.

It is extremely difficult for men and women schooled in the various religions of the day to set aside their fear of dire consequences should they be found even considering any idea which is not "absolutely correct" in a doctrinal sense. Yet common sense should tell them that their own religious beliefs, whatever they are, comprise but one of thousands of sects or divisions of sects.

The average Christian is bound to the tradition of the historical Jesus being the chosen, anointed, and "only begotten" heir of the favor of God. He does not seem to realize that God created *only* favorites in all his children and that he expects all of his sons and daughters to strive for the one supreme standard of perfection which is innate within the divine image of each and every one. This is the true image of the Christ out of which all were made as children of the Light.

Jesus' "I AM" affirmations were spoken of his Christ Self, the Universal One who is the true and only Son of God. The image of the Son "with us," the Immanuel[3] (manifest as each one's Christ Self), is the true Self, i.e., the *true Light* which lighteth every man that cometh into the world.[4]

When the Master said, "I AM the Light of the world,"[5] he affirmed the Son Presence as that Light. And he promised that as each one would lift up this Son (i.e., Sun or Light) of man within himself, he would also know that Son in Jesus:

> Then shall ye know that I am he—and that the I AM in me, as the I AM in you, is the Light of my world and your world and is the All of cosmos. Then shall ye know that I AM He—that I am the incarnation of the Word, the Christ. When ye have lifted up the Son of man, then shall ye know that I do nothing of my (outer) self; but as my Father, the Mighty I AM Presence, hath taught me, I speak these things.
>
> He that sent me—the Mighty I AM Presence—is with me: the Father hath not left me alone. When ye shall have lifted up the Son of man within your own soul and temple, then shall you also know the Father, as I do, through the Presence and Person of the I AM THAT I AM. And *this is* the Word that is made flesh in me. Hence, I am Jesus *the Christ.* I AM He.
>
> If ye continue in *this Word,* then are ye my disciples indeed. And ye shall know the Truth, for you shall have become the Truth that I AM, and that Truth shall make you free. [6]

"I AM the Resurrection and the Life: he that believeth in me, though he were dead, yet shall he live" [7] is spoken of the Holy Christ Self, who is

not a historical figure or even a human person-
age but rather the Divine Person, or Personhood,
of every child of the Light.

This Divine Person is an 'electronic' manifestation of the Presence of God, vibrating at
times at a rate beneath that of the Presence (the
Father) in his role of reaching out to assist the
evolving soul directly, being capable of both
ascent and descent in vibration whenever necessary. Thus, the Holy Christ Self of each son
and daughter on earth is able at will to become
one with the absolute Presence of God above (the
I AM, or Father)—or the embodied soul below.

When the soul realizes the full impact of this
gift of love, it is like a beautiful melody which
amplifies over and over with each listening that
GOD IS LOVE[8] and that He is quite unwilling
to have men and women perish, to remain in
delusion, or to be forever bound by unhappy
situations.

Know, then, that by concentration upon the
Holy Christ Self, anyone can let go of the delusion of separation—which, as Ecclesiastes declares, is only vanity (a human conditioning of
the human consciousness). Anyone can rise
above the need for psychoanalysis or for soul-
saving by the sawdust trail or the *via dolorosa,*
finding instead in his beloved Christ Self, who is
the Light-manifestation of God which never fails,
the hope of the universe in unending portion
freely given for the integration of the whole man.

The human problem of self-love, self-pity,

or self-delusion (and this includes every addiction, binding human habit, and predilection to sexual perversion) is no longer of concern to those who abide in the true knowledge of the indwelling Father and Son. No malady of over self-concern exists for them—with its attendant sinful state and sense of struggle—to hinder or further delay their progress or trap their energies while they painfully speculate, and woefully, as to whether or not they have found favor with God and man. [9]

It is much easier for those completely free from self-love to spread the balm of happiness everywhere than it is for those who are still bound by this dreadful disease (dreaded, that is, only so long as one is its slave; unreal and unfeared when one is its master).

Thus, souls on the path of selflessness, overcoming their too, too self-importance, become lost in a giant concern for both the Love and the Plan of God (which they know is waiting revealment in their own Christ Self). These seek to be like the little brothers of Jesus, or to unite with the little brothers of Saint Francis, or to be even a little unknown brother of love, simply loving the blessed earth, the trees, the sky, the sound of sweet music, and the song of the Lord. Such as these have found peace, have found God.

Listen, then, to the voice of your Holy Christ Self, the Father's gift of eternal salvation to you. The Christ is all these things: the wise Masterbuilder whose name is called Wonderful, whose wisdom (wise dominion) makes him Counsellor, whose vibrations make you feel so peaceful and calm because they emanate from The Prince of Peace. [10] His omnipresence is the ever-nearness of The Mighty God, saying, "He that has seen me has seen the Father" [11]—the Everlasting One, your own individualized focus of divinity, the Mighty I AM Presence!

Try to be ever full of joy. Magnify the LORD in silence or audibly as your heart dictates, but let all be done with the wisdom of God in reasonable perfection before men, so that all may glorify God as they behold you. Let this be your goal.

So do beloved Jesus and I, as World Teachers, direct you. So do thou and so teach, that all men may smile even at themselves—at the human because they should not take it too seriously, and at the Holy Christ Self because they ought to take it very seriously—with an ever-present smile of welcome.

So is Love extolled, so does greater love exert its power of elevation upon your spirit. So is the Father revealed on the path of sainthood.

I AM Wisdom's fount of heavenly affection, kissing your pathway daily with peace and spiritual light which knows no wane.

Gently but fondly,

Kuthumi

Corona Class Lesson 9

Example

". . . And the Father Is in Me"

Eager Ones Who Rejoice
　　in the Transfer of the Father's Flame—
　Go ye into all the world and proclaim the good news! [1]

　It is generally accepted, blessed ones, that the proclaimers of great truths ought themselves to follow them. This is logical inasmuch as all men love the comfort of assurance, which blessed assurance always brings release from the pain of uncertainty with its wavering and instability.

　True though it be that the best teaching is the good example (Latin, *ex* 'out of', and *sample* denoting a representative portion of the whole; hence, a part drawn out of the whole of the teacher's life and consciousness), vacuous individuals, devoid of a spirit of justice or fairness, whether by ignorance or carelessness, often excuse their own shortcomings by finding fault with the teachers of Truth, thereby impugning their service.

Beloved ladies and gentlemen who would teach Truth, I am certain none of you intend to be anything but the perfect example; yet until you have attained, you must either have the courage to do your best, knowing you have made a few mistakes, or else do nothing. Now, I think better of those who know they have made mistakes and yet dare to do their best than of those who fearfully hide their talents in a handkerchief, feeling that the law of God is too harsh or exacting and their own personal errors too gross.

Blessed teachers, do not expect any quarter from the misguided ones who would not summon the courage to go out and proclaim the love of God themselves yet have the rashness to decry the conduct of those who do even though they retain a few petty shortcomings. Let each one strive for the highest and the best. So shall freedom come more quickly to all!

All souls created by the same God were originally endowed with an equal portion of his power, his wisdom, and his love—no matter how far they have wandered from the moment of their cosmic birth.

Concerning offenses, the question has often been asked, "Shall I forgive my brother indefinitely for continuing wrongs against me?" When I spoke in Judaea and Galilee on this subject, my answer recorded in the Gospels was all-embracing, taking into account every situation—both

the sin of foreknowledge and the sin of ignorance. The timeless message "Forgive them,
Father, for they know not what they do"[2] and
"Forgive them even seventy times seven"[3] is
plainly uttered, and yet much understanding is
needed on the matter.

The best way to forgive others is first to
forgive oneself for all errors and then to expand
this forgiveness infinitely to all. Be sure to cover
every circumstance, make no exceptions. If God
be a flaming fire and all of his offspring divine
sparks, why should not one spark forgive
another, no matter how much the sacred fire
may have been misused?

True, one requires special wisdom in the
solving of certain problems—and, whereas forgiveness is in order, one ought to wisely avoid
exposing oneself unnecessarily to the dangers
inherent within human vanity. Yet love must
and will prevail when the Presence is wholly
relied upon.

Now, not everyone has or holds the same
balance of love, wisdom, and power. Some have
an excess of one and much lack of the others.
For example, if men lack wisdom, no matter
how much they may love, their well-intended
acts may seem to go amiss. If they lack power,
no matter how wise and loving they may be,
their good may not be far-reaching to the mark
or as effective as they would like it to be. If they
lack love, no matter how much wisdom and
power are manifesting, they may find that their

acts are oft aborted, their energies rendered partially or wholly useless to the great cosmic
purposes.

Find your balance, then, in a triangle of
perfection, a holy trinity which produces the
most intense action of all three within the heart
of man and the heart of creation. Here the great
wisdom of the discriminating Holy Christ Self
calls upon the mighty light rays of the Presence
to draw forth and focus the God-power which in
itself is invincible.

Here the all-loving heart of the Presence
seals the balanced flame of wisdom and power
in a penetrating sheath of divine love which can
never be requalified with human nonsense or
avarice. Free, then, from deceit, the threefold
flame represents, as beloved Morya so often
says, "a thrust for a purpose." (Let all who deny
purpose in creation take heed!)

Certainly, then, no cosmic teacher of Truth
should be unduly criticized. I do not say that
their fruits should fall far from the parent tree;
yet remember, it is easy to see in others the very
same qualities that are acting in one's own
world. Even when I manifested perfection, some
wise men (intellectually wise) and some quite
devout men (religiously devoted) saw me as
possessed with an evil spirit and profane. [4]

All who would teach men the Great Law of
God must even in this day be prepared to suffer
some misunderstanding and false accusation. [5]
If there is no cause to bring this to pass, the
sinister force will try to manufacture one and,

having so done, will begin to fabricate its chain of lies. If there be even the slightest cause, this unrighteous force (mentally aggressive and seething with malice) proceeds to distort and twist facts by gossip so as to disturb as many people as possible and thus prevent the saints from carrying on their great mission and service of love to Life.

Take heart and be diligent! Be wise to this deception—hold the faith. The life of the Light is, above all, transcendent and worthy of any suffering or inconvenience for the sake of my name, I AM.

After two thousand years of Christianity, the clamor and confusion centering around "What must I do to be saved?"[6] still rages, and seekers for more light often become so engrossed in the search that the goal itself is lost sight of.

Beloved ones, your ascension is your goal! It is that simple. If all the energy you have ever misqualified by misusing Life's precious substance is requalified and transmuted by the violet fire of freedom's love and by forgiveness in action, what then can prevent your ascension or the attainment of your goal? Yet your own Presence alone knows the day and the hour when it shall occur.

How can any action take place except the Great Law be aware of it? The visible and invisible universe is the Body of God, and surely he in all his wisdom and intelligence is ever aware of every transaction, no matter how insignificant it may seem.

Did I not say, "The very hairs of your head are all numbered"? Did I not declare that not even a sparrow falls to the ground without the awareness of God the Father (the I AM Presence)?[7] Hence, all so-called accidents are, without exception, actions of the law of cause and effect. And this is the law of karma, which one day you will come to understand as the instrument of your freedom from bondage.

Those who would do as we did and attain their own cosmic victory must be willing to govern Nature and themselves by the power of the Godhead. (*Govern: G* equals God, *over* signifies dominion, *n* denotes Nature; hence, *God-over-Nature.* Thus, the sons of man are commanded by God to *govern* by taking dominion in the earth through the light rays from the Presence, according to natural law.) This includes taking God-control over the action of causes (and causation) in your life in order to achieve the desired effects. The cause of your ascension is the victory of your Presence called into action *by you* in all your affairs!

Now, if individuals feel they can best instruct the Presence in how to govern their affairs, I am certain that the Presence will carry out their instructions as a 'blind action' of the Law; yet the individual, not the Presence, will be responsible for causes set in motion by this misuse of God's power producing the effects of human ignorance. This abuse of the Law and the Divine Decree is the cause of all trouble and confusion yet remaining in the world today.

And never in all eternity shall the children of God change for the best and return to the fold until they prove the Law for themselves by giving all power and dominion to the Presence of God. The Father automatically gives full illumination to every mind and heart just as swiftly as he is called into action to perform his perfect work and will.

This is how I attained my own victory. I knew that I came forth from God and that I must return to him. I perceived that the surest way to do so was the I AM way; hence, I declared: "I AM in the Father and the Father is in me. He that hath seen me hath seen the Father. The words that I speak unto you I speak not of myself: but the Father that dwelleth in me, he doeth the works."[8] This is the true and only formula for the exemplar who would demonstrate his dominion over "these things" of the earth.

Surely, the Great White Brotherhood needs teachers who can be good examples, yet even the best examples do not of necessity draw men to the divine course. For the element of free will comes into play, and some do not even respond to miracles. However, if the Ascended Masters and the cosmic hierarchy were to await the full manifestation of absolute perfection before sending out teachers to proclaim the truth of God's light and love, mankind might have to wait a long time to be free!

I am grateful, therefore, for those who are both honest and humble enough to admit to mistakes, yet zealous and hardy enough to submit to human criticism by going forth to do the best they can to serve in the Father's vineyard. Many of those who suffer the most severe criticism shall go further to attain their victory than man may think.

Their heart's right motive and prayerful attitude, seen and heard at higher levels, will in due course attract a higher state of perfection until at last they attain the cosmic consciousness of the immortals—though their critics remain sidetracked and bound in limitation and self-created confusion. Yet we would have none thus fail. Let all be vigilant!

Ours is a universal service of love to the whole earth. The Christ message is alive! The search for peace on earth, good will (God's will) toward men[9] goes on in all exalted pursuits— both religious and secular. The goal of universal brotherhood has even today mightily invaded the very political framework of society.

I am once again standing in the temple (of God's high estate and purpose) to reinforce the bulwarks of freedom's holy light against every godless communistic scheme, whether altruistic-appearing or not. The hearts and minds of men, women, and children have unfortunately become a battleground where the media of press, television and radio, and the personality cult seek to capture and indoctrinate the people of the earth with biased concepts and human nonsense, served up as a gargantuan commercial cocktail—heady, high-minded, deceitful, and full of greed.

Once again I, Jesus, take the scourge in hand to purify the people of the earth so that as heaven's instruments they will unite to seize the pen and spiritual sword (even the two-edged sword [10] which involves personal victory) while they continue also to fight in the worldwide conflict for the triumph of Good over Evil.

Only by taking heroic measures to counter-act the apathy and godlessness of the present day can my disciples give to my message and mission of two thousand years ago a new and effective voice in this hour.

Let them win the hearts of today's men and women for the radiant personal love of God, their own Mighty I AM Presence.

Let them win for the worldwide dawn of peace in the golden age, when goodwill shall blaze forth through all hearts from the magnif-icent cosmic heart of God—who even now loves the whole earth as one great Son (Sun)! So *shall* it be!

With the entire hosts of heaven, I AM beckoning my Christ-filled soldiers *Onward!*

Jesus the Christ

Corona Class Lesson   10

Heart

"Ye Are the Light of the World"

Beloved Who Would Form the
        Diamond Heart of Mary and Morya—
    The reverberations of the bells whose sweet and solemn tones gently stir the hearts of men continue to ring out a higher message of Love's own voice calling the sons of men to an eternal Angelus. And God's peace settles over cities, towns, and villages covering all with a gleaming mantle of splendid and holy light whose weaving waxes stronger with each passing year unto that perfect day when the perfection of Christ shall rule in every human heart.

    This can be a reality when trust in God (as freedom's motto states, "In God We Trust") becomes the watchword of every man and woman who will firmly, wisely, lovingly reach out through the dense fog of human calamities toward the peace of spiritual calm. When called into action, this calm produces hallowed feelings of unity and the sweet whisper of Life's ever-new opportunities.

Beloved ones, peace and love are presently evasive to humanity, whose continuous generation of turbulence has delayed their perfection both personally and on a planetary scale. When these qualities reign in the heart, the beauty of human teamwork in loving cooperation with God will make men their own architects in the golden age.

To the end of maintaining world peace and love, I have spent countless hours before the magnificent organ in my home here at Shigatse, in Tibet, consciously uniting the love of my own heart with that omnipresent love of God which blazes through the entire cosmos and is the life-energy of every star in the vast starry sea of sky.

Drawing this universal energy into my own being in almost infinite quantities, I have created music of a sublime character, full of healing love rays, which magnetizes myriad lovely angel devas who travel joyfully on wings of song with my music. Seated at my organ, I consciously direct and radiate (broadcast) through my heart tender, uplifting and powerfully transforming strains to all who are bowed down with depression, sorrow, pain, and every enclosing material force.

As you well know, these conditions shut out the Christ Light and prevent God's healing peace from manifesting for my many little brothers—from those with weary, dust-covered frames to those anointed with sweet oils and such fragrant perfume as is reminiscent of the first Christmas with our special gifts of gold, frankincense, and myrrh. [1]

Many dear hearts have wished one another a merry Christmas while others have thought about the need for an eternal Christmas which abides through the whole year. Know, blessed ones, that the Christ Mass, the tangible focus of invisible yet spiritual Light, or Christos, is ever within all men. As beloved John the apostle declared, "This is the Light which lighteth every man that cometh into the world." Hence, this Light of great magnitude who is the Christ of every man shall one day be to all people the salvation of the earth. [2]

Every day increasing numbers of God's followers are beginning to understand his greater plan for them and can therefore more readily fathom the so-called mysteries of Christianity and other world religions. Thus, religious study is emerging from a mode of relative obscurity (full of mystery to many) to one of almost popular appeal among those willing to face the reality that tradition is no substitute for Truth and that general acceptance is not either.

The simple yet beautiful idea of each one's heart as a crèche (cradle) into which the tiny Holy Christ Flame descends to abide and guide (as the "hidden man of the Heart," [3] i.e., the hidden *man*-ifestation of God) further reveals that the heart of man has focused within it God's Life on the human level (in the physical octave), making it truly a Holy Grail constantly brimming with the effulgence of divine love. When this Love is set free to flow unhampered by human thoughts and feelings, it will wash away every error, correct every adverse condition, and act with a healing resurgence of unlimited compassion.

Today some correctly perceive the role of beloved Jesus as the drama of every man's quest for Godhood. If people accept the negative idea that God requires human or divine sacrifice as a propitiation for world sin (karma)—whether they see the crucifixion as a vicarious atonement, retroactive, for their sins committed after the fact or they accept the idea that they, too, must undergo the agony of Gethsemane and Calvary—they ought to be compelled by the logic of their belief system to accept vicariously every positive expression of the Christ as well.

And thus, they ought rightly to prefer above all to ponder these words—"Thou art my beloved Son; this day have I begotten thee"[4]—as also applicable to themselves and to their reality as sons of God.

I am certain that when men fully enter into the kingdom (consciousness) of God, they no longer have tears or a sorrowful heart but dwell continually in a state of listening grace where the positive love of the Holy Spirit for all creation is the only music heard in the heart or mind. In this great spiritual sensing, death is swallowed up in victory.[5] On such as these does the complete meaning of *God* as synonymous with *Good* dawn as reality.

In lesson 8, I pointed out the dangers of selfish overconcern which keeps people bound to a round of self-condemnation. Blinded by pre-occupation with self in any form, talent goes unused for God's glory while people ride the human merry-go-round, and opportunity for true God Self-realization is denied its rightful place. Wrapped in a napkin of selfish exclusive-ness, those yielding to the impulses of self-love frequently deny themselves true freedom and justice.

Determining to have their own way apart from God's, they carve out a life of idolatry and pleasure, oblivious of the planetary needs or the fields white to the harvest[6] of countless millions awaiting our message, praying for the chance to learn more of Truth and the cosmic purposes of Almighty God.

The greatest measure of spiritual and—I can rightly say—even material security is vouch-safed to those who turn to serve the Light; for one day, when least expected and wholly unan-nounced, all will see in fact that the Light is actually serving them!

Sometimes people unknowingly forsake the guidance, temporarily, of their own God Presence I AM, hoping to find in some other phase of life's complex experiences and educational offerings the assistance they require to overcome their problems and get ahead. I say in absolute God Truth, your own God Presence is the fullness of all that you desire. And should you weary of hearing this, your own Christ-intelligence will try to reach you and lovingly say, "Be still, and know that I AM God."[7]

You see, your Presence wants to help you to do all things well. Therefore it directs you through your Christ Self to silence mere human qualities and to develop that vital quality of listening grace where, in love's meditation upon God, you diligently seek to know and be his will and wisdom in action. Precious ones, if you would overcome as the saints have done, not vain effort or undue strain but the practice of a gentle submission is the requirement whereby you welcome the gift of heavenly virtue—responding always to the heavenly constraint of the gentle Presence, whose guidance is unfailing when your desire for Truth is uncompromising.

Everyone persisting in selfish error stands out in bas-relief, as did Lot's wife (who became a pillar of salt), as an example of misplaced human attention. Instead, lift up your eyes to the hills, as the people Israel have chanted for thousands of years: "I will lift up mine eyes unto the hills, from whence cometh my help. My help cometh from the LORD . . . the I AM THAT I AM, who is my Light, my Beloved, my I AM Presence"[8]—never late and never in short measure, regardless of human concepts; for the Divine Helper is an agent of cosmic law and must perforce answer the all-compelling call of souls in distress.

Beloved Morya and other Masters of the Great White Brotherhood are desirous of creating a worldwide spiritual unity through the activity of The Summit Lighthouse. Naturally, the opposition will try to defeat our very purpose, which is all for the Light. However, *the Light of God shall not fail!* (That is why Micah, the angel of the LORD, the blessed Angel of Unity, recently stood tangibly on the platform of the Washington National Cathedral.)

Therefore, the truehearted—our blessed, most determined chelas—will readily understand the need for loyalty to a cause and to a purpose. Likewise they will understand with clear intentions, a correct perspective, and common sense the need for group decrees for the protection of the fulfillment of this goal.

The Darjeeling Council is sponsoring the activity of The Summit Lighthouse to be a great clearinghouse of light, a haven of refuge in future days for all who love the Christ Light and are able to see the need for such a central agency holding within its framework the dedicated services and purity of the Order of the Diamond Heart. You see, a heart is universally needed as a focus through which to channel energy to any body or group effort. This is true from the Great Central Sun down to the centrosome of a cell or the nucleus of an atom.

Therefore, you will understand why the light rays of this diamond heart of planetary dimensions are to be under the direction of the blessed Mother Mary and the Chohan of the First Ray, El Morya, whose purpose it is to bring about as speedily as possible the edicts of those angels who under divine guidance long ago chorused, "Glory to God in the highest, and on earth peace, good will toward men."[9]

Those who understand the need for an organization to serve as a framework or structure through which the Ascended Masters and their chelas can function, those who can also understand that some organizations once under our guidance have suffered from the hardening of their spiritual arteries and are no longer entirely useful to us, will then lovingly and joyously give their obedience to the Light and will offer themselves to be the backbone, the heart, and the radiance of our purpose to externalize the Christ Light and to teach all peoples how to do likewise—especially those who seek and want the whole Truth. Thus, our diamond heart will be God-chosen and it shall manifest to the benefit of all.

Teachers who will honor the Christ 365 days a year will by and by see shining down the avenue of the years a blazing sun of Love's wisdom radiating large and beautiful through the trees of life. True-blue chelas of the will of God who have taken up the path of the Second Ray of Illumination in order to fill the urgent need of the hour to be teachers of Jesus' calling unto the lost sheep of the house of Israel[10] and Judah will be personally crowned with the rays of the Corona Class.

When our lessons are meditated upon by you (from the first through the forty-eighth), they will give you such insight and in-depth understanding of the path of individual

Christhood as The White Lodge* deems essential to your victory in this life and to the opening of heaven's door thereby unto the multitudes through the blessed Summit Lighthouse.

Taking the completed work as a manual in hand for study and reference as you first try on, then wear with dignity and compassion the mantle of the ministering servant, you will have a solid foundation of knowledge and a cornerstone of justice to assist you to be both wise and effective in helping us guide and direct the spiritual affairs of God's children. By your conscious cooperation with us, we shall together lead all children of God to greater planes of advancement, soul progress, and personal development free of the pitfalls of the past.

With the holy Christmas season drawing nigh as this is being written, I trust you will recall that we have often referred to your calling amongst God's people. You are indeed called to represent the ascended host and the Darjeeling Council to the many; and therefore, you ought to apply to El Morya for training that you might perform this service in wisdom's way. Most men are no more familiar with us than they are with the angels! With all due charity, teach them the way of the Ascended Masters.

Blessed ones, through your Holy Christ Self (by ample adoration poured out to the Beloved as "the only begotten of God,"[11] i.e., the only part of you created solely by God, in contrast to your human consciousness), you ought to seek diligently to externalize the treasures of Higher

*synonym for the Great White Brotherhood

Consciousness upon earth, knowing that you will thereby draw forth the identical benedictions and ministrations of the angels as blessed Jesus did and as every Ascended Master has done in his final embodiment on earth.

Then men will see your good works; [12] for the light of your aura glowing in strength like Jesus' aura will draw to itself, by the power and radiance of God's love poured out without limit upon the whole cosmos, those spiritual realities which took tangible form long ago one wondrous night in Bethlehem of Judaea, and which today—this day—await rebirth in you!

O angels of God, our holy brothers, bless all children of the Light and especially our readers. Bless all seekers for Truth and especially all doers of Good who shall bring Peace to this loving earth.

I AM your friend and celestial musician,
My melodies are unceasingly yours to command—

Kuthumi

Corona Class Lesson 11

Innocence

"God Sent Not His Son to Condemn..."

To My Own Who Seek the Powers
    of the Holy Ghost Lawfully—
    An outlook to the future with the expectancy of a better tomorrow is the only hope that many people have. This is all well and good, providing their future does not manifest, through carelessness in the present, as a mere mirage on life's desert.

I am reminding all of the obligation Love keeps to the present through the vibratory action of your own God Presence. Your beloved I AM Presence is flooding your world daily—yea, even hourly—with a beautiful stream of God's consciousness blazing into your world through the silver cord which connects you with your own Divine Self, conveying to your heart and sacred centers (chakras) manifold blessings of the Light.

Blessed ones, today is yesterday's future. It is already here. You do not have to wait for it. This is Life—eternally present.

When I was a small boy playing and working in the carpenter shop at Nazareth, like many of the children in the neighborhood, I developed a real affection for the tools and equipment we used. I learned to take sweet delight in fashioning various objects suitable as gifts or household articles for the use of my dear mother or others in the spiritual community. By applying myself to carving wood or constructing purposeful items, I became quite skillful in the trade.

The point I would make is that no matter how engrossed I was in the action of mind and hands, how delighted my eye with the creation unfolding before me, I was always able to listen and to hear the hum of the universe and my heavenly Father's heartbeat, to feel the waves of his love sweeping into my being and then flooding back on the return current like the ebb and flow of the tide.

Much later, when the woman who needed healing and had searched everywhere for it without success touched the outer hem of my garment, my childhood meditation stood me in good stead; for I felt the instantaneous response to this pull on my life in the surge of God's consciousness which, like a charge of electricity, flowed from the heart center of my being into hers to give her immediate relief and complete healing. [1]

You see, the sensitivity of my soul was the means to keep me in tune with the Father's heart and to build up the charge of his great love and power in my body and sacred centers. So must all do who would be healers and comforters to

Life—keep sensitive to God and oblivious to human hurt, and hold a sense of God's omnipresence as the only reality, when all around are concerned with the baubles and glitter of mere mortal intelligence, popular opinions, and human feelings that wax hot and cold.

The message of the Holy Christ Self does not bespeak condemnation, blessed ones. If sometimes you read into our messages what may seem to be a criticism of human qualities, bear in mind that we are essaying to develop in you Christ-discrimination whereby you can learn to choose the best and highest alternative, not by trial and error but by attunement with the will of God. You must be God-taught what is right and wrong in order to claim victoriously as God's children your rightful heritage—a culture of the Spirit where you can make right choices because you have learned to distinguish between what is constructive and what is destructive to your divine plan, what is helpful to the soul's re-creative process and what is distressful and detrimental to the immediate or future endeavor.

None really know what the meaning of Pandora's box is until they see that all pain and sorrow were released upon mankind when people began to regard life as an admixture of good and evil.

Holy innocence, dear hearts, was never the state of being naïve or gullible; otherwise, God himself would be considered to be so. Rather, holy innocence is and always will be the outpicturing of the Christ Mind in the soul's search for the fullest expansion of the infinite Mind of God. This is the rapture of real Being! Innocence is the *inner sense* of the little child, one with the Spirit of God.

In order to accomplish the 'outpicturing' of the Christ Mind, one must translate the stream of messages from the infinite Mind and Heart of God into practical action in one's daily affairs. This requires attunement—the inner sense of right and wrong, i.e., 'innocence'—and discrimination, another faculty of innocence which is the wisdom to choose by the inner standard of the Christos: "This, not that."

If you will assiduously exercise attunement with your I AM Presence and discrimination through your Christ Self, you will increase your inner sense of the divine will as well as your discernment of what is right or wrong for you as you follow the path of the ministering servant.

The goal of your striving, blessed heart, is that the song of the Holy Spirit proclaim its message of goodness and ever-unfolding joy to the world through your own sacred labor, so that through your effort many may be freed from the power of misqualified energy and from a distorted viewpoint of everything and everybody— much of which has been brought about through dabbling in the shadowed forces of psychic phenomena and the introversions of psychoanalysis without benefit of Ascended Master guidance.

Those who have entered the heart of Christ and been assumed unto the I AM Presence through self-identification with that God Self in the ritual of the ascension—we who are the *Ascended Masters*—are the most qualified teachers available to illumine the mind and heart of those whose goal is reunion with God and who are determined to achieve it by attunement and discrimination applied to the path of Love.

Blessed ones, holy innocence is that state of listening grace referred to by my magnificent colleague Kuthumi in his last release. It is a state to which men are happy to return even as they are happy to be free of their outworn earthly perspective of persons, places, conditions, and things. This freedom is true holy innocence and the pure quality of God's own mind.

This state cannot be compared to that of an ostrich with its head in the sand or a condition of naïveté; but if it could, then I should hope that more people would become so! You see, I well know of the existence of scribes, hypocrites, and Pharisees—having had my share of dealing with them through the centuries—whose malice aforethought was surely the antithesis of holy innocence. They would have made far less karma had they been more naïve than evil. But such was not the case.

Blessed ones, all of this yet remains in the human octave; therefore I must remind you again that when you are busybodying, discussing people from the critical human viewpoint, analyzing their motives and conduct from some superior chair,[2] predicting what they will or will not do under a given set of circumstances, deploring their mistakes, et cetera, you are certainly not very able to find time to be really happy!

If, however, you do find happiness in deprecating others, I tell you quite frankly, it is but a carrion appetite which mankind develop through gossip momentums and by going against nature in lusting after exotic or occult satisfactions which are far from the Christlike path.

The nature of God's Spirit, of the angelic hosts and the Ascended Masters and cosmic beings, is the true image and inner pattern in which every living soul embodied upon earth was originally created. This lovely image is your own God Self and, as your God Self, it is the most powerful magnet to raise you to the plane of your Real Self and to draw you toward heaven's exalted purposes which can be fulfilled on earth right now, today, as the most transcendent goal of all eternity.

I know that the whole world is aware of the so-called shadow of death, yet most all seem to find comfort in the Psalm of David, "Yea, though I walk through the valley of the shadow of death, I will fear no evil: for Thou art with me." [3] Blessed ones, to live daily in the Thou-art-with-me consciousness is to live in the certain knowledge that your own Mighty I AM Presence is walking right within you and helping you to do the perfect thing always.

Oh, I know the human inclination well. It wants you to be angry, to say sharp things, to be exalted because of the virtue you have already externalized or the skills you have developed— yes, and for many other subtle reasons which make people strut like peacocks with their human pride! And then later, by the law of the circle, they meet face to face the energy they have so misqualified. This is the round of human karma from which I AM able to deliver you.

How many of my readers and auditors can see that this message is for you today? How many of you can see that it is not intended merely to tickle your ears or cause you to have a false sense of security so that you will not know your own God Presence when he cometh? The Holy Christ Self is the bridegroom indeed, and the marriage feast is the communion by the Sacred Heart with all similarly exalted hearts of Light. [4]

The imminence of that hour, which is portrayed in my parable of the five wise and five foolish virgins, [5] is intended to keep people alert to initiation and awake through the inner sense of Life, so as to watch with their own Holy Christ Self every hour. It is our intent that through the Corona Class Lessons you will learn to build two ways: one, through creating good karma by doing good works; the other, by keeping the heart flame blazing through steadfast attunement with, and dynamic decrees to, the great God Source, our beloved Father.

By humility and steadfastness of purpose, through thinking faith, hope, love, and God (Good), you will soon begin to outpicture in greater measure the things of the Spirit upon which your heart meditates and dwells. You will not long remain a helpless introvert dwelling in a world withdrawn from reality; neither will you be a callous, selfish extrovert dwelling in the surface foam of life. Instead, you will be balanced, capable of reaching up mind and heart to God and yet with love and tenderness able to reach down with helping hands, free of pride, to your brothers and sisters yet in a state of bondage.

Herein lies the failure of most religious activities in the present age. The sobering message from my blessed mother, Mary, which was released at Fátima (to be opened in 1960 in Rome), concerning the failure of Christianity to espouse the motto "I AM my brother's keeper," was her response to that condemnation heaped upon condemnation by those corrupt ones in Church and State who walked in shadow. And, to a far less degree, it was her rebuke to the credulous who succumbed to the tactics of the brothers of the shadow due to their lack of holy innocence.[6] For holy innocence is the natural immunization of believers against the wiles of serpents who have invaded the religious societies of the world.

Religion in some quarters has become an accomplishment of pride wherein some men look coldly upon others as fallen ones and, like the Pharisees of old, call out in prayer, "God, I thank thee that I am not as other men!"[7]

The need, then, for the innocence of noncondemnation[8] is so apparent and almost pitiful that I hope many who do not have it will be led into acquiring the true and right perspective which I gave to my disciples, quoted in the scriptures as "The Son of man is not come to destroy men's lives, but to save them."[9]

All condemnation is of the destroyer and not of me or my own. It is anti-Christ in that it moves against the delicate developing soul and its internalization of the Christ consciousness through its native holy innocence. The Satanic source of condemnation is not innocent but malicious in its murderous intent, cunning to destroy hope, honest effort, and the zeal to overcome one's shortcomings on the road to self-perfection.

Ministering servants, I send you forth in the name of God as Sons of Light to deliver my children from the wiles of Serpent; therefore remember your calling, "for God sent not his Son into the world to condemn the world; but that the world through him might be saved."[10]

It has often been said that the greatest men are the most humble, that the best contacts are to be had not with minor officials, puffed up in self-importance, but with the highest representatives of a company or government, who have a broader world view. This has often proven true. Thus, be ever magnanimous and shun rigidity and intolerance.

Teach men the way of the Christ so that through communion with the Holy Spirit they may go out and acquire the power to heal, the power to open the blinded eyes, the power to cast out demons of misqualified energy (which have returned to their sender and bound him), the power to command the elements and the forces of Nature, and, above all, the power to ascend while affirming to all men, even as I did: Lo, I AM with you alway, even unto the end of the (Piscean) age (the age when your karma shall be outplayed and fully balanced if you will it so)![11]

O beloved ones, all mysteries shall be revealed unto the humble who are truly meek, who fear not, knowing they shall inherit not only the earth[12] but also the kingdom of spiritual power to exercise dominion over all the creation. You see, when the Father calls, "Come up higher"; when the Father beholds your true inner compassion, your longing which is only for God-victory over human causes and effects; when the Father sees the vital, absolutely determined intent of your heart to be one with your Holy Christ Self and Mighty God Presence I AM, then I do not think it shall be long in coming! I know it was not for me.

Whom God loveth he sometimes chasteneth,[13] but he will never allow or give you to bear more than you are able. By preserving everlasting glory through serving God's name I AM, you yourself will find the hidden meaning of the words of my own beloved Teacher: "He who loseth himself (the life of the lesser self) for my sake shall find himself (the Life of his Higher Self) again."

Did I not once declare that he who seeks to save his life shall lose it, but he that loseth his life for my sake (letting go of, i.e., 'loosing', the human tendencies for the sake of the Light) shall find his true Life again (in the renewing of spiritual momentums)? [14] This meaning should now become clear to all.

The Life men claim by free will, the Life they selfishly grasp and hold on to with clenched fists, is already lost through misqualification. The Life which the personal consciousness of each one releases and sets free to obey the loving fiats of his own blessed God Self shall return to the giver—the blessed one who has learned at last the first principle and lesson of God:

It is more blessed to give than to receive. [15]

These have understood the character of our Father who art in heaven. Such I call "brother." Together let us scale the stars, God's radiant orbs of twinkling hope, love, and Life—his many mansions! [16]

Thank you for your attention upon my words. It has enabled me to give you my Christmas gift—the gift of my own Self...

For lo, I AM with you always.

Your Counsellor and Prince of Peace,

Jesus the Christ

Corona Class Lesson 12

Recognition

"My Kingdom Is Not of This World"

Blessed Ones Growing Up
        to Be King of Your Own Domain —
    What is the real wonder of you? Have you
ever thought about the heavenly gift of individual identity that you have been given which
makes it possible for you to choose to be either a
little or a big brother to all Life?
    Many have said, "If I were king..." Specu-
lating in this wise, people think that they could
run the universe better, or at least that they
would run it differently, if they were king — not
realizing that they are already king of their own
world, possessing, as they do, the potential to
master the Father's gift of Life and individual
identity.
    The gift of absolute dominion belongs to
men and women with the faith, the will, and the
wisdom to accept and externalize this God-given
right — this choice to individualize the God flame

uniquely, to shape one's destiny according to Life's profound purpose.

Those who govern themselves well, managing their resources of time, space, and energy as sands in the hourglass—particles of light descending the crystal cord—are more fitted to rule a kingdom than those who do not; likewise, those who do not attempt to control the happenings of their personal worlds are surely unfit to govern the universe. These remain among the learners, no matter how much they may think they are qualified to show others how to live.

Nevertheless, growing up into the Christ-estate—once the soul determines to change for the better and organize the endeavor—need not be a long process; for some saints have achieved this (not unaided) almost overnight. Truly, self-mastery is the intended unfoldment of every man's original God-given endowment.

A sense of limitation, fear of many different things, depressions of the mind and emotions as well as every unhappiness arise solely because the lifeline of cosmic supply guaranteeing light, illumination, abundance, and love to all is pinched, whether by ignorance of the Law or by selfishness. Seeking their own gain, the short-sighted choke off the material or spiritual supply of others, sometimes knowingly (selfishly) and at times unknowingly (ignorantly), and in the process (by the law of karma) clamp their own arteries.

Circulation, blessed ones, originates in the heart of God and is designed to provide for the unceasing flow of light through the universal body—the entire matter cosmos. The Great White Brotherhood has long held the tenet of *Unity* as expressing in one word the essential quality of God, teaching Oneness as the identifying quality of Be-ness: "I AM the eternal Source of all Good and your unfailing supply of every good thing."

The wonder of the Christ message—which caused the morning Stars to sing together and all the Sons of God to shout for joy, [1] while the angelic hosts rang out their glorias, touching the hearts of shepherds and blazing from the East in the nova of Bethlehem drawing the Wise Men from afar [2]—was wholly its universality!

Here mere drops of hope became streams, and streams of hope swelled into mighty rivers, and rivers carried men's souls into one great ocean of an infinite parental care. That "God is Love" was believed when Christ was born. Hope was alive in the beating hearts of mortals and the cup of Love ran over; they danced for joy and piped their songs of delight across the hills and valleys of Judaea.

The knowledge that all men can be king— and that the only "if" is the one which humans accept or create for themselves—taught to the present day by the true shepherds of the people, gives to all an untarnished hope which we of the Ascended Masters' realm have already realized (outpictured in the physical), following in the footsteps of the Master Jesus to achieve our own ascension in the Light.

That the consummate Christ-intelligence within you has already begun the process of maturation is a sign of hope for the appearing of the full identity of your God Self in the flesh. Remember, some men are yet in the infant stage, others are in spiritual boy or girlhood, while still others face with equanimity the multitudes' fickle cries of a joyful "Hosanna!" (acceptance) or an angry "Away with him!" (rejection).[3] Bear, then, with the evolving spirit of man; so shall all receive help as the need be. Be kindly, be tolerant.

God has given to all, whether they are aware of it or not, a most precious gift of himself: eternal Light. The Light seems brightest in contrast with the deepening darkness; and at the Mithraic time of the year, at winter solstice, men celebrate with joy and feelings of peace the coming of the greater Light.

Beloved ones, recognition is the key! Recognition chorused by the Sons of the morning, echoing over the fields in the harmonized rapture of the angels. Recognition nestled peacefully in Mother Mary's heart to be long pondered; recognition steady as a rock in the strong arm of Joseph.

Let all learn recognition of God's gift. Yes, it is more blessed to be God and give than to be man and receive. Yet, as God receives the precious gift of man's love sent to him in boundless awareness of the gifts he has already given, God himself becomes the recipient and all creation receives the greater blessing.

In this shining circle of Light's unity drawn around all people of goodwill on earth, the Christ in all is fairest!

Humbly, I AM

Kuthumi

Mission

"A Priest Forever after the Order of Melchizedek"

Blessed Disciples of Today Who Recognize
          the Mission for What It Truly Is—
The significance of the journey is never found in the transient joys of scenery or pleasant companionship along the way, enjoyable though these may be. The real meaning lies in the defined goal whose very process, self-realized at journey's end, assists all Life in climbing cycles' infinite stairs.

The mission of every life is twofold. First there is the universal purpose in which God intends all his creation to share; then there is the unique contribution of each lifestream based on those special inner qualities which only the individual can give.

Blessed are the lovely pine, spruce, and evergreen trees which men take into their homes to inspire them with remembrance this holy season. I am ever and always with you, and to draw very near to me you have but to draw close, by recognition, to the Christ flame within you which is the animating principle of your life.

As the highest mountains are not scaled by one leap but by many well-placed footsteps of small victories and great, so in your patience possess ye your souls. [4] Place your feet wisely on the rock as you also pray—looking neither downward nor backwards but fixing your gaze upon the summit heights—and you shall see that the "corona of hope" is in all, externalizing and becoming step by step the nimbus of the Son of God, the radiance around the head of a Christ in action.

To our holy order of Sons of the Most High, priests of God with Melchizedek [5] and brothers of Light, I, Jesus, welcome all. Kneel to your own God Presence I AM, drinking daily into the communion of saints. For to this end were all borne by the Holy Spirit from realms of Light— that fair flowers though we may be or become upon earth, fairer still shall we be in the heart of the Father.

As your hearts now beat with his higher hope, maintain our communion spirit. Hold fast to the image and guidance sent to you daily by your own Holy Christ Self; then shall each day be for you a natal day of cosmic expansion into ever-new birth.

As you toil in our vineyard, you shall soon see that the thin veil now separating us is becoming more gossamer until in the victory of the golden age the glory of the Light shall bid welcome to the LORD with the beauty of a daily Christmas. You shall see that the stir within every heart shall be the holy hush of man's sunset as mere man—and a rising sun for all who love and adore as I do the divine image, the Christ of every man!

Lo, I AM your brother always,

Jesus the Christ

Transfiguration

trans·fig·u·ra·tion \ (ˌ)= ˌ= = ˈrāshən \ *n* -s [ME,
fr. MF, fr. L *transfiguration-, transfiguratio,*
fr. *transfiguratus* (past part. of *transfigurare* to
transfigure) + *-ion-, -io* -ion] **1 a :** an act,
process, or instance of changing or being
changed in form or appearance **:** METAMORPHOSIS
⟨the autumnal ~ had just begun —*New Yorker*⟩
⟨astonished people by becoming a society man . . .
a ~ —Norman Douglas⟩ **b :** an act, process,
or instance of undergoing an exalting, glorifying,
or spiritual change ⟨in poetry and art may be
seen the ~ of nature⟩ ⟨a new elevation of the
mind of man . . . in this ~ the arts have a noble
and vital part to play —Sir Winston Churchill⟩
2 *usu cap* **a :** a church feast observed in some
branches of the Christian church on August 6
in commemoration of the Transfiguration of
Jesus recorded in the New Testament **b :**
an artistic representation of the Transfiguration
trans·fig·ure \ tranzˈfigyə(r), traan-, -n(t)ˈsf-, ÷
-gə(r) \ *vt* [ME *transfiguren,* fr. L *transfigurare,* fr.
trans- + *figurare* to shape, fashion, form, fr.
figura figure] **1 :** to change the form or appearance of **:** TRANSFORM ⟨her face was *transfigured*
by uncontrollable passion —Arnold Bennett⟩
⟨his will has been *transfigured* by association
with the wills of others —B.N.Cardozo⟩ — often
used with *into* ⟨his . . . special gifts led him
to ~ the wasteland into a circus —C.J.Rolo⟩
⟨nationalism was *transfigured* into international-
ism —C.B.Forcey⟩ **2 :** EXALT, GLORIFY, SPIRITUALIZE
⟨the great cliffs and domes were *transfigured* in
the hazy golden air —John Muir †1914⟩ ⟨music
. . . will ~ plain meanings and clothe the verbal
substance with a kind of incandescence —
A.T.Davison⟩ ⟨the same sacrifice *transfigured* the
communicants who shared the mystery —Oscar
Handlin⟩ — often used with *into* ⟨her beautiful
face was *transfigured* into the ravishingly angelic
—Arnold Bennett⟩ ⟨the moment when good verse
. . . is *transfigured* into a thing that takes the
breath away —C.D.Lewis⟩ **syn** see TRANSFORM

Light

"God Is Light"

I AM the Resurrection and the Life! Yes, and
I AM also the preceding Transfiguration!

Blessed and Beloved Ones Who Love Light
    As Though You Were Adoring God—
      How right you are, for God is truly Light,[1]
and in him is no darkness at all![2]
      Now, I am certain that thoughtful men and
women will immediately recognize the difference between the uses of light in Nature and the
uses of spiritual light in man. I refer to the fact
that in Nature the outline of manifestation is
achieved by a little more shading here and a
little more light there, thus portraying on the
canvas of life scenes of heaven and earth
painted in a variety which is outpictured in
sunlight and shadow, green leaf and bright
marigold, and the marine blue of the deep—
white foam and cloud, eternal movement of sky
and sea.

Yet, blessed ones, this is a phenomenon entirely different from the vibrations of the Holy Spirit manifesting within and about man as the essence of God, the Mighty I AM Presence, in cosmic action. For in the perfection of God's light, there is no darkness whatsoever—no shading, no subtlety—only the pure radiance of the Most High.

Nature requires that atomic matter be clothed with various molecular patterns locking in vibratory levels which define every type and combination of material manifestation necessary to the evolution of a peculiar lifewave. You see, divine Law originally intended the creation to unfold in the physical octave that cosmic beauty which was outpictured in the Mind of God and given from God's own hand to the Silent Watcher* on behalf of child-man.

The reason the sons of God consider their God to be a flame or a universal fire (Moses identified our God as "a consuming fire"[3]) is that, whereas Nature exhibits vibratory changes by a light stimulus or force from without, the soul of the son of God has the potential to self-realize the pure God-power of the cosmic fires from within himself.

The creative fires are at the very core of being, and the ancient memory scored in electronic life is that the spirit of man was born out of the very sacred fires by which Elohim gave birth to cosmos. The sons of God simply cannot forget that they came forth from the Great Central Sun

*one at the Elohimic level who holds the immaculate concept out of the divine image for the whole of creation

to sow the fires of the Christic seed everywhere in the matter worlds—and to endow their Father's creation with the light of Life.

Because they are made of the same stuff, they know their Father is a consuming fire. Were they not essential fire beings, the sons of God would not have survived "all the fiery darts of the wicked"[4] (fallen angels' sendings of malice) to the present hour—nor could they have been successful co-creators with Elohim throughout their long trek through the galaxies. By divine direction, therefore, the son of God can draw around those inner fires of the heart that specific God-activity which his I AM Presence gave to the Silent Watcher to externalize for his lifestream alone, made wholly in the divine image.

In the immaculate purity of this perfect light and perfect image, the birthright of every soul born of God, there is no darkness whatsoever— nor any of the gradation required in the natural manifestations of the footstool kingdom.[5]

However, some of the 'gods' have wrested the secrets of creation to alter the inner nature of man (both his soul and his genes) to conform to an inverted pattern. Through his inharmonious habits of thought and feeling man became vulnerable to this treacherous violation of the nucleus of self. Therefore, because these gods were dishonorably motivated in their genetic enslavement of lesser endowed evolutions to a mechanistic control, when I was embodied as Jesus of Nazareth I spoke unto these manipulators of life, saying, "You are of your father the devil, and the lust of your father will ye carry out."[6] (This lust was for the Light of the Christ sealed in the blood of the children of Elohim and equally for the Light of Christic attainment radiating from the chakras of the sons of the Great I AM.)

I referred, then, to the abortions of cosmic principles by the godless, the deadly inversion of divine Law by the fallen ones who used the sacred gift of free will to turn God's purposes upside down at human levels and, with malice intended, created pain and sorrow for the children of God. By such devices, they added to their heavy burden a karma self-incurred by prior disobedience to the LORD God and to his subsequent Edenic judgments rendered upon the race through the Great Initiator, Lord Maitreya.

Contradicting and rebelling against the divine intent, Atlantean archdeceivers, as well as geneticists who had begun their synthetic imitations of the creation of Elohim in pre-Lemurian epochs, moved to subject mankind to the whims of their diabolical will.[7]

Transfiguration is the means devised by the Godhead to free man from (1) all manipulations and degrading changes intended to de-evolutionize the race and (2) all that is not in complete unity with the seed-essence of God himself and with the sacred fire of the Mighty I AM Presence.

Through the acceleration of the electronic fire rings of the Presence that occurs during the initiation of the transfiguration, individuals are

HEALING
through the
Transfiguration

"We Seek Healing by the
Power of the Flame of the Transfiguration"

*L*et us think upon the moment when Jesus took Peter, James, and John apart and was transfigured before them. That transfiguration was a prelude to his resurrection and his ascension. It was the celebration of the Light in his heart filling all his temple, even the very cells of his being. And so we contemplate the words of Jesus recorded in the Gospel of Mark:

> Verily I say unto you, That there be some of them that stand here which shall not taste of death till they have seen the kingdom of God come with power.

Mark wrote this as the first verse of the ninth chapter of his Gospel, preceding his description of the transfiguration.

It is a tremendous prophecy of the power of God's Light with us today. It means that we need not pass through the transition called death before we have received and internalized the kingdom of God—*with its power.*

God's *kingdom* is his consciousness. It is all-light, all-power, all-wisdom, and all-love. It is the Trinity in manifestation—yours to claim through the divine spark of your God-identity—the threefold flame in your heart. It is yours to exercise through the science of the spoken Word.

Taken from a Healing Service Conducted by Elizabeth Clare Prophet

*I believe Jesus demonstrated
the transfiguration to prepare his disciples to
undergo the same eventual transformation.*

When we invoke the transfiguring Light of God, it intensifies his kingdom within us and increases the magnitude of the divine spark, one day to become the full manifestation of our own Higher Consciousness dwelling in us bodily.

Beloved Jesus has taught us that each one must seek for and find the transfiguring Light. This begins with a meditation upon the Light, establishing our soul's contact with the Light. And a very profound oneness with God the Father, who is represented in this chart of your Real Self as the Mighty I AM Presence (the upper figure)—the Presence of God with you always.

The power of the I AM Presence to deliver this Light to you is stupendous. You have but to open the door of your heart and call for Light in the name of the Son, represented in your Holy Christ Self (the middle figure in the chart), to receive that power which is the power to transfigure.

I believe Jesus demonstrated the transfiguration to give his disciples a foretaste of the kingdom of God and to prepare them to undergo the same eventual transformation in their own souls and bodies. To accomplish this the Master transported them to a higher dimension of God's consciousness, parting the veil that they might see divine personages and a divine event not normally beheld by mortals.

The event is the initiation of Jesus by the Father in the presence of exalted witnesses—natives of both heaven and earth. It is a solemn, high and holy occasion that marks the major turning point on the path of his personal Christhood. Its message to his students carries the full weight of all his healings and miracles which are to come, as the Master said:

> He that believeth on me, the works that I do shall he do also; and greater works than these shall he do, because I go unto my Father.

One of "these works" is the transfiguration. From this moment on, accept the reality that God desires to see you transfigured—both daily and in the ultimate sense, when he shall initiate you personally as surely as he did Jesus.

> After six days Jesus taketh with him Peter and James and John and leadeth them up into an high mountain apart by themselves; and he was transfigured before them.

> And his raiment became shining, exceeding white as snow, so as no fuller on earth can white them. And there appeared unto them Elias [Elijah] with Moses, and they were talking with Jesus.

We see the testimony of heaven in the presence of the Ascended Master Elijah—who had already come (reincarnated) and gone (been beheaded) in the person of John the Baptist—and the Ascended Master Moses. The prophets, by their very real and living presence (they talked with Jesus), bore witness to the incarnating Son of God.

On each occasion when God gives you his glory, you can be certain that angels and Masters who have transcended the woes (karma) of time and space are confirming that Light and celebrating that moment with you, even as those on earth, your friends of Light, do also celebrate the joy of the divine union when your soul is singularly touched by the Spirit.

This marvelous account that we find in the New Testament gives to us an understanding of the term *Ascended Master*—one who has walked the earth and balanced the elements of karmic circumstance while demonstrating the power of God. Truly, Moses, as well as Elijah, comes under this dispensation. Both walked the earth, performed miracles, and were the instrument of God's word, his prophecy, and his law.

Many are asking, Where have they gone? We need not wonder any longer, for in the moment when Jesus takes the disciples into a high mountain—raising their consciousness—he opens the portals of heaven and reveals that there are those who ascended, such as Enoch, who "were taken up" to heaven prior to the ascension of our Lord. None other than Jesus himself, with the Father's approbation, ordained for us personally as Christ's disciples this communion of the saints. Yes, my beloved, the Father and the Son took the occasion of Jesus' transfiguration to reveal both the path and the teaching of the Ascended Masters.

These are the immortals. These are our elder brothers and our teachers. And we follow them by going and doing likewise—by expecting, as Jesus told us, that if we believe that the Light of

The Chart of Your Real Self

God is in them, when they are consummated in that Light, they with God, working through our own Higher Self, will perform the same works and greater works through us—heart, head, and hand—multiplying the Light and increasing it in every age and dispensation.

> Peter answered and said to Jesus, Master, it is good for us to be here. And let us make three tabernacles, one for thee and one for Moses and one for Elias.

Peter, to be sure, made known to Mark, who wrote down the Gospel, the very words he spoke on this occasion. We see that Peter wanted all to know of the presence of Moses and Elijah—so much so that he would have built a tabernacle (a tent sanctuary) to each of them. (I suppose with the same devotion that has prompted the saints to build cathedrals on the very site of the apparition of the Blessed Mother.) But before Jesus could answer him

> ...there was a cloud that overshadowed them. And a voice came out of the cloud, saying, This is my Son, the Beloved, hear ye him.*

The cloud is the cloud of Sinai, the same power of the I AM THAT I AM that was also upon the tabernacle throughout the forty-year journeying of the Hebrews in the wilderness. The cloud enfolds your I AM Presence as rings upon rings of light radiating the rainbow rays of God. (It is the causal body, the Shekinah glory surrounding the upper figure in the chart.)

Yea, the LORD's I AM Presence went before the children of Israel in a pillar of a cloud by day and of fire by night to give them Light—to lead the way. Thus shall your I AM Presence go before you without fail to direct, to illumine, to transfigure you. As the cloud enveloped Moses when he communed with God, so the cloud also envelops you when you are one with God in prayer and meditation. You may not see it, but it is there—the glory of God enfolding you in the presence of immortal love.

It was God the Father who spoke to the disciples on the Mount of Transfiguration—signifying his sponsorship of Jesus' mission. And the LORD spoke out of the cloud of the I AM THAT I AM,

*See The Jerusalem Bible, Mark 9:7; Matt. 17:5.

commanding the students to listen to their Teacher, the beloved Son of God incarnate. *This* then is the vital message of the transfiguration:

> This is the One I have chosen to bear the Christos, the anointing of my Light. He is the Exemplar of the path of your own Christhood. *Listen to him.*

Therefore, we, the disciples of Jesus Christ, must pursue that oneness with our Master whereby we learn to put on the cloak of his Christhood, learning as he teaches us through the Holy Spirit. For he told us that he would send us the Comforter who would teach us all things, bringing to our remembrance "whatsoever I have taught you."

This is a promise for today and for all ages to come. There is no time and space with our Lord. If it were not so, it would not be written "Jesus Christ, the same yesterday and today and forever!"

J esus *is* with us. There is *no* time and space. We are with him on the Mount of Transfiguration, in the hour of the crucifixion, and in his resurrection. We are with him when he heals by forgiving sin and by the command: "Rise, take up thy bed, and walk!"

This moment of the oneness of God the Father with the Son, with the disciples, and with the Ascended Masters will forever be unto us the understanding of the saints robed in white—verily the mystery of the Great White Brotherhood—Ascended Masters communing by divine ordination with their unascended disciples.

> Suddenly, when they had looked round about, they saw no man any more, save Jesus only with themselves.
> And as they came down from the mountain, he charged them that they should tell no man what things they had seen, till the Son of man were risen from the dead.

Here we are witnesses to what some might call a miracle. But what is the science of God if not to exalt our spirits, to elevate our souls, to raise the consciousness and the perception of our minds and hearts to see the glory of God as a foretaste of heaven? The message is clear: then and now all disciples following in the footsteps of the immortals must realize that the prophets and the saints were people like ourselves who had human frailties and burdens and fears, yet whom God called and empowered with his Spirit.

The prophets and the saints were people
like ourselves who had human frailties, yet God
called and empowered them with his Spirit.

And they became extraordinary men, carrying the burden of the LORD, which is the mantle of his Light. And they walked the earth and faced the same tests and tribulations we face—and greater. With Elijah's mantle, Elisha smote the river Jordan, and God parted the Red Sea through Moses, performing miraculous, yet spiritually scientific, works before Pharaoh and in the wilderness. All of these things God is able to do through the one or the many he may call and anoint and use unto his purposes.

You are here to receive the message that God can raise you up and use you at any moment of the day or of the night when there is a need. The Great Lights of history, East and West, had one thing in common: they prepared themselves to be instruments, they expected to be instruments, and they gave themselves to that calling.

It is difficult for God to find instruments when those instruments assign to him only a few hours here and there. When God needs you, he needs you—just as when you need him, you need him.

To be the available instrument is one of the great keys in the path of discipleship. The disciple is the disciplined one who is always ready—"Here am I, Lord, send me!" said Isaiah.

Thus, the one who is available and pursuing the mysteries of self-purification by the Holy Spirit is the one who may be chosen because *he* has chosen and elected to be God's servant. (But not necessarily, as in the case of Saul of Tarsus, persecutor of Christians, whom the Master Jesus confronted, converted, and raised up to be his mightiest apostle. When the record of Paul's past lives is made known, his extraordinary devotion to God, temporarily misdirected as Saul, will clearly reveal why our Lord chose him.)

As God's servants—all of us desiring to be better servants each day—we come together, then, to consider the mystery of healing—healing through the power of the transfiguration. And we know that Jesus said, "My Father worketh hitherto, and I work."

Jesus gave us our Father's Word in order that we might perform his Work. And therefore, we affirm the Word in order to increase the Light of the Presence of God with us. We would capture the Light of Sinai and the Light of the Mount of Transfiguration—because it is lawful—because both Father and Son ordained us to be disciples entering into this level of communion—because our Teachers have explicitly set the example.

Therefore, because our God has covenanted it, this evening we seek healing by the power of the transfiguration flame, blistering white—so white that when it fills your aura, even your garments will shine. Preparing the vessels to receive that Light, we call to the Holy Spirit for the violet transmuting flame of our God, whom Moses testified to be "a consuming fire."

The violet flame is the heart of Elijah 'healing' the barrel of meal and the cruse of oil and the widow's son. It is the God of Israel washing Naaman's leprosy, visiting it upon the dishonor of Gehazi—by the hand of the prophet.

The violet flame is the cup of Easter communion. It is the wine of forgiveness. It is Jesus breaking bread with us. The gift of the violet flame fulfills all of the promises of God in the Old and New Testament, 'erasing' the records of sin so that it shall come to pass that the LORD will say, "I will remember their sin no more."

As we prepare to make healing supplications to the Light and the Cloud and the Fire of the LORD upon the mountain, let us give the simple affirmation of God with us (Immanuel) in the "Heart, Head, and Hand Decrees." These dynamic devotions to God's I AM Presence in our lives are taught to us for our commemoration of Christ's mission by the Ascended Master El Morya (who was embodied as Saint Thomas More).

See yourself standing in a pillar of violet flame as shown surrounding the lower figure in the chart. Your heart, head, and hands are your instruments for the trinity of Life in expression. The work of heart, head, and hand in balance is intended to express the love of the Son in the heart, the wisdom of the Father in the head, and the power of the Holy Spirit in action through the work of your hands. Only when the triune manifestation of your heart, head, and hands, serving harmoniously as the vessel of your Higher Consciousness, are balanced in the flow of love, wisdom, and power can there be a corresponding balance in the

Delivering her message. Elizabeth Clare Prophet reveals techniques you can use to heal yourself and others through the transfiguring Light.

threefold flame. This balance is the means (and the spiritual magnet) whereby you ascend the golden spiral up the Mount of Transfiguration.

We call now to Almighty God to release the violet flame to purify and intensify the Light of the heart through this our decree. Let us offer it together:

> Violet fire, thou love divine,
> Blaze within this heart of mine!
> Thou art mercy forever true,
> Keep me always in tune with you. (3x)*

As you demonstrate the science of the spoken Word with devotion in this manner and as you visualize the power of the violet flame in your heart, you will magnetize it (draw it down) into this dimension from your I AM Presence. It is at the point of the 'third eye' (at the center of the brow) that your inner sight is focused. So you go within and you 'see' your physical heart enfolded in the violet flame—a veritable fire that is purple and violet and pink—blazing within.

By the Word of God—spoken and affirmed aloud by you—this spiritual fire penetrates your physical heart until you can actually feel the power of the Holy Spirit burning in your heart *chakra.*† This flame of the Holy Spirit melts, transmutes, and dissolves the fears and sorrows that come upon the heart, the burdens of the day, even hardness of heart and ancient records of the karma of past lives that stand between you and your full integration with your Real Self.

You have seen Catholic pictures of the sacred heart of Jesus or the immaculate heart of Mary depicted with a flame burning in the heart. That's the idea. The beautiful sacred fire that symbolizes the devotion and the holiness of the saints can be yours. Jesus and Mother Mary sanctified their hearts to reveal to you that you also have a divine spark in your heart which can be expanded to become a powerful force for God in the world—a pulsating threefold flame which God will use to transmit his healing love to others.

Therefore, let us take this mantra again with intense love and adoration of Christ and his Mother and the saints who have

---

*(3x) means repeat three times. Give the mantras three or four times or as many times as needed to draw down the Light of your I AM Presence to "cut through" any problem.

†Spiritual center. See "Integration: The Missing Dimension in Physical Fitness—An Exercise in the Toning of the Chakras" and "The 'Spinning Wheels' of the Yogi," *Heart: For the Coming Revolution in Higher Consciousness* (Autumn 1983), pp. 52–68. Write for your copy, $4.00 ppd.

gone before on the path of the sacred heart. See this flame clearly as we decree again. Practice the power of your imagination—which is the faculty of your third eye to create an image in the mind, or to duplicate a frame of reality on the screen of the mind—and simply 'see' the flame in action.

O Jesus, Mary, send thy violet flame!

> Violet fire, thou love divine,
> Blaze within this heart of mine!
> Thou art mercy forever true,
> Keep me always in tune with you. (9x)

Having established the violet flame within the heart by our decree, let us concentrate our visualization of its alchemy in the head. This is for the purification of three chakras (spiritual centers) which we have in this part of the body: (1) the power center, known as the throat chakra (you can feel it at the suprasternal notch at the base of the neck), focuses the gift of the creative Word and the power of the Word in speech; (2) the crown chakra at the center top of the head is the focus of wisdom and illumination; and (3) the third eye, which we have already mentioned. The 'exercise' and spiritual purification of these chakras is essential for the expansion of the consciousness of God in these vital centers.

Now we call forth the violet flame to blaze into the entire head area from the base of the neck upwards. We desire the violet flame to pass through the mind, to clear the debris of all concepts that are not clear, truthful, or founded on the science of Being. The apostle wrote, "Let that mind be in you which was also in Christ Jesus." The violet flame, as the agency of the Holy Spirit, is the means whereby your physical, mental, and spiritual vehicles can be restored to manifest the mind of God.

> I AM Light, thou Christ in me,
> Set my mind forever free;
> Violet fire, forever shine
> Deep within this mind of mine.
>
> God who gives my daily bread,
> With violet fire fill my head
> Till thy radiance heavenlike
> Makes my mind a mind of light. (4x)

The violet flame is the means whereby your physical, mental, and spiritual vehicles can be restored to manifest the mind of God.

Now let us visualize the intense action of the violet flame passing through our hands. Did you know that you have centers (chakras) of healing in your own hands? Visualize the violet flame burning in the center of each palm. The laying on of hands taught by the prophets, Jesus, and the apostles was given so that the hands as two—focusing the polarity of Alpha and Omega—could conduct the healing Light to one sick, bereaved, burdened.

The Light that is conducted through the hands has an origin and a source. It comes directly from the threefold flame in the heart, whose spiritual energy descends over the crystal cord directed by your own Higher Consciousness (illustrated as the middle figure in the chart). We do not self-generate this Light which is our very 'lifeblood'. It comes from the heart of God whose Presence you feel and know as the I AM THAT I AM, always with you.

The I AM Presence releases the Light which descends over the crystal cord (shown in the chart) as the perpetual flow of the River of Life. It is the Light of your 'lifestream', i.e., the stream of your consciousness. It is the sustaining power of your self-aware-ness that always has been and ever shall be "hid with 'Christ' in God." (This universal Christ present with Jesus is also your own Higher Consciousness whom we address as the Beloved, the Holy Christ Self.) This perpetually flowing fount of sacred fire is your life, your energy, and your consciousness. It's all yours—to qual-ify, to direct, and to increase for the blessing of all Life every-where! And the well never runs dry because the Source is infinite!

As beloved sons and daughters of God, your temple is in-tended to be the temple of the Holy Spirit, as Jesus and the apostles taught. You have free will. You may call upon God to use your lifestream, your temple, your heart and soul to transmit the Light of your I AM Presence to those in need.

Thus, with a heart full of love, with a head understanding the wisdom of God, and the hands as the instrument of the transfer of power, you may effect the same healing Light and currents that passed through Elijah, Elisha, Moses, Joshua, Jesus and the apostles, and many saints who have had the "gift" of healing.

Remember, God is no respecter of persons, but uses any among his pure sons who prepare the vessel for his coming.

Now let us affirm, "I AM the hand of God in action." Please visualize intensely the violet flame 'burning' in your hands. Hold them as cups and see the flames of the Holy Spirit dancing in your palms.

> I AM the hand of God in action,
> Gaining victory every day;
> My pure soul's great satisfaction
> Is to walk the Middle Way. (4x)

Let us take these three calls again, giving them consecutively—heart, head, and hand—with the accompanying visualization of the violet flame:

1. Violet fire, thou love divine,
   Blaze within this heart of mine!
   Thou art mercy forever true,
   Keep me always in tune with you. (3x)

2. I AM Light, thou Christ in me,
   Set my mind forever free;
   Violet fire, forever shine
   Deep within this mind of mine.

   God who gives my daily bread,
   With violet fire fill my head
   Till thy radiance heavenlike ·
   Makes my mind a mind of light. (3x)

3. I AM the hand of God in action,
   Gaining victory every day;
   My pure soul's great satisfaction
   Is to walk the Middle Way. (3x)

Now let's try the dynamic decree that pulls down the transfiguring Light. When we affirm the spiritual alchemy of God's transformation (transfiguration) in our daily lives, we do so by the use of his name I AM which he gave to Moses for all generations to come. His name I AM releases his power into action in our lives.

> I AM changing all my garments,
> Old ones for the bright new day;
> With the sun of understanding
> I AM shining all the way.

I AM Light within, without;
I AM Light is all about.
Fill me, free me, glorify me,
Seal me, heal me, purify me!
Until transfigured they describe me:
I AM shining like the Son,
I AM shining like the sun!

It is a wonderful moment when you realize that by the power of God's name I AM THAT I AM you can change your old garments—old habits, old manifestations—and put on the garment of the living Christ. This is part of the ritual of God's forgiveness, his gracious offering to his own of ultimate mercy. Let us give it again and again with great joy. (Repeat mantra above.)

You are shining in the likeness of your Mighty I AM Presence, the Sun of your own true being! You are shining like the Son of God who is the Great Mediator* between your immortal Spirit and your evolving soul personality. (Represented as the middle figure in the chart.)

As Jesus used the forgiving aspect of the glorious violet flame to free all from past karma resulting in present mental illness or disease, let us give the call for the Holy Spirit's alchemy of forgiveness.

Please visualize your whole body filled with the white light and the blazing violet flame penetrating through to the etheric memory (even to the subconscious record of trauma, violence and your reaction to it, creating knots in the psyche that cause malaise), to the mind's conception of any illness or disease, to the emotions (the fear of it, the feelings of it, the pain of it), and finally to the physical manifestation.

The violet flame is the Holy Spirit's baptism "with fire" foretold by John the Baptist. Moses witnessed: "Our God is a consuming fire." This sacred fire belongs to the sons and daughters of God; it is the gift of God to us, unlocked by our call to the I AM Presence. We use it for healing and for the upliftment of the whole world, but we must begin with ourselves.

I AM forgiveness acting here,
Casting out all doubt and fear,
Setting men forever free
With wings of cosmic victory.

*See "The Great Mediator: His Role as Transformer," *Heart: For the Coming Revolution in Higher Consciousness* (Autumn 1983), pp. 72–79.

I AM calling in full power
For forgiveness every hour;
To all life in every place
I flood forth forgiving grace. (5x)

Let us return now in our meditation to the center of the heart where we invoke Christ's Presence. Through the heart we speak to the Real Self (who is our Christ Self)—one with the Christ of Jesus, one with the Cosmic Christ and all sons and daughters of God who have overcome the world as he did.

If you will look at the chart of your I AM Presence, you will see the figure of Christ as the Son descending from the Father. The Son is the Light-emanation of the Father. And the Person of the Son is our Teacher, our Friend, our Saviour, our Christ—our own Higher Consciousness.

Let us call to the Beloved:

Thou Holy Christ Self within my heart
    Help me to manifest all thou art
Teach me to see thyself in all
    Help me to show men how to call
All of thy glory from the Sun
    'Til earth's great victory is won
I AM we love thee, thou art our all!
    I AM we love thee, hear our call!

Now listen as your Beloved Christ answers.

I hear thy call, my children dear
    I AM thy heart, so never fear
I AM your mind, your body, too
    I AM in every cell of you.
I AM thy earth and sea and sky
    And not one soul shall I pass by
I AM in thee, thou art in me
    I AM, I AM thy victory.

In the name I AM THAT I AM, let us command the power of Light to intensify in our hearts. We shall then proceed to direct that Light to the diseased area. Remember, the threefold flame in your heart is your personal focus of God's power of the transfiguration to *heal* all thy diseases. Its Source is absolutely unlimited. The eternal God can transmit to you this very hour the eternally transfiguring Light for thy wholeness.

Keep my flame blazing
By God's love raising—
Direct and keep me
   in my rightful place!

I AM Presence ever near me,
Keep me mindful of thy grace:
Flame of Christ, ever cheer me,
In me show thy smiling face!

At this time, it gives me great joy to be able to offer invocations in your behalf for your personal healing, for that of loved ones, or for conditions in your cities and nations or around the world that you would like to bring to our attention and to this altar.

You may come to the altar and briefly state the nature of the problem, the name of the disease, or the description of a burden on the planet. And I will give the invocations while you remain in prayer until the calls for you have been completed.

Thus saith the LORD, the Holy One of Israel, and his Maker, Ask me of things to come concerning my sons, and concerning the work of my hands, Command ye me!

MS: My name is Michael. A cancer developed in my body and a tumor developed in a lymph node near my spinal cord and sufficiently damaged it to effect paralysis. I was originally paralyzed from my chest down. But I fought my way back, and the paralysis is now from my hips down. I am confident that with the Light of God I will make it back all the way.

I would also ask for healing for a very sweet child from our study group in San Diego, Jamaica, who had cancer also and who has just undergone surgery and is on the road to recovery herself.

ECP: Thank you, Michael.

Exorcism of Demons and Discarnates of Cancer*

Howbeit this kind goeth not out but by prayer and fasting.

Beloved Mighty I AM Presence from the heart of God, we command the sacred fire to descend as the full power of the Holy Ghost to now exorcise the demons and discarnates focalizing cancer in the bodies of Michael and Jamaica and all other Keepers of the Flame worldwide.

*These calls given by Elizabeth Clare Prophet at healing services conducted in the Chapel of the Holy Grail are printed here for your use as prayers for healing. Discover their power for yourself by giving them aloud, as you speak in the name of God with the authority of his Christ.

*The threefold flame in your heart is
your personal focus of God's power of the
transfiguration to heal all thy diseases.*

Blaze the Light of the transfiguration! *Burn* through, O living sacred fire! *Bind* the demons and discarnates of cancer! *Bind* the virus and every cause and core in all planes of consciousness!

Burn through and bind the cause and core of that disease! *Burn* through and let God's transfiguring Light expand within the temple and the spine of Michael and in the very brain and the pituitary of Jamaica! *Burn* through, O holy Light of God!

Legions of healing angels, angels of the transfiguration, we welcome thee. Beloved angels of the Holy Spirit, angels of the Blessed Virgin Mary, come now into the temple of being. Come now into the homes of those who are burdened with this disease of cancer.

Bind the very cause and core of it! *Bind* it now, mighty Archangels of the LORD! *Blaze* the Light through! We *demand* the binding and the exorcism of cancer from the physical body, the emotional body, the mental body, and the memory body—and from the memory of the cells!

Burn through, and therefore let the healing Light replace now all that is damaged in the central nervous system, in the brain, in the pituitary, in the lymph system! *Burn* through into every heart now and *expand* the Light!

In the name of Jesus, we say:

> Light expand! Light expand!
> Light expand, expand, expand!
> Light I AM! Light I AM!
> Light I AM, I AM, I AM! (9x)

In the name of Jesus Christ, I command the transfiguring Light of God that never fails: *Descend* now! *Burn* through! *Heal* now these four lower bodies of Michael and Jamaica and all other Keepers of the Flame who so call!

Burn through, O living Light of the Word. From the heart of Brahman, *Descend!* Beloved Father, show forth thy grace, according to thy Law of Love, according to the law of wholeness! Violet-flame angels, now transmute the cause and core of these conditions in each and every Keeper of the Flame.

Blaze the light of Archangel Michael! Beloved Archangel Michael, raise your sword of blue flame and cut out the very cause and core of that disease in the finer bodies before it does manifest. *Burn* through and let the blazing light of freedom and the power of the resurrection now restore and make whole that which is injured by this condition!

In the name of Jesus, we say: I AM the resurrection and the life of every cell and atom of my four lower bodies now made manifest! (5x)

In the name of the Father and of the Son and of the Holy Spirit, in the name of the Mother, I accept it done this hour in the full power of the transfiguration of Jesus Christ! Amen.

MS: Thank you.

JA: I am so glad to see you. This is Max. He's had a problem with his right leg since he was 18 months old. The doctors say that it's something that he was born with that's coming from inside of his body and manifesting on the outside. It goes from his feet to his buttocks. And it causes him tremendous itching and problems. Sometimes it bleeds. It's like a birthmark, only it occurred when he was 18 months old. It came from inside his body. That's what all the doctors I've taken him to say.

ECP: And what do they state is the cure for this?

JA: Well, one physician said to put cortisone cream on and give him oral cortisone. I didn't do that because I'm fearful of cortisone. And the next physician I took him to, because I wanted a second opinion, said that if I had given him oral cortisone, he might have had a problem with stunting of growth. I've done a lot of home cures. Nothing's worked.

And God said, Let the earth bring forth grass, the herb yielding seed, and the fruit tree yielding fruit after his kind, whose seed is in itself, upon the earth: and it was so.

ECP: Max, I would like to know if you would begin to drink the juice of wheatgrass in quantity. You can mix it with pineapple juice or apple juice or carrot juice. Wheatgrass is chlorophyll. And chlorophyll contains the healing Light of God. God places in chlorophyll the gift of the light of the sun for our healing. And when we take it in and it goes into our bloodstream, it begins to make all of our cells whole.

I'm going to pray for God's transfiguring Light to come into your leg, but you also have to drink God's elixir which is that wheatgrass. And when you drink it, you take your glass and you put your left hand under it and your right hand over it.

These are your healing hands. This is how God transfers his Light from your Mighty I AM Presence, through your crystal cord, through your heart. And so your hands become the instrument to charge the wheatgrass with the spiritual Light of God.

And so, you call to God in this way and you say: "Dear God, in the name of Jesus Christ, use my hands to charge this wheatgrass with the spiritual Light for the healing of my whole body and mind and soul and especially this condition in my leg. I accept it done this hour in the name of Jesus. Amen."

Will you do that?

Max: Yes, Mother.

ECP: Now I'm going to make the call for you. Will you hold your hands like this, cupped to receive God's transfiguring Light?

For Consuming the Cause and Core of the Imperfect Matrix

Every valley shall be filled, and every mountain and hill shall be brought low; and the crooked shall be made straight, and the rough ways shall be made smooth.

Beloved Mighty I AM Presence, beloved Father, beloved Holy Christ Self of Max, I command the action of the sacred fire through his very own heart flame. *Blaze* through the body temple now! *Blaze* through the four lower bodies and the sacred centers! *Release now* the power of the transfiguring Light for the consuming of the cause and core of that matrix!

I command the consuming *now* by the sacred fire, by the violet flame, of the cause and core of that condition in the physical body. *Burn* through and dissolve it in the etheric body, the astral body, the mental body, the auric sheath, and the physical manifestation! *Burn* through to the very cause and core of the physical cells! Let it be consumed now by the power of the Holy Spirit from within, from without, and in answer to his own prayer. By his faith, he *is* made whole in this hour!

I accept it done in the name of Jesus Christ, Amen.

God bless you.

IS: Beloved Mother of the Flame, I have two requests to make. One is on behalf of my son, Darryl Ramirez, who's a Montessori student. He wants a blessing for the children of the world that are born with dyslexia, mongolism, mental retardation,

The Threefold Flame of Your Heart

Your heart is one of the choicest gifts of God. Within it there is a central chamber surrounded by a forcefield of such light and protection that we call it a 'cosmic interval'.

It is a chamber separated from Matter and no probing could ever discover it. It occupies simultaneously not only the third and fourth dimensions but also other dimensions unknown to man. This central chamber, called the altar of the heart, is thus the connecting point of the mighty silver cord of light that descends from your God Presence to sustain the beating of your physical heart, giving you life, purpose, and cosmic integration.

I urge all men to treasure this point of contact that they have with Life by giving conscious recognition to it.

You do not need to understand by sophisticated language or scientific postulation the how, why, and wherefore of this activity. Be content to know that God is there and that within you there is a point of contact with the Divine, a spark of fire from the Creator's own heart called the threefold flame of Life. There it burns as the triune essence of love, wisdom, and power.

Each acknowledgment paid daily to the flame within your heart will amplify the power and illumination of love within your being. Each such attention will produce a new sense of dimension for you, if not outwardly apparent then subconsciously manifest within the folds of your inner thoughts.

Neglect not, then, your heart as the altar of God. Neglect it not as the sun of your manifest being. Draw from God the power of love and amplify it within your heart. Then send it out into the world at large as the bulwark of that which shall overcome the darkness of the planet, saying:

I AM the Light of the Heart
Shining in the darkness of being
And changing all into the
  golden treasury
Of the Mind of Christ.

I AM projecting my Love
Out into the world
To erase all errors
And to break down all barriers.

I AM the power of infinite Love,
Amplifying itself
Until it is victorious,
World without end!

With this gift of infinite freedom, I give you my never-ending promise to assist you to find your immortal freedom as you determine never to give up and never to turn back.

Remember that as long as you face the Light, the shadows are always behind. And the Light is there, too, to transmute them all.

SAINT GERMAIN

any kind of karmic condition, and for their parents to understand their condition so they can help them bring forth the Light. And for myself I ask for the healing of my feet and my eyes which have been quite bad since I was a child.

I've had four operations for bad muscle tone. The muscles of the bottom of the feet just weren't right—very wide feet. I can't stand for long periods of time. And I'm blind in my right eye, and thank God I got sight back in my left eye some years back. I had lost it temporarily.

For Healing of the Eyes and the Feet
Heal the Record and the Mind's Conception of It!
the Feelings and the Physical Body

If therefore thine eye be single, thy whole body shall be full of Light....

How beautiful upon the mountains are the feet of him that bringeth good tiding, that publisheth peace; that bringeth good tidings of good, that publisheth salvation; that saith unto Zion, Thy God reigneth!

Beloved Mighty I AM Presence from the heart of God in the Great Central Sun, in the name I AM THAT I AM, in the name I AM THAT I AM, in the name I AM THAT I AM, Be *still* and know that I AM God! Be *still* and know that I AM God! Be *still* and know that I AM God!

O Thou Transfiguring Light of God that never fails within my Christ, descend now into the body temple of Iris! *Burn* through! *Burn* through! *Burn* through for the healing of the eyes and the healing of the feet. *Burn* through by the power of Elohim! *Bind* the cause and core of that condition! *Bind* the discarnate! *Bind* now the cause and core down the record of her lifestream in this and all past lives.

Burn through, and let the light of restoration, the healing flame of resurrection, manifest by the power of the mighty feet of Jesus and of Moses and of Buddha. *Burn* through, and let the feet of the Divine One of the pilgrims of peace now appear and manifest in the physical octave, in the etheric, mental, emotional bodies. Let the pattern be corrected, O God!

Let the all-seeing eye of God appear now by the power of the resurrection flame, by the power of healing. Let that fire descend to the four lower bodies until each, in its own fashion and time and space, receives the power of the sacred fire.

O Mighty Power of the Transfiguration, *Heal* the record!

Heal the mind's conception of it! *Heal* all in the feeling body, the astral belt, the electronic belt! *Burn* through and then heal the physical body!

I command the healing of the whole man. Let the whole man be made whole by the sacred fire! By the power of the sacred fire, I accept it done this hour. In the name of the Father, the Son, the Holy Spirit, and the Mother, Amen.

For the Healing of Children with Congenital Birth Defects

Suffer little children, and forbid them not, to come unto me; for of such is the kingdom of heaven.

Mighty I AM Presence, in the name of the child, I call forth the transfiguring Light. In the name of the One Sent and in the name of the Child Jesus, I call now for the power of Almighty God to mitigate and heal, where the great karmic Law will allow, children born with congenital birth defects of every kind.

Burn through, therefore, O Thou Light that does not fail! And let there be the binding and the arresting of the cause and core of those conditions in the earth which are the afflictions of the children of the Light bearing world karma and world sin. Blaze forth this night the Light of the all-transfiguring Christ wherever the Great Law will allow.

I call forth the presence of Archangel Raphael. *Blaze* the light of Raphael and Mother Mary! By the power of the Cosmic Christ, *blaze* thy light into the hearts of children everywhere! Let them be raised up to perform their mission.

Beloved Ascended Masters, beloved Lords of Karma, beloved Cosmic Christ, intercede on behalf of the children of God on earth. *Seal* them in the power of healing! *Seal* them in the divine image and in the resurrection fire! We accept it done this hour in the full power of the transfiguration of our Lord.

In the name of Jesus, I am transferring that Light by the very power of his hand and light and heart. Sacred heart of Jesus, minister unto thy children in this hour. We say it, and we ask it in the name of Darryl. We ask it in the name of the Light that does not fail. In the name of Jesus, Amen.

CB: I'm asking for a personal healing, Mother, from records and momentums of rebellion and disobedience and fear and death and hell experiences, and also from feelings that I've had a lot in my life of not wanting to be in embodiment.

Rebellion against Life: the Suicide Entity

Master, we saw one casting out devils in thy name and he followeth not us; and we forbad him, because he followeth not us. But Jesus said, Forbid him not; for there is no man which shall do a miracle in my name that can lightly speak evil of me. For he that is not against us is on our part.

Beloved Mighty I AM Presence, beloved Holy Spirit, *cast out* now the demon and discarnate of rebellion, fear and doubt, death and nondesire to exalt Life in that temple! *Burn* through! Be *out* now, thou cause and core of death and all demons of death! *Burn* through, Almighty God, and bind all suicide entities! *Bind* the cause and core of fear! *Burn* through! In Jesus' name, it is done!

CM: About two and a half years ago, I was told I have a demyelinating disease. And it's been a great burden to my body and has interfered with just about every part of life, being a mother and everything. The tremors and the weakness and the fatigue that overcomes the muscles is quite a bit.

ECP: Could you state once again the name of this condition?

CM: They haven't named it as multiple sclerosis; but I wouldn't be surprised if that's what it is. It's the breakdown of the myelin sheath of the nerve fibers. It's just constant discomfort. And I'm grateful through vitamin therapy and juices to be able to be here now.

ECP: Are you taking a great deal of wheatgrass? Wheatgrass therapy is marvelous for the maintenance of health. You should be starting with a teaspoon, building up to ounces—10 ounces, 20 ounces—which you mix with apple juice or carrot juice or pineapple juice, if you wish. And always charge your juices with the power of God's Light. Always know that Alpha and Omega transfer the blessing through your hands as you take the glass, your left hand beneath it, holding it, your right hand cupped over it.

And the myelin protective sheath of your nerves can be healed. You must visualize this taking place as you direct the power of the transfiguring Light from your I AM Presence into the nerves daily. You have to do God's work, using his Word. You have a glorious opportunity to prove his life in you and to show that God is the means of the healing of MS, of demyelinating disease, and every other condition. It has no power in your temple, and you *will* focus the powerful Light of Jesus' transfiguration in your temple for your wholeness.

Elizabeth Clare Prophet in intense meditation
on the inner sound while offering healing invocations.

CM: The other thing that is a real burden to me is that I think I could bear the disease except I feel that I should always be manifesting perfection. And it's very difficult for me.

ECP: Say, "God is perfect in me now!"

CM: God is perfect in me now!

ECP: I AM manifesting his perfection now!

CM: I AM manifesting his perfection now!

ECP: Naught else can manifest here!

CM: Naught else can manifest here!

ECP: I AM God's perfection manifest in body, mind, and soul!

CM: I AM God's perfection manifest in body, mind, and soul!

ECP: We're all going to give that healing mantra for "Christ Wholeness" together with you. I want you to give this every day and command your cells to be whole. Will you do that?

CM: Yes.

Arrest the Spiral of Demyelinating Disease and Multiple Sclerosis

Be ye therefore perfect, even as your Father which is in heaven is perfect.

Beloved Mighty I AM Presence from the heart of God, *enter* now this form! Arrest the spiral now! Arrest the spiral now! Reverse the spiral now of the cause and core of this condition! *Burn* through, O Thou All-Transfiguring Light, and consume the cause and core of it! *Reverse* the action now! *Heal* the damage! Restore the myelin sheath!

Burn through, O Light of God! Manifest now in the very physical cells! *Heal* now! *Heal* now! *Heal* now the cause and core of that condition!

I call unto the Great Central Sun Magnet: demagnetize this body of the cause and core of this demyelinating disease by the power of the Mighty I AM Presence. I *command* Light to flow from the Mighty I AM Presence! I *command* the atoms, cells, and electrons to intensify the Light of the Messiah in the very center! *Intensify*, accelerate, and throw off all disease manifesting, known or unknown, in the physical, astral, mental, and etheric sheaths!

Blaze the Light through! *Blaze* the Light through! *Blaze* the Light through!

In God's holy name, we now decree for Cynthia:

Christ Wholeness

In the name of the beloved mighty victorious Presence of God, I AM in me, my very own beloved Holy Christ Self and beloved Jesus the Christ, I pour forth my love and gratitude to her beloved body elemental for her faithful service always. (Pause to visualize the precious body elemental in an ovoid of the pink flame of divine love.)

I now command her body elemental to arise and take complete dominion over every imperfect condition which may be manifesting within her physical body! Beloved body elemental, move into action now to mend the flaws in the functioning of the nervous system affecting the muscles and the entire body under the guidance and direction of her own beloved Holy Christ Self, beloved Jesus the Christ, and the immaculate design of her life-stream released from the heart of her own beloved Mighty I AM Presence—O Thou Great Regenerator!

In the name of the mighty Presence of God which I AM and by and through the magnetic power of the sacred fire vested in the threefold flame burning within my heart, I decree for the healing of the myelin sheath and all related diseases in the body of Cynthia:

1. I AM God's perfection manifest
   In body, mind, and soul—
   I AM God's direction flowing
   To heal and keep me whole!

Refrain: (repeat after each verse)
   O atoms, cells, electrons
   Within this form of mine,
   Let heaven's own perfection
   Make me now divine!

   The spirals of Christ wholeness
   Enfold me by his might—
   I AM the Master Presence
   Commanding, "Be all Light!"

2. I AM God's perfect image:
   My form is charged by love;
   Let shadows now diminish,
   Be blessed by Comfort's Dove!

3. O blessed Jesus, Master dear,
   Send thy ray of healing here;
   Fill me with thy life above,
   Raise me in thine arms of love!

4. I AM Christ's healing Presence,
   All shining like a mercy sun—
   I AM that pure perfection,
   My perfect healing won!

5. I charge and charge and charge myself
   With radiant I AM Light—
   I feel the flow of purity
   That now makes all things right!

Your body is alive. It has intelligence. And it is waiting for your command. This body is continually changing—cells are dying, cells are being reborn in the normal state of living. So, you see, you must maintain a vigil of perpetual prayer and meditation.

Very often you must command the cells to obey the inner matrix of your Christ Self because these are self-renewing cells. But they are newborn life, and they must be commanded to obey the matrix of your Christhood rather than the matrix of disease which in turn must be broken.

So we see that healing is an ongoing process of God-mastery. And it is a scientific action that you take with God. It is not a one-time event of coming to the altar.

All of us are being reborn daily. We have old habit patterns. Our energies tend to fall into those patterns and to outpicture in the same old way. So if we want change, we must renew ourselves daily. We are daily dying with Paul and daily being reborn. (I Cor. 15:31) And this is the season when the resurrection flame passes through the earth body and all her evolutions with rejuvenating power.

So you speak now to that disease and you say to it:

—You have no power! Your day is done! In God's name, I AM, be thou dissolved and transmuted into light, illumination, and love forever!

—The only power that can act is God's law!

The Word of God is healing you now, but you must say it, you must give the command. You must speak it into every cell of your being. You must reverse the course of death and hell encroaching upon you. It has no power! You must fight the good fight and win. You must not let down your guard.

Two thousand years ago Jesus Christ overcame the last enemy, which is death, and he within you and you in him shall overcome this enemy today. All power to Christ's Spirit of the resurrection flame in your temple!

In the name of the Father, the Son, the Holy Spirit, and the Mother, I accept it done this hour in full power, Amen.

Remember to ask your friends to pray with you these prayers, for Jesus said:

> If two of you shall agree on earth as touching any thing that they shall ask, it shall be done for them of my Father which is in heaven. For where two or three are gathered together in my name, there am I in the midst of them. . . .
>
> Whatsoever ye shall ask of the Father in my name, he may give it you.

ES: Beloved Mother, I would like to ask healing for the nation of Hungary from the oppression of World Communism—it's like a cancer that eats their bodies, minds, and souls—and also for their misuse of the science of the spoken Word, and their criticism, condemnation, and judgment—their negativity toward life and one another expressed because of their depression under the Communist system.

For the Flame of Freedom in the Hearts of the Hungarian People

The Spirit of the Lord GOD *is upon me, because the* LORD *hath anointed me to preach good tidings unto the meek; he hath sent me to bind up the brokenhearted, to proclaim liberty to the captives, and the opening of the prison to them that are bound.*

Beloved Mighty I AM Presence from the heart of God, draw the mighty solar ring around Hungary this day! Our God—Thou who art a consuming fire: *Burn* through and cut free a nation and a people from World Communism! *Burn* through and let there be a mighty power of the explosion of the flame of freedom in the hearts of the people of Hungary!

Burn through! *Burn* through! *Burn* through, O Thou Transfiguring Light! *Bind* the cancer of World Communism! *Bind* the beast of World Communism! Come, let Thy sacred fire, O God, burn through to the very cause and core right now this day!

Blaze the light of freedom! *Blaze* the light of each one's divine spark, of free will and the free enterprise system! *Burn* through and blaze the freedom of the sacred labor of Almighty God, of the Father in the Son performed freely—heart, head, and hand—unto his glory and by his grace!

Bind the totalitarian movements and the totalitarian state in Hungary! Overthrow it now by the mighty power of Saint Stephen! *Burn* through by the mighty power of Saint Stephen! *Burn* through by the mighty power of Saint Stephen, by the communion of saints in heaven and on earth, and by the cosmic cross of white fire of beloved Jesus Christ! *Bind* all condemnation within and without! *Burn* through, O Holy Ghost, and raise them up to the vision of the Son of God!

I call upon the entire Spirit of the Great White Brotherhood, Ascended Masters, Archangels, and legions of the sacred fire for the LORD's judgment this day upon World Communism for the 1956 slaughter of the Hungarian people in their homeland by the enemies of Freedom.

They Shall Not Pass!
by Jesus Christ

In the Name of the I AM THAT I AM,
   I invoke the Electronic Presence of Jesus Christ:
They shall not pass!
They shall not pass!
They shall not pass!
By the authority of the cosmic cross of white fire
   it shall be:
That all that is directed against the Christ
   within me, within the holy innocents,
   within our beloved messengers,
   within every son and daughter of God
Is now turned back
   by the authority of Alpha and Omega,
   by the authority of my Lord and Saviour Jesus Christ,
   by the authority of Saint Germain!

I AM THAT I AM within the center of this temple
   and I declare in the fullness of
   the entire Spirit of the Great White Brotherhood:
That those who, then, practice the black arts
   against the children of the Light

Are now bound by the hosts of the LORD,
Do now receive the judgment of the Lord Christ
   within me, within Jesus,
   and within every Ascended Master,
Do now receive, then, the full return—
   multiplied by the energy of the Cosmic Christ—
   of their nefarious deeds which they have practiced
   since the very incarnation of the Word!

Lo, I AM a Son of God!
Lo, I AM a Flame of God!
Lo, I stand upon the rock of the living Word
And I declare with Jesus, the living Son of God:
They shall not pass!
They shall not pass!
They shall not pass!
ELOHIM   ELOHIM   ELOHIM

I accept it done this hour in the full power of Almighty God by the prayer of the One Sent. Let the saints of God in heaven move through the saints of God on earth for the victory of freedom in every nation. We accept it done in the name of Saint Germain.

Beloved Jesus Christ, beloved Saint Germain, beloved Mother Mary, beloved Father, beloved Son, beloved Holy Spirit, hear my call and answer for the healing of the body of God upon earth. *Heal* them, therefore, of all their diseases! *Heal* them, LORD God Almighty, as thy servant David said: "...Who forgiveth all thine iniquities, who healeth all thy diseases, who redeemeth thy life from destruction."

'stepped up' in vibration and clothed with the seamless garment[8] of electronic light. This transfiguring light comes from the heart of God and passes through all illusion and human density which, cloudlike and cunning, seeks to conceal from their gaze, in a thousand allures and subterfuges, the latent divinity of the seed of Christ.

When this action of the transfiguration is initiated by the Presence and received by the soul in the fullness of God-awareness, a state of consciousness is entered into by the disciple wherein he no longer considers himself Christian, Jew, Buddhist, Mohammedan, or a member of a separate religious sect. Neither is he conscious any longer of racial characteristics stamped on the outer form; but, in the joy of the divinely blessed transfiguring experience, he is one (as I AM) with the pure, electronic white light of God's sacred fire. This is the true initiation of the Holy Spirit through each one's Holy Christ Self.

The effect of God's light upon man's consciousness is great joy and peace. When the light and fire of God flow through him like a crystal-clear river of Life,[9] washing away the former impressions of unhappiness, the glory and freedom he feels are boundless!

Every son of God can and should pass through the initiation of the transfiguration—not merely as an Easter ritual, but as the once-in-a-lifetime mountaintop experience with the Ascended Masters Moses, Elijah, and myself, witnessed by the apostles.[10] This is the gift of God to permanently change one's life and to prepare the soul for succeeding initiations on the path of Christhood ere the resurrection can be attained.

The power of the transfiguration to change one life exemplifies the action of the sacred fire, whose transforming light is the miracle worker day by day, until the soul and four lower bodies of the disciple are prepared for the fullness of the all-enveloping transfiguration.

Such as these, proving the Law of Love step by step, descend the mountain and go forth (return to service at human levels) better equipped to render real assistance to their own friends, loved ones, and a world that hungers as never before to be filled with righteousness— the knowledge of the "right use" of all God's powers. These are truly the meek who, full of divine strength, shall inherit the earth.

I AM showing the Way to eternal Life,

Jesus the Christ

Corona Class Lesson 14

Acceleration

"We Shall All Be Changed . . ."

Beloved Who Would Teach Men
        the Way of Transfiguration —
    Beloved Jesus has told you of the need of
every son of God for personal transfiguration
such as he experienced both day by day, with
the Spirit making all things new,[1] and on the
mountaintop when the anointing of the Piscean
avatar was attended by ascended and unascended initiates witnessing in heaven and on
earth to his commission as World Saviour and
Teacher. Spoken directly from the Father, the
divine approbation was heard: "This is my
Beloved Son, in whom I AM well pleased: Hear
ye him!"[2] (This is the incarnation of myself, the
One Sent to you in whom the I AM Presence
dwells. Be God-taught of me through him and
follow him all the way in the regeneration.[3])
    Jesus emphasized that the intensity of this
wondrous whiteness of the sacred fire, perme-
ating the consciousness with God-happiness

and freedom from the bondage of the senses, would, as a side effect to the permanent change wrought, engender the soul's desire to retain the Light and to remain in its God-exalted estate. The Master also stressed the need to descend the mountain after each successive exaltation in God, once again to enter into loving service to a world in great need.

I am desirous of giving assistance to all who truly desire the rite of transfiguration to take place in their own being and consciousness as a genuine cosmic initiation which is ordained by the Father for all of his children.

First, it is well to understand that the verb *transfigure* breaks down into the prefix *trans,* meaning "change" (across, beyond, through, so as to change), and the word *figure* from the Latin, meaning "to shape, fashion, figure." Hence, to transfigure is "to change the form or appearance of," or "to metamorphose."

Figure, in our analysis of the soul's preparedness for this initiation, refers to each one's state of being as he approaches the event. The form or appearance currently manifesting shows that portion of the figure of Christ, the image of the hidden man of the heart, actually being outpictured by the soul—representing each one's present spiritual state.

To transfigure thus connotes the shedding of the human image as the soul identity is accelerated in the putting on of a tangible electronic garment, or life-essence, which can never be requalified (or lowered in vibration) to the level

of the former state. In the ongoing transfiguration process our disciples experience the spiritual substitution of every human failure with
God-dominion, God-creativity, and God-victory,
as every manifest virtue and attribute of the
Godhead displaces habitual submission to the
synthetic programming of the human.

Those who have been stuck in the mud
know how tenacious the soggy earth can be,
how relentless it is in not releasing anyone from
its grip. When the release comes and one
emerges into the sunshine and wind, there is
usually a drying of the caked dirt on clothing
and skin, necessitating a thorough washing so
the clumps of mud will not remain to spoil the
day. Even so, the one so blessed as to find
escape from earth's binding habits through a
divine experience must not allow the clods to
mar the temple garments.

Now, in transfiguration there is an actual
expansion of the light of God that never fails.
From within every cell and atom of the physical body, this expansion occurs under circumstances whereby the mud of one's former sullied
state is itself dissolved and cannot cling
longer round the atoms and cellular structure,
for it is permanently changed (transmuted) by
the Light.

Every thought, whether of conscious direction or unconscious drift, whether personal,
racial, or cellular (yes, there is even such a
thing as a subconscious cell thought!), is then,
through transfiguration, brought to a state of

God-bliss, and the millions of thoughts that are the components of consciousness become as cups of light running over with cosmic joy and divine wisdom. Each God-thought, then, becomes a radiating orb charged with the radiance of heaven which the Father desires to share with all Life in the entire cosmos— through you!

The Sun of God, the Christ within and above, continues to pour into the chalice of your heart (chakra) its Life-giving properties. This concentrated action of the sacred fire flushes out from the innermost regions of the mind (including the subconscious) every quality less than Light itself and releases any and all tenacious misqualified substance from each one's world.

In the ritual of the transfiguration, there is a cosmic release to all other unascended beings so fortunate as to be near the initiate when he is passing through the divine experience. This transfer of light surges to a peak, tapering off only after adjusting the body's electronic structure to its high frequencies. The purpose of this acceleration is to prepare each one for his own ascension in the Light.

We are acquainting our students with this knowledge for a good and sufficient reason. We trust that those who think they already know these things will meditate more deeply upon them, while those new to the concept of the personal transfiguration seek understanding from God, their own Mighty I AM Presence.

Thus, let all seek divine assistance in preparing for this most blessed experience of the expansion of the Light (Christ) in the four planes (four lower bodies) of their own personal world.

Remember, you must ask for heaven's treasures if you would truly receive them!

I AM your cosmic teacher in God's love,

Kuthumi

Corona Class Lesson 15

Possibility

"Arise, Shine! for Thy Light Is Come"

Beloved Who Walk in the Light
    As I AM in the Light—
    In the midst of man's preparation for entrance into his cosmic victory and the state of life God intends all to enjoy and to have, I am confident that sincere souls will understand the need for faith, the need for persistence, or constancy, and the need for devotion combined with intense gratitude.

    My own manifestation of the eternal radiance upon the mountaintop was but a prelude to the victory of my ascension. Blessed ones, the drama of Good Friday, the hours in the tomb, and the resurrection[1] were made comparatively lighter because of the blessing of the transfiguration. I hope that having accepted the reality of this initiation in my life's history, you will see its possibilities in your own life and will make it a part of your history, too.

It is a perfectly natural spiritual manifestation—as simple and sweet as the sunshine itself. It is quite effortless, for once you get the full realization of just what your own Mighty I AM God Presence can actually do for you, you just stand back and let the Presence act in your world as it is wont to do.

Then, when you call to your own dear God Presence, you will sense God's interest in you as your own heavenly Father—even as I did—and you will know, first of all, that God wants to transfigure you. Being convinced that this is so will help you journey from the consciousness of possibility to the state of realization.

Let no man tell you otherwise, for I know and have experienced these glorious transitions from human thought to divine reality. When I say, "Lo, I AM with you alway," I speak from eternal realms of existence where I am still able to reach out and contact your own world of thought and feeling.

Blessed ones, did I not say that every plant which my Father did not plant must be rooted up?[2] This is the meaning of the change that takes place when God's light glorifies you. You see, no matter how much glory we of the ascended hosts may sense or absorb, the only way for you to enter completely into a state of God-victory as we did is through the conscious way which I AM—in other words, the "I AM" Way! This puts each individual squarely before the door of his own beloved Holy Christ Self that he may knock and be admitted. [3]

Being itself is the "AM" of existence, my beloved. But in order for you (the "I" individualized) to enter in, you must become the "I" of the "I AM" and experience for yourself the wonders of the glory of God. Do you see, blessed ones? Oh, do meditate on this point of the Law!

Let your whole being become, therefore, increasingly conscious of God's great light! Be conscious that his light is a reality all around you at all times and that it is the reality of existence.

Sense that you can contact the Light and that it can contact you. Sense that it is the life-force in every budding flower, every sweet scent, every ray of sunshine, every feeling of hope in the human heart. Sense that it is the eternal bond between heart and heart, that it is the avenue of Ascended Master communication, that it is the light of thousands of suns shining in their strength. Sense that God can—by the power of making himself large or small, by the power of the "I AM"—put all of this radiance of himself into every cell of you and into your whole being!

Call for the intensification of the cosmic flame of the transfiguration and for the amplification of your faith in it. Be constant in your application. And then, with heartfelt devotion and gratitude, await the sudden expansion of the perfect love and light that casts out all fear.[4]

Welcome into your lifestream with open arms and grateful heart the flow of God's light without limit until, like me, you abide in God's arms of transfiguring mercy where you always know the full meaning of God-freedom which all of you should share—and one day shall!

All blessings of the cosmic dawn to you!

Your

Jesus the Christ

Corona Class Lesson 16

Obedience

"The LORD Is My Light"

Beloved Who *Are Light* in the LORD
      and Walk as Children of Light—
    I especially want the students of the Light everywhere to attain a conscious awareness of the real meaning of transfiguration. To have this experience is a blessing of great magnitude! Think of it, blessed ones—only a comparatively few unascended beings have *ever* experienced it! Nevertheless, it can be called forth from the Great Law by the faithful living in a high state of God consciousness.
    When your devotion to Love reaches a certain intensity, the yearning of the Light for itself automatically moves the light within each cell to expand from the center outward in concentric spirals to contact the divine radiance present in the very atmosphere. This takes place, beloved, when the Presence of the All-Father issues the command.

Some do not fully comprehend what the real meaning of this blessing is. Simplicity is necessary in order to grasp the principle and fix it firmly in mind; but when this understanding comes to you personally, it is not through a mere conscious willing but by the direct gift of the Father himself, your own beloved I AM Presence.

Blessed one, the ascension is the final sacred rite that enables you to enter into your eternal God-estate with beloved Jesus and those of us who have won our freedom; when it takes place, the change is permanent and the victory is complete over everything human. Therefore, transfiguration is made possible to unascended beings as *a prelude* to their being raised into the high estate of the ascension.

Every so often we hear people say they prefer to remain in embodiment or to reembody upon earth because they know that someone has to do the work and anchor a focus of light among mankind for the Ascended Masters to work through. It is true that we need calls from your octave in order to take action in your world or to intercede on behalf of humanity — for cosmic law demands that the call which compels our answer be forthcoming from unascended mankind in *physical* embodiment. But, blessed ones, far too few from this planet have won their ascension victory, and the whole world is waiting for the sunrise when thousands ascend in one day to fulfill their God-destiny!

Do you know what it will mean to our dear

earth and yours when so many attain their victory? The increase of our ranks, the swelling of
the cosmic chorus, the soul-touching gratitude
and praise poured out to God the Mighty I AM
Presence by the ascending ones—going forever
out of mortality into immortality, out of all
shadow into the glory and comfort of the absolute Light of God[1]—will be beyond words to
describe.

The net gain of light to the cosmos and all
sentient beings is incomparable! Why, every
molecule of matter is charged with the currents
of the ascension flame released through the
ascending ones! Those who witness their everlasting victory in the rapture of Love may then
claim the mantle (attainment) of their brothers
and sisters who have advanced beyond mortal
dimensions (for the laws of mortality could no
longer bind them).

This transfer of light, as in the scenario of
Elijah and Elisha,[2] can take place only if some
make the 'sacrifice' to "come up higher" and
others remain to "teach men the Way." While
both fulfill the law of the Master/disciple
(Guru/chela) relationship, their mutual acceleration impels the remnant through the Doorway
of Light.

The momentum thus generated as each lifewave, each graduating class, ascends will provide a continuing upward pull until one day in
the not-too-distant future (as cosmic cycles are
reckoned) all earth's evolutions will be ascended
in the Light and free, and earth herself shall

ascend into golden octaves of light and peace—
worlds without end. May you invoke the divine
timetable for your ascent, for God knoweth the
hour of your translation.

I want to convey, then, to those who now see
the transfiguration as the next step in their
soul's fiery destiny, the first essential to becoming transfigured as beloved Jesus was: it is
obedience to the Voice and the Law of your own
beloved God Presence, as applied by your Holy
Christ Self—the Teacher—to meet every situation and test, human and divine.

You see, some students do not feel the need
or the desire to surrender their will completely
to God, thinking to retain, by right, some control. Blessed ones, in examining the cosmic
record of centuries, I have never found one case
in which human control exceeded or even
equaled the wisdom and perfection of God-
control and God-guidance. And I do not think
I shall!

However, the most humble, ordinary-
appearing persons may be vested with such a
radiance as the result of being God-guided that
even the worldly, steeped in human concepts,
can sense that there is something very special
and wonderful about these devotees who do
surrender their will to God and are blessed in
return with the power of the greater will.

This investment of God (notice, I say "in-
vest-ment") is an act of the supreme guiding intelligence that controls every star in the sky. Here
God's investment becomes man's investiture

as the Father invests the power of his will in his sons and daughters who surrender their will to him and *vests* them therefore with a mantle of authority and responsibility to expand his kingdom below as above. This precept is still taught by Jesus in his parable of the talents: Thou hast been faithful (i.e., obedient, responsible, trustworthy) over a few things, I will make thee ruler (a co-creator with me) over many things. [3]

Thus, obedience is the first simple step that *must be taken.* It is the threading of the eye of the needle for God's handiwork to come—cosmic Selfhood, divine, illumined, free. Truly you create yourself by allegiance (obedience) to your inner blueprint and the Voice within who so lovingly guides you into all Truth.

When working in harmony with God's will, you must consciously think on Light from a divine standpoint. By and by, quite suddenly, you will find your whole being feeling lighter. This is because what you think on, you shall become. In this case, through thinking on God's light you are becoming that light in action everywhere you move.

This is an automatic process which can attune your mind to God's Mind as well as tune the mind like a spiritual instrument, a divine harp, to harmonize with every other 'instrument' in the cosmic orchestra. When the light streams radiantly forth in a brilliant outpouring of harmonious music, and heavenly choruses travel on lightbeams from your God Presence directly into your world and affairs, you will know that the Initiator draweth nigh.

At first you will begin to develop the sense of the transfiguration as Jesus did, and then you will begin to know, as he did, that this sensitivity to the daily transfusing light of the Presence, this attunement with the flow of the creative Word, is an experience drawing you nearer unto the Father, your own God Self, and to the full-orbed initiation of the transfiguration through beloved Lord Maitreya.

May it be so! I bless you with this knowing. May your heart make it plain!

In Illumination's Flame, I AM

Kuthumi

Corona Class Lesson 17

Power

"All Power Is Given unto Me . . ."

To You Who Must First Be Transformed
      by the Renewing of Your Minds—
    When I stood on the mountain with blessed Peter, James, and John, the world seemed far behind and God very near! That is the beauty of mountaintop experiences.

    Because I learned how to still the sounds of all human discord, it was possible for me to speak the words "Lo, I AM with you alway." These words were my promise that the I AM of me, focused on earth in the flame of my 'sacred heart', would remain constantly with each disciple as the guardian Light.

    And truly the I AM of me is with you today as you seek and find me through your own threefold flame. And I AM the Saviour *of* that Light, even as I AM *in* that Light. And that threefold flame *is* "the true Light which lighteth" every manifestation of God which descendeth into the physical plane!

Some feel that I did not struggle to attain. Blessed ones, everyone who has ever entered the atmosphere where human discord (evil as the energy *veil*, or maya) dwells has had to face some measure of struggle. But, as your blessed Saint Germain has told you, it is the sense of struggle that makes the struggle. [1]

Hence, the immaculate concept my blessed mother held for me, the periods of solitude when I withdrew from the discord of the mass mind, the interludes of fasting and communion with the Father were contributing factors that enabled me to draw from my God Source, whenever I needed it, the energy to heal, the strength to escape human limitations, and the wisdom to constantly keep in tune with the Power from on high.

Blessed Kuthumi told you last week of the first step to transfiguration. He said it is obedience to the Voice and the Law of your own beloved God Presence. We both know that the human ego does not like to be told the simple and blunt Truth. But only Truth can make you free! Therefore study the Law and learn to know the Voice of God which speaks from out the flame of your heart.

In this activity of The Summit Lighthouse, the Darjeeling Council has determined to set forth a high standard. The goal of your ascension is the highest goal of life. It demands excellence of striving and character—above all, the keeping of one's word; therefore do not give it lightly.

We have already attained the goal of the ascension—my blessed mother has attained it, your blessed Saint Germain has attained it, and when you attain it, it will make you one with the immortals. I do not think, then, that anyone should gamble with such an opportunity.

All of us were obedient to God as we made our way up the mount of transfiguration. We counted it the highest honor to so be and to so attain, and so it is.

Kuthumi also spoke of thinking on Light, and that is the second step. The third is like it—thinking on Power. This Power is never human and must never be humanly appropriated: it is the all-Power of God. It is his "omnipotence." Doing these three things while repeating the "I AM" Lord's Prayer as I am reciting it here with you can raise your consciousness greatly:

Our Father who art in heaven,
Hallowed be thy name, I AM.
I AM thy kingdom come
I AM thy will being done
I AM on earth even as I AM in heaven
I AM giving this day daily bread to all
I AM forgiving all Life this day even as
I AM also all Life forgiving me
I AM leading all men away from
     temptation
I AM delivering all men from every evil
     condition
I AM the kingdom

I AM the power and
I AM the glory of God in eternal, immortal
   manifestation—
All this I AM.

The Light of God within you and the Power of God within you will assist you in expanding the Light (Christos) in every molecule of your being, until your own Presence floods forth its light rays to the center of each cell and to your heart center itself to glorify you as a Sun of God even as was done for me!

What I tell you may seem to your outer minds but little, yet it is enough, blessed ones. The wise shall use it to attain transfiguration. After all, the Voice that spoke saying, "This is my beloved Son in whom I AM well pleased," was the Voice I had long obeyed.

Peace be unto you, my peace I give unto you. *Be*, then, that peace!

I AM the living Christ,

Jesus

Corona Class Lesson 18

Wisdom

"Give Thy Servant an Understanding Heart"

Beloved Who Would Approach
        the Mount of Transfiguration with Him—
    Ascended Master words are cups of light
indeed—of this you may be certain. Beloved
ones, our Pearls of Wisdom on this vital subject, transfiguration, have not been as long as
usual. This is for a reason. We are more interested in your getting the feeling of what this
blessing will mean to you personally and to
those fortunate enough to be associated with
you when you have this experience (which
automatically attunes you more completely
with God) than we are in your intellectual conception thereof.

    We realize that some men and women who
read these words may not fully understand the
scriptures on these sacred subjects or even the
purposes of God, due to the unfortunate effect of
early training in this lifetime. Then, too, bitter

lessons learned in the schoolrooms of life have left their scars upon their natures.

Also, the truths of heaven have grown dim within their soul memory, whispering in syllables that seem forgotten symbols to the outer consciousness. Yet they are so rich in meaning to the immortal consciousness of the Holy Spirit who feeds the inner man [1] with the true manna (spiritual bread) of God that expands all that is of God within the soul.

Blessed ones, to have our guidance may not seem important to those who like to feel that they are a law unto themselves (and they usually are). But you who have truly utilized the knowledge we have conveyed have almost always found it possible to avoid pitfalls and to make a more rapid as well as a safe progress in the perfections and wonders of the Divine. Not the least of man's gifts is wisdom. Solomon sought it above all and received in addition all the treasures of earth. [2]

Following from afar in admiration of the Christ and the Ascended Masters may be interesting and informative, but to practice the laws of God as we did and to attain to a practical demonstration of our spiritual techniques is the surest path to victory and freedom—not only for the individual but for the entire planet!

Those who wish to continue to think in the thoughtforms of children may do so; those who are not content with such a gait are the more energetic builders who rank among the constructive people of every age. These come into the vanguard of divine experiences and become either potential candidates for the ascension at the close of this embodiment or future saints and sages to show the way back Home to other seekers everywhere, who are also God's children.

To change, then, from the limitations of human thought and feeling and to unite with your own God Presence before your ascension is to contact the Light that initiated all creation, both material and spiritual. It is to provide untrammeled avenues of thought to the radiance of God and to deny the waves of discordant energy entry into your feeling world. It is to transform this energy by the violet flame's transmutation, charging it with such a magnitude of God's light, love, and power that it shall never again be requalified with human conditions or limitations.

This is a permanent, wholly constructive initiation which, once experienced, brings new understanding to the scriptural passage referring to Jesus' garments during the transfiguration, "white as snow, whiter than any fuller could white them."[3] The transfiguration is a living gift to each man and woman so honored, so immaculately clothed by God in the white light!

Together, blessed Jesus and I await your externalization of this gift. May the excellence of

the Light and the Power be yours, our pupils
who shall soon be, by your example, qualified
instructors of the Christian mysteries.

I AM your progressive attainment
in the unfailing Light—

Your brother,

Kuthumi

Sin

¹**sin** \ 'sin \ *n* -S [ME *sinne*, fr. OE *synn, syn;*
akin to OFris *sende* sin, OS *sundia,* OHG *sunta,*
suntea and perh. to L *sont-, sons* guilty; prob.
akin to L *est* is —more at IS] **1 a :** a transgression of religious law **:** an offense against God
⟨making her dream. . .of the ~ which he resolved
to allure her to commit —Daniel Defoe⟩ **b :** a serious offense **:** a violation of propriety ⟨colleges
which glorify research and publication. . .are
guilty of a grave and perhaps irreparable ~
against civilization —Millicent McIntosh⟩ ⟨the
rhetorical ~ of the meaningless variation —Lewis
Mumford⟩ **c :** a serious shortcoming **:** FAULT ⟨the
English ~ has always been. . .a lack of social co-
herence —Herbert Read⟩ **2 :** violation of religious
law **:** disregard of God's will ⟨thought about the
nature of ~ in general —H.E.Fosdick⟩; *specif* **:**
violation of proscription of fornication ⟨accused
. . .of living in ~ with her fiancé —Leslie Rees⟩
— see ACTUAL SIN, DEADLY SIN, MORTAL SIN, ORIGINAL
SIN, VENIAL SIN

²**sin** \ " \ *vb* **sinned; sinned; sinning; sins**
[ME *sinnen, singen,* fr. OE *syngian;* akin to MD
sondigen to sin, ON *syndga;* denominative fr. the
root of E ¹*sin*] *vi* **1 :** to violate religious law **:**
commit an offense against God; *specif* **:** FORNI-
CATE **2 :** to commit an offense ⟨critics often
sinned against good critical sense —C.I.Glicks-
berg⟩ ~ *vt* **1 :** to perform sinfully ⟨there
remains so much to be *sinned* and suffered in
the world —Nathaniel Hawthorne⟩ **2** *archaic* **:** to
drive by sinning ⟨we have *sinned* him hence —
John Dryden⟩ — **sin one's mercies :** to show
ingratitude

Law

"With What Measure Ye Mete . . ."

To All Who Condemn Not the Word,
         but Hope in Him—
    The smoking censers of sweet incense
swinging in the wilderness tabernacles of the
children of Israel often commingled in the wind
with the odor of sacrificial burnt offerings.
These were sacrifices offered to appease a supposedly wrathful God in atonement for the
many sins of the children of Israel committed
during their wilderness wanderings. [1]
    The desire to appease God, the wish to find
release from feelings of guilt and its attendant
oppression, and the idea that forgiveness is possible occupy the minds of millions of God's
children to the present day. Understandable,
then, is the contrast between the sweet incense
symbolizing prayer, love, and adoration and the
somewhat odoriferous idea of animal or human
sacrifice.

Under the guidance of the Darjeeling Council of the Great White Brotherhood, beloved Jesus and I are currently releasing this series of lessons in order to create a climate of greater understanding of what sin *is*, what sin is *not*, and what effective countermeasures can be taken to neutralize its effects by removing its cause and core. The involvement of conscience and consciousness with sin, the high expectations God has for his offspring, and a general clarification of this entire subject is to be compressed into our Corona Class Lessons, sent to you with all our love.

This sending should prove highly beneficial to those who carefully assimilate our instruction, for we are determined to put into it much needed assistance for all disciples who would teach Truth to the child heart. We are, however, well aware of the fact that some of our new students retain biased concepts or some religious bigotry. These we admonish to keep those old thought and feeling momentums under control until the completion of the course, in order to forestall any negative interference that would block the flow of our divine ideas into their worlds.

For some this will not be difficult, but for others who may feel a false sense of loyalty to this or that doctrine or its proponent (as I did on occasion, prior to my ascension, when identified with various religious faiths), it may require greater restraint in order to attend that understanding which, by its nearness to God, will be the best self-evident proof of our teaching.

Blessed ones, in connection with such matters as belief systems and religious faiths, remember that long before you reached your present understanding in this life, your concepts underwent change many times—and it is always possible that they will do so again in the course of the journey leading to the circle of understanding of the so-called mysteries of Life.

These matters may seem "cut and dried" to those who are grounded in a specific teaching; but in order to obtain freedom from *any* or *all* error inherent in a human system, the price you must be willing to pay is simply to keep an open mind and heart. Pause, then, both to consider new ideas and to reexamine old ones in the blazing light of the forthcoming divine knowledge.

In the world of science, the true scientist must be willing to keep open the avenues of receptivity and to constantly reevaluate long-established theories about the matter universe. By his eagerness to examine new evidence, even if it invalidate his former conclusions, he becomes a reliable channel for the progress of all men.

Spiritual values and principles must also stand the supreme test of validity *and demonstrability* in time and eternity. It should be recognized, however, that people's concepts concerning the application of eternal truths can be both accurate and inaccurate. Admitting that to err is human, then, the ministering servant must examine his own spiritual progress as it corresponds to the new thoughts that flow from the heavenly octave where I AM—that there ye may be also. [2]

The sincere students of Christian literature may well recall the biblical scene when beloved Jesus stooped down and carefully wrote in the sand those words which freed the supposedly sinful woman from the scorn of her would-be executioners. His statement, "He that is without sin among you—let him first cast a stone at her," [3] is a classic reminder of the 'humanness' of sin and firmly supports the later remarks of Saint Paul who declared, "There is none righteous, no, not one." [4] David's statement in the Psalms "In sin did my mother conceive me" [5] is also apropos the idea that "all have sinned and come short of the glory of God." [6]

Now, blessed ones, dear Jesus often declared while yet embodied in physical form that the Son of man came not into the world to condemn the world, but that through him the world might find the path to eternal Life. [7] It is reasonable to assume that whatever sin may be, all men have either been guilty of it or have submitted to it at one time or another.

It is correct—and I say far more so—to conclude that God as Spirit, as Law, and as the manifestation of the Shekinah glory [8] is not at all interested in the condemnation of earth's evolutions or in singling out individuals because of their present or past condition of sin. Rather is he supremely interested in *freeing* them from the ignorance of sin (and sinful ignorance) and the wiles of the Tempter.

Usually when pondering the doctrines of sin formulated by men, people engage in one of two misconceptions: either they excuse themselves while condemning their brothers for the same error, or they create the image of an angry God made in their own likeness, sustained by their own feelings of guilt and the consequent need for punishment or atonement.

The carnal mind derives satisfaction from contemplating this false picture of God only because it reinforces its own synthetic image and world view and allows it to hate and kill and maim in the name of its god. But the soul, knowing that the Father is in reality all-wise and all-loving, acts accordingly when free from the indoctrination (condemnation) of the serpent mind.

It is true that before the birth of beloved Jesus much of the karmic retribution portrayed in Old Testament scriptures did tend to support the idea of an angry God (the harshness of the Law untempered by the grace of the Divine Mediator); and the carry-over from the old to the new dispensation, because of Christianity's roots in Judaic tradition, has in some quarters affected Christian thought to the present.

If the eyes of men were opened to perceive the immensity of world pain returned upon them daily (by the law of karma) for redemption; if they could see that this pain and their attendant suffering is caused by their erroneous

concepts concerning sin and condemnation—
they would understand the urgent necessity for
us to shed light upon every shadowy, unhappy
thought concentration on the matter.

Sincere study and the correct explanation
from the office of the World Teachers removes
from erroneous concepts the sting and strength
of error. The orthodoxy of many religionists
(most of whom are sincere people) may be trod-
den upon in this dissertation, but in the spiritual 'ivory tower' of my own ascension, I have no
fear of human censure.

And thus I am determined—with a fervor
beyond the usual gentility imputed to me by
many of the chelas—to alert the responsive and
receptive ones to these accurate probings in
Ascended Master Truth which lead to the promised land of freedom. There the milk and honey of
spiritually sweetened thought is become that understanding which creates greater harmony with
God, peace within oneself, and the power to pro-
mote goodwill among the blessed people of earth
whom we dearly love in God's name, I AM.

The biblical statement "the sting of death is
sin; and the strength of sin is the law"[9] is then
brought forward for clarification. The idea that
"the strength of sin is the law" is a key idea
and contains the understanding which beloved
Hilarion, as Saint Paul, recorded in his great
wisdom.

From one standpoint, the law of which he
spoke is the law of mortality, man-made—
which itself is strengthened by the law of

karma. Death has a sting only where the individual has sustained his own mortality through
his failure to absolve the record of sin. This he
is obliged to do through balancing his karma
by good works and the application of the violet
flame in dynamic decrees. [10]

The relative strength of sin is subject to the
law of transmutation whereby through repentance and remission of sin one can transmute by
the sacred fire the cause, effect, record, and
memory of all error and thereby no longer be
under the karmic weight of prior acts. Sin loses
all power over the individual once he subjects it
and himself fully and finally to the Law of Love.

As you know, beloved ones, it seems there
are as many motives as there are people, yet
this is not true. For the itemizing of human motives soon terminates and it is quickly perceived
that outside of a subtle shading in variety,
human motives are quite basic. Furthermore, it
will be found that for the most part human
attitudes and motivations originate in a misunderstanding as well as in an understanding of
the laws of God.

Excessive feelings of hopelessness often
overtake men when they contemplate the need
to forsake their so-called sins. This, in turn,
generates the feeling that they cannot live up to
the high standard of the Law. Their perception
of the "rigidity" of the Law seems to favor continuing in so-called sin and the way of all flesh
because the goal of sinlessness appears nigh
impossible. Thus at times it is, in fact, the

blessed Law misunderstood, and its apparent inflexibility, which encourages and strengthens both the sense of sin and the act of sin!

Now, we of the Great White Brotherhood in no way desire to see shadow amplified by false doctrine or false teaching, nor would we do aught but assist each soul to find its way back Home. Blessed ones, it is results that count in spiritual matters as well as material ones. And so, in divine practicality, I should point out that the blessed Law is in reality neither weak nor rigid: It is the statement of the purity of eternal Truth. It is the codification of immortal values and standards which by their very nature cannot be compromised by lesser principles—the latter by contrast, appearing at times almost evil.

In truth, the Law is the greatest security in the universe, protecting the righteous and commanding the unrighteous to forsake the sinful unreality of their ways and come up higher. While affording ample opportunity for all to mercifully dismiss sin and the law of sin from their worlds, the Great Law also promises absolute God-justice to evildoers[11] who persist in their evildoings, blasphemous towards Christ and his Call.

Your deliverance from all self-delusion is our goal in these Corona Class Lessons. In relation to the foregoing, your freedom from sin and the sense of sinfulness should liberate your soul from an oppressive apprehension of the hurdles of the Law—and what has seemed to be your own limitation in jumping over those hurdles.

Understand, then, that there are eternal as well as temporal values. Surely God who is wholly perfect could not permit his permanent Law to uphold a standard less than absolute perfection. Life on earth reveals countless examples of the great mercy of God, daily bestowed with the infinite patience he extends to all his creation.

Therefore, let none wrongly conclude that God is angry with them or with any part of Life. Neither let them foolishly conclude that, because he is not angry, the Lords of Karma who follow the perfect promptings of the Father of all will let pass deliberate or wanton acts of malice carried out against another part of Life.

For Justice declares, "With what measure ye mete, it shall be measured to you again." [12] This is an operative law and relates to the conduct of men in their dealings with one another. However, in their personal relationship to their own Mighty I AM Presence and the eternal Law of Perfection, there is ever the guiding hand of the patient Father (extended through the Son) who without condemnation adores to see his children know the Truth that makes them free.

No longer permit the high hurdles of the Law or your own temporary limitations to hinder your demonstration of the Law. Let the reach exceed the grasp, and strive by illustriousness of spirit to magnify your God-power for the accomplishment of righteousness—the *right use* (instead of the wrong use) *of the Law* among all children of the Light.

Know that each small strength you summon expands the victory of your soul, measurably increasing the Light that illumines, blesses, and heals you. Each act which reinforces the honor of the Law strengthens the manifestation of the great causal Law of Love as it moves the entire creation, in measured cadence, into eternal tabernacles of the Spirit.

It is the sweetness of Love immortal, like fragrant incense rising, that requires no shadow of animal or human sacrifice—only Christ-accomplishment which fulfills the whole Law for you, His grace multiplying your good words and good works.

I thank you.

Kuthumi Lal Singh

Corona Class Lesson 20

Love

"Thy Sins Be Forgiven Thee!"

To the Blessed
  Who Have Suffered Guilt Too Long—
  The power men have given, inadvisedly, to the whole idea of sin must be broken ere the full perfection of God can be fully known. Humanity through force of habit continually re-creates feelings of guilt which mar the soul, shading the brilliant stream of divine illumination passing through, as it were, a pane of glass and depriving the 'lightstream' (lifestream) of the wondrous luminescence of God.

  I am determined to assist the beloved chelas and every sincere student of earth's schoolroom in bettering their understanding of the transcendent laws of Life by which the universe operates. For far too long the race has continued in a round of ceaseless condemnation of themselves and others, resulting in a habitual misqualification of energy. This has caused a false conscience to be created within the subconscious, inculcating feelings of guilt and unworthiness in self and others. These feelings reinforce in turn the false conscience which then overrides the inner voice of the Divine One, who is the only true and reliable conscience.

My parable of the prodigal son[1] portrays God's true relationship with his beloved children. It makes clear that our Father never intended his sons and daughters to eat the husks of sin or to dwell in the limitations of sin as presently measured by human thought and feeling.

Surely our Father never intended to see his son waste his energy in riotous living; yet by making wrong choices, the son did in fact enter into karmic conditions of servitude and bondage. This is not to say that whenever the erring one determines to arise and shake off his carnal shackles, the powers of Light will not immediately blaze forth the required assistance to welcome that beloved one Home, where forgiveness is complete. Indeed, it is so.

Through the whirlpool of human consciousness, the downward pull of the senses, and the oft-repeated failure of the human to look up, mankind completely overlook this divine intent; and God's love, our love—which is a precious ointment—is often spilled in wasteful self-pity and selfish self-love. And more's the tragedy when one considers the loss of entire segments of a life-span and the misappropriation of energy which should rather have been used to fulfill the sacred mission of a life.

The solution is simple: the misdirected attention must be refocused upon the Great God Source and kept there. By placing it on their problems, mankind have only multiplied them instead of diminishing them by the universal love and care which heaven is constantly pouring forth. This they have frequently failed to see simply because they were looking in the wrong direction—down, not up!

While feelings of guilt may spur men to seek confession and penance, these feelings are never the means of setting them free. Do not be deceived by human foolishness! If guilt were from God who is all Good, the end result of this feeling would itself be good; but if it stem from human error, no matter how real seeming, it cannot produce any permanent good whatsoever in your world.

Guilt is a vibration which is related to condemnation of self and others; and when you accept it or entertain it in *any* form, you become disturbed unless the thought be swiftly changed.

Now, there is a voice of conscience and I certainly do not mean to discourage its use. I am, however, interested that the true chela understand the difference between that which alternately self-condemns and self-justifies and that which correctly instructs, inspires, and guides into all Truth, all Love, all Righteousness, and the fulfillment of God's divine plan for each precious life in accord with the Law of Love.

You see, codification of the Law has been a

human requirement. Moses' labor of love in communing with his own Mighty I AM Presence brought forth the Ten Commandments from the heart of the Ancient of Days. These have been and continue to be a mighty assistance in the development of human law and order, constricting human behavior so as to cause less destructive (and more constructive) world karma.

Today the Law requires that individuals develop for themselves the inner sense of the Law of Love and then outpicture it in living for Truth. This I advocated during the final embodiment of my earthly mission and I remain constant in stimulating its emphasis in everyone's affairs. Now the Ten Commandments and much more are read from the inward parts of man where God has written the Tablets of the Law of personal Christhood built on the ten.

Humanity's incorrect assimilation and practice of the divine plan may be compared to a misuse of the photographic process. First, in clicking the shutter they do not admit enough light. Second, in developing the divine image they adulterate the process so that the finished proof is altered to resemble laggard qualities more than the righteous expressions of the Divine One.

Even today many people live in a primitive state of consciousness insofar as the Law of Love is concerned. Neither riches nor education can guarantee men's spiritual integrity. By sincere attunement with the law of harmony and the education of the heart through a mighty demonstration of the real love of God, the disciple is relieved of the severity of the dos and don'ts of the Law. Thus, by personal application the great warmth of the Law of Love acts to expand the spirituality of each lifestream.

Endued with the fullness of the Spirit, the soul will naturally obey the Ten Commandments in an attitude of joy and freedom. Through the spiritual exercise of the Law, the security and protection of the Law is guaranteed to all who obey it. Beyond this, the grace and mercy of the Law also extend the blessings of higher octaves to the gracious and the merciful servants of the Law.

The spiritual senses are best quickened by a pure spirit free from feelings of condemnation and guilt. To all sincere chelas of the Great Law, I AM therefore saying, Thy sins be forgiven thee!

Greater peace in the feeling world and an intense desire to be in attunement with the omnipresence of God will be the first signs following your acceptance of this intercession of my grace. From the center of Christ-forgiveness, there blazes forth a delightful inner confidence that God's abundance is all around you—a feeling that God's love in you is so magnificent that sin and the record of sin are completely swallowed up by it! Thus are death and the "wages of sin" swallowed up in total victory.[2]

While the world debates the politics of the day and hopes to obtain salvation in the social order, the power of the kingdom of heaven continues to express divine justice individually to each person on earth. America's spiritual destiny in the "inner world government" is to be the cupbearer of Light (of the Christ consciousness) to the world, the fount of Divine Liberty for the earth. By rightly understanding his divine Sonship, akin to my own, each disciple will help to make this universally possible for all nations and peoples. Thus, each life mission is important to the Father.

It must be realized that distortions in connection with my mission have been almost overwhelming. The divine doctrine of the remission of sins, taught by John the Baptist before me,[3] is little understood. My words uttered both before and after my crucifixion conferring upon my apostles the power to remit or to retain sin[4]—to thus exercise the law of forgiveness as well as the law of the judgment—would indicate that even at that time blood sacrifice was not the necessary ingredient in this process. Quite the contrary, forgiveness is an alchemy of love, of repentance, of cleansing by the Word and of the healing of the desire to sin again.

I spoke to many, saying, "Thy sins be forgiven thee,"[5] and again, "Go and sin no more"[6]—yet the world's religious delusion to which countless millions pay unfortunate allegiance (believing they do my will and the will of the Father) centers around this false idea that propitiation in the form of a painful punishment is required by a vengeful Deity. These see my crucifixion as sacrificial, my mission as unique, and my Sonship as greater than all, whereas to God every son is already one with the Father.

You see, whenever error is accepted as though it were real, it becomes by the pressure of its acceptance a flaw in the foundation of the temple which each one is building. Such a flaw can throw the entire structure off plumb for a lifetime (and succeeding lifetimes) unless and until it is corrected. Let me begin, then, this correction on behalf of Truth.

The "way of the cross" pertains to the meeting of God and man. It depicts the manifestation of God in man who is in the process of obtaining the perfection of his own ascension in the Light, even as I did. Eventually this "outer man" will be completely absorbed into his perfect Selfhood, but were he to merge prematurely with his God Self, which is an all-consuming fire,[7] it would destroy the very fabric of his soul-identity.

Therefore, it is the mercy of the Great Law, which never lowers its standards or fails in its compassion, to create a wide spiral in the eternal cycles of time and space where the becoming God-likeness of man is nurtured by the wisdom-love of God. Hence, in the cruciform of life man finds an avenue leading to permanent victory, and the reality of the Father becomes known and understood as an act of complete, enduring love.

If any sacrifice be required for man to return to his natural, spiritual Sonship, it is the sacrifice of wayward and willful human qualities. As beloved Kuthumi and I have stated

before, the path to God is never so much a
sacrifice as it is a sacrament, never so much
sacrificial as sacramental.

Go, then, and sin no more—to the best of your
ability. But do not be tense about it, blessed
ones. You see, your increasing spiritual strength
and understanding ought never to be sapped by
condemnation of self or others. If you abide in
loving forgiveness, it will be much easier for you
to find your complete freedom in the way of the
Christ, through right understanding and the
fullness of God which surrounds you now and
forever. As the Psalms declare, "Whither shall
I flee from thy presence?"[8]

Therefore, in truth ye *do* know the Way: for
I AM the Way, I AM the Truth, and I AM the Life.
No man cometh to the Father (his God Presence)
except through me (the Holy Christ Self of each
one),[9] and this is the universal plan—the same
for all.

Face and overcome sin, condemnation,
false conscience, and fear. To all these declare
fervently and know that:

> I AM the fullness of God/Good!
>
> I AM walking into daily oneness with
> the Father.
>
> I AM made ever new in God's image,
> the similitude and likeness of all that is
> Good.
>
> I AM the justice of the divine Law
> which reaches out to fulfill the true spirit
> of both human and divine Law.

I AM the manifestation of that sacred Law, and in the joy of the ascended Jesus Christ consciousness,

I AM illumined to know that this living, inner Law is the Golden Rule!

May peace and power attend thee always.

I AM in Truth thy elder brother,

Jesus the Christ

Conscience

"As a Man Thinketh in His Heart . . ."

To the Dear Seeker
      after the Thread of Consciousness—
    The consciousness of every man is keenly linked to memory, and it is the memory process which files an orderly sequence of events in the storehouse of being and ties together the past and the present (and even the future) into a rationally self-realized whole. The stream of consciousness flows into the mold of memory, and it is the resulting image which, when formed with the proper intensity of thought and feeling, becomes preserved as a record.

    We shall now show the relationship between consciousness and conscience. Using thought and feeling processes, man individually and collectively has evolved so-called behavioral norms which he regards as good or evil. Although the formula may change over the years, man persistently holds many basic concepts about what is and what is not acceptable.

These evolve into social mores which, when reinforced by racial and religious habit patterns, become tradition. Tradition itself stems from both right and wrong attitudes of thinking and feeling, and is the result of human logic wrapped in emotional overtones which shape the emerging pattern. The results are never final and often lack both objectivity and equity. Seldom do they show forth the luster of either real humanity or divinity.

Apart from these pressures of thought and feeling, there is a still stronger influence at work. This is the eternal voice of each one's own God Self. The God Presence of each lifestream ever strives to make its righteousness known by seeking to penetrate every human density and to correct every wrong idea.

Bear in mind, blessed ones, that the perfection of the eternal spheres surrounds the material creation and is always amplified without limit by the wonderful angelic host, the devas and cosmic beings, including the entire hierarchy of heaven.

This benign influence affecting all planes of being is marvelous to behold at inner levels, whether or not people are outwardly aware of it. (Of course, if they are, it makes cooperation easier! Hence, our explanations are forthcoming for all who require this instruction in order to make the most of Life's seen and unseen opportunities and blessings.)

I am certain you are aware that in various ages, including the present, a number of these wonderful beings have appeared to the few and sometimes to the many in order to encourage them and to create in them a more resolute faith.

Dear ones, divine conscience is the preceptor of each lifestream; it is activated in a special compartment of consciousness linked with the memory of inner-level experiences. Its function is to record within the soul and the outer self guiding reins from divine levels. These constraints emanate from the Holy Christ Flame—even the golden-yellow plume of illumination distilled by the 'hidden man of the heart'—assisting all who intuit its gentle but firm leadings to better fulfill their divine plan.

The true divine conscience is sensitive to the intimations of the Christ Self, but sometimes (and quite often in many lifestreams) the human conscience responds to the pressures of the mass mind. Humanly accepted norms—those thought to be socially correct or religiously righteous—have a marked influence on many, which accounts for the differing levels of tolerance in various peoples and cultures.

Thus, amplified and standardized through the human media, the mass mind has built up a set of values all its own. Though often mechanistic, these send forceful influences through the radiating power of the human aura which impinge upon that God-directed guidance ever-present within each one's true conscience, whether readily apparent or beneath the threshold of awareness.

Because this admixture of the humanly acquired and the divinely endowed conscience is to be found in the majority of souls presently embodied, it is important in the face of pressures from all quarters for each disciple to understand the action of conscience, memory, and consciousness in his own being. If he will rightly understand this teaching and apply its knowledge, it will help much to eliminate a senseless round of personal criticism, condemnation, sin, and self-judgment.

Dear students, realize that your God Self has given you the power of free will so that you will lovingly, joyously choose to meditate on your own life plan—to think about it, to invoke it, to pursue it, and to will it into manifestation. This process is intended to stimulate your own realization of and respect for divine values and enable you to more effectively establish in consciousness that conscience which is a truly sensitive instrument. This inner voice does not induce self-torture and anguish but offers guidance and comfort that enables you to decipher the true will of the Father and the Son always with you in your own I AM Presence and Holy Christ Self.

Out of consciousness attuned to Divinity arises the right idea which transmutes the wrong idea, supplanting erring thought and emotions with the eternal banner of Truth, Light, and Right. This triple reinforcement of your Christ Self frees the soul from all past mistakes based on ignorance, dogma, doctrinal controversy, ecclesiasticism, 'situation ethics', the woeful misunderstanding of the life and mission of beloved Jesus, and all so-called evil vibrations. Then there is quickened within the heart the holy image of God revealed in each one's purified and true conscience as that reflected radiance, the divine gift to all who listen to God's voice of loving intelligence within.

Foremost among the erroneous concepts of mankind is the ever-present memory of wrong-doing which causes them to equate that wrong with sin and then to suffer self-damnation from their conclusion. Beloved Jesus knew that on earth only the few are intentional wrongdoers. He taught that if men really understood the Law and the far-reaching consequences of their misdeeds, they would not persist in their gross violations of conscience. His prayer "Father, forgive them, for they know not what they do"[1] embodies his merciful understanding toward the misguided multitudes.

In the centuries since his blessed ascension, through his cosmic service to the earth, the Master has evolved many spiritually sound approaches to manifold human problems. With the objective of giving greater freedom to the children of the Sun of Righteousness, the offspring of the Most High, the World Teachers are desirous of communicating these solutions to all who will read and run with the good news, both hearing and doing His word. One of our grand solutions is to correct, one by one, every wrong idea of sin held in mind.

Perceive: As a man thinketh in his heart, so is he;[2] therefore, one's thought, as the thinking process, held in mind and memory is ever a powerful part of one's consciousness as pertains to individual identity. This thought which so molds and limits the human personality includes all opinions, faulty premises and conclusions blindly held, as well as outright lies, fabrication and fantasy stubbornly adhered to regardless of all reason or evidence to the contrary.

Consider the intense feelings of scorn held in the desire body which coalesce around many nonsensical notions concerning people, politics, mores, and religion! Inasmuch as all warping of reality exists only in human thought and feeling, it is from these areas of the conscious and subconscious mind that sin and the sense of sin must be cast out.

Beloved, the correct thought about God is not always enthroned in the conscience of man. For example: God is eternal, Life is eternal; therefore God is Life and Life is God. By a like reasoning one can see that God is Mind and Mind is God and, as such, He is not only conscious, but He is also Consciousness itself.

This Mind who *is* universal Consciousness embodies the Law and the Truth of being for every manifestation of Himself—made in his image and likeness. As the center of all Self-awareness, including that of his offspring, this Mind, then, is also the Divine Conscience—the discriminating intelligence of good and evil, right and wrong, Himself exercising (and enabling man to exercise) free will.

Now, these thoughts are the correct thoughts *about* God. Going one step further, we see that the correct thought *of* God in man (i.e., the thoughts God thinks in and through man) is, then, man's only true or necessary conscience. And this Divine Conscience is God! With this understanding which thou shalt surely gain through oneness with the universal Mind, the first and only commandment the disciple would ever need is "Thou shalt have no other Conscience before me!"[3]

God is all-powerful, all-wise, wholly pure. Sin can never be a part of this God who is your life, your spirit, your being. It can only be a part of you if you make it so by indulging the sense of sin, revolving states of error long forsaken and forgiven, or engaging in acts forbidden by the Great Law. Sin has only as much reality as your own mind or the mass mind gives it.

A false conscience is a tinderbox piled high with theological, psychological, and illogical illusions. Many of the erroneous Judeo-Christian teachings are centered on the idea of sin, punishment, and propitiation by human or animal sacrifice. In the absolute Love of God for and in man, sin is entirely nonexistent. From the standpoint of the immaculate image held in the universal Mind, *sin is not real!* regardless of how many scriptural verses refer to it.

Sin exists in the dead past, in pagan and superstitious ideas colored to look real—often distorted, mark you, by well-meaning and sin-cere people who, though acting in good faith, are full of misplaced loyalty. All of this unholy error must be transmuted by holy Truth.

If the energy people have given to the wrong concept of sin, binding forever and forever bind-ing the Father's beloved children to hellfire and damnation (think of this dreadful, truly sinful, doctrine!), had been used to reinforce the true metaphysical concepts of the soul's innate vir-tue, the earth would long ago have been free from the stain of repetitious sin—dyed in the wool, believed in, and therefore committed over and over again.

Outworn traditions handed down from par-ents to children have for too long deceived the very elect. [4] Even those well grounded in the spiritual truths, who ought to know better, will through force of habit start the condemnation process all over again in their silent scorn—erupting now and again with vituperation and contumely.

Frequently, such as these become depressed by their own self-condemnation periodically heaped upon others and they begin to believe that their lives are falling short of the mark. A moment's reflection on the thought that God is all around them and that in reality they can-not live life solely unto themselves (except it be in a delusory, vapory, human-miasma-type existence) will soon evaporate their self-deceit—sown in the bitterness of constant criticism—without a trace. So be it!

Until the doctrine of sin is removed from the world, and especially from the world of the disciple, how can he successfully hold an immaculate concept of himself and of those to whom he would teach the way of forgiveness through noncondemnation? So long as one thinks that vile people exist anywhere in the realms of God's perfection, how can one's thought be immaculate?

The false belief that sin or evil has a life of its own perpetuated by God must be cast into the sacred fires of Truth. Once you have fully and finally transmuted by the violet flame of purity the karmic debris and residual effects of this damnable concept, you will be ready to take the next step on the path of the ministering servant. As an act of grace, the God-magnificence of Life will come to the fore in your consciousness and, by the power of the Holy Spirit and your own joyousness, express itself through you to all who yearn for the sunshine of liberating Truth.

Beloved, God is the high standard and the best rule by whom the creation and selfhood come into being. One who does not express the highest that he is capable of often permits himself to indulge a care-less attitude. Through the misuse of free will people remain entrenched in the lesser, or prodigal, role. The Golden Rule establishes the standard through your own Holy Christ Self that every motive and act be one of love by each part of Life toward every other part of Life.

Sin, then, is *never* real. It is a laggard idea dealing in the blacks, whites, and grays of human consciousness, whereas God's consciousness, which is your Life, is all Light!

Sin is never real, and therefore in obtaining freedom from it, men must identify *it* as nothing and *God* as all. There is a karmic ledger that must be balanced, and by karmic law human error must be adjusted and adjudicated before the Lords of Karma.

Serving to set free every part of Life that has suffered by one's mistakes, healing old hurts, mending fences, and displacing human conduct by divine conduct is in accord with the justice of God meted out at human levels, and none shall escape so much as a jot or a tittle of the Law or his responsibility for each and every ungodly act toward any part of Life.[5] Mercy's flames give freedom to all through the diligent application of the violet fire and through hearts burning with eternal love which imputes not sin to any who truly love God and care for his flock, as did Abraham of old.[6]

Build, then, in consciousness the celestial Christ-concept of all Good, and secure your victory. Such thinking will not lower your standards or carry you into byways of delusion; for by simple, direct contact with your own God Presence, you will unloose the limitless power to achieve the goal of sinlessness—without spot or blemish[7] marring the garment of the soul. The divergent angle between the human and God is best closed by realizing that with God all things are, in truth, possible.[8]

True self-preservation is to keep active the divine Principle which animates the temple of being with the eternal heart flame of God. The perfection of God will become a sacred Eucharist on the heart's altar, where the sacred fire imbues each one with the tender truth of a loving Father dwelling in the loving heart of his obedient son.

This is the revolutionary idea that makes of mortals immortals; of men, gods—and casts all, in Mercy's love and name, upon the Life of the eternal plan and the Wisdom of the eternal Good.

I AM loving you free from all sin.

In Wisdom's holy name,

Kuthumi Lal Singh

Sacrifice

"Without Shedding of Blood . . ."

To the Deserving of the Path of Joy,
      Abundance, and Happiness—
    Foremost among God's ideas scintillating in the universe is the ever-living love that radiates joy to the world. The poor in spirit[1] as well as those deficient in this world's goods will always find enough in the cup of Christ's consciousness that runneth over.[2] His abundant Light fills every human need—and divine.

    I AM the source of all joy, of all abundance, of all! Why, then, do men seek to find happiness elsewhere? It is because in their sense of lack they amplify their need to possess that which in reality is already their own. This is a misunderstanding of the divine vision of universal Love which gives without limit to all.

    Religious movements are conceived in order that people might be happy in God in the present and that they might find happiness in God in the future. The security of heaven is an anchor for which men yearn. I am certain, then, that the Spirit of the Father flashes out in response to each blessed lamb with an intensity beyond that soul's yearning.

God's love can be perceived shining through the foliage of Nature, in the electronic composition of matter, and as a light in the eyes of men. So little understood is God, so little is he known or realized by most men, that scarcely can they conceive of his outpouring of power which lies latent within their being.

You see, blessed ones, by the law of the circle, when you apply limitation to another it returns to you for adjustment. When in ignorance people apply limitation to God, to others, or to themselves, this practice, which is most dangerous, causes the Great Law to withhold from them the very powers of Light which would give them their freedom.

The statement that "truth is stranger than fiction" is often true. Just think of the hundreds of years that Christendom (which means "Christ's kingdom") has contemplated the sacrificial aspects of my crucifixion! But in this case, the truth about sacrifice could not possibly be stranger than the fiction that has been handed down concerning the crucifixion.

Biblical writers, saints, prophets, and holy men have written and taught about the idea of appeasing an angry God through the blood sacrifice of his Son. Although these have acted with great sincerity, they have nevertheless been influenced by the strictly pagan practice handed down from distant days when men departed from the ancient religions of Atlantis wherein true communion with God was taught and experienced as the interchange (sacrificial emission) of light between the soul and the Spirit.

Subsequently, the true art of sacrifice (self-giving unto God) degenerated into the sinister and perverted uses of the sacred fire in sexual rites performed at the altar. As a substitute for the ritual of self-sacrifice of the synthetic image (shedding the snakeskin of the serpent mind), the false priests offered temple virgins (in place of themselves) in sacrifices of appeasement to the gods. (It came to pass prior to the flood that young men were offered in place of women.) The malpracticing priesthood encouraged the bizarre and sensual in their subjects and, magnetizing the denizens of the astral world through nefarious incantations, cooperated with the black magicians who created the conditions which led to the Noachian deluge and the sinking of Atlantis.[3]

The Canaanite idea of child sacrifice, "burning their sons and daughters in the fire,"[4] temple prostitution, and burnt offerings and sacrifices to Baal, imitated by the Israelites, recalled the last days of a decadent Atlantis. These abominations, of Nephilim[5] origin, were denounced by Jeremiah and Ezekiel, as well as by Isaiah, Amos, and Micah.[6] By and by, the substitution of the blood of sheep and other animals for that of human beings was deemed preferable in the rites of atonement practiced in the cultures of the Fertile Crescent. Yet, to this day, human as well as animal sacrifice can be found on the continent of Africa.

In the knowledge of the foregoing historical facts and self-evident spiritual truths, consider how unreasonable it is that a formula for human or animal sacrifice or the shedding of blood could have been required or ordained by God for the propitiation (atonement, expiation, balance) of sin (i.e., karma).

If, then, sacrifice is *not* required for the remission of sins, what *does* Life demand in order to balance humanity's debts? I am happy to clear up this point for all who adore the Truth that will make them free from such smoldering error which blind theology has kept active, thereby mutilating both the human and the divine image in man which would otherwise have been universally outpictured upon earth long ago.

Let us together examine the mystery of the blood of the Lamb as the acceptable sacrifice which, we are told, meets with the divine approval in remitting the sins of mankind. [7]

Life and *God* are synonymous terms and denote interdependence in the interchange between the divine and the human, for the life of man is God and God's Life flows in man's veins. The term *life* is equivalent to blood in the scriptural sense and is preferred to *blood* by the spiritual student, who rejects the idea of the shedding of blood as abhorrent and inconsistent with true humanity and certainly with Divinity.

The scriptures declare that "without shedding of blood there is no remission" of sins.[8] I am declaring to you and to all men forever the truth concerning this biblical statement, herein quite simply revealed: without the shedding (casting off) of that life, or life-force, which has been misqualified with human foolishness, the sins of man can never be remitted (requalified with the love plan of God). Moreover, without the release of the life-essence (i.e., 'blood') of the Lamb who is your Holy Christ Self, you cannot balance your karma.

Hence, it is by a continual requalifying, mastering, governing and controlling of energy through the Ascended Master Light of the individualized Holy Christ Self that men and women shall rise to the point where their former sins, which are solely error recorded in memory, are blotted out[9] by the Holy Spirit. This ritual of true sacrifice takes place as they invoke the violet fire of forgiveness, the white radiance of God-purity, and the comforting assurance that as they put off the old man with his deeds, the new man— the firstborn Son made in the image of God— comes into manifestation in the glory of reality.[10]

The idea that God, your beloved I AM Presence, favors one child and rejects another is totally inconsistent with divine Law. My own life was offered to God to epitomize the Cosmic Christ, to prove that man and woman in physical embodiment can ascend out of Matter and remain close by in octaves of light (invisible, yet co-occupying the physical plane at a higher frequency) to mightily assist the earth and its evolutions in returning to the original divine plan of the abundant Life.

This I am doing to the present day. Well may it be spoken of me—as it should be of every soul who is destined, whether one knows it or not, to be a Christ—"I AM" (the I AM Presence in me *is*) the Way, the Truth, and the Life: no man cometh unto the Father but by the same path of personal Christhood which all who have embodied the Word have demonstrated.

In the purified state man "sheds the light" of the I AM Presence through his sanctified (sacred) heart and other spiritual centers (chakras) for the transmutation of world sin (karma). In this release of light the initiate discovers the true meaning of the remission of sin by the "shedding of blood," noted by the mystic writer of Hebrews. However, the full force of this initiation is not experienced until after the records of personal *sin* (violations of the law of grace) are consumed by Love nor until personal karma (the obligations to Life incurred through disobedience to God's laws) is balanced by sacrificial service (words and works, including dynamic decrees for world transmutation).

"Without *shedding of blood...*" is then seen to be the flow of Life from God through the purified soul and temple of man. The pure life-essence of the Holy Christ Flame is released in "rivers of living water" from the 'belly'[11]—and this refers to the *solar plexus,* or *place of the sun*—which becomes the fount (chakra) of

Christ-peace in all who also believe in the Christ of me as the God-power in themselves.

Yes, without the shedding of this 'blood', there is no world remission of sin by the Son of God incarnate in you! And for this cause you and I came into the world—to take upon the office of our Christhood the burden of world karma so that the lost sheep gone astray from the House of Reality might experience a deferment of their karma and a certain relief from suffering while they learn of me and my true burden, which is Light. [12] This Light, when internalized by themselves, will enable them in their turn to take full responsibility for their own burden of karma as they, too, follow the selfsame path of discipleship you are on: personal transformation through integration with Christ, the Light of your world.

How fallacious is the idea that God respects men's persons or favors one of his sons while dishonoring another. Some do not see that it is mortal men who dishonor themselves, doing despite to their own cause before the courts of heaven. Yet I am not concerned with the changing human but with the changeless God Self and his intentions, which are to endow the *Son of* his *man*ifestation with every honor and blessing that the soul prepares itself (qualifies itself) to receive.

One of the first requisites the aspirant to Christhood must meet is to acquire the inner knowing that God is no respecter of persons [13] and that he is willing to bestow his powers without limit upon all of his children when they prove themselves trustworthy. Then he must accept the reality that Life is already manifesting through him with the fullness of Life's blessed God-powers.

The knowledge of the correct use of these powers to the glory of God and for the healing of the whole Body of God from the cause and core of every disease and discomfort must follow. It is the Law!

I AM the Christ-gift that lifts karmic burdens, heals all souls, and lights your way!

Jesus the Christ

Atonement

"Go and Sin No More!"

To Believers in the Memory of God
    Who Would Quaff the Royal Liquid—
    All the love of God would have long ago abolished the mists which have clouded the human consciousness had man not abused his free will and persisted in basing his salvation on erroneous interpretations of the scriptures, codified by the blind leaders of the blind.[1] The introduction of error has made doctrinal accuracy difficult, and confusion has concealed God's plan for his creation.

Neither beliefs nor belief systems can lend eternal verity to wrong concepts. The power of God unto every man's salvation lies in the Sun of God[2]—illumined Truth which alone can make man free.

Because sin can have no real existence in the consciousness of God or, for that matter, within the divine nature of his offspring, it retains its quasi reality only in the memory process. In the human sense, the record of sin which is semipermanent is merely a chronology of the negative, or anti-Christ, acts of each lifestream.

Anti-Christ here signifies that which is "against the Light" or impairs the full radiance of Light by densified shadow. This shadow is created solely by lowering the vibratory rate of thought or feeling to a point where it becomes gross, or dense, in nature.

When energy is negatively qualified, the natural law determines that it should be returned to the Great Central Sun for repolarization; however, in magnetizing human qualities and sustaining them through habit, desire, restlessness, vanity, fear, doubt, et cetera, mankind continues to misqualify the newly 'reclaimed' energies of the Sun according to the old patterns of negativity. This repetitive process explains how sin (although confessed) is re-created over and over again.

Therefore, it must be pointed out that the memory of man is at present not the memory of God, for the old patterns and records of sin occupy its compartments. It must likewise be recognized that the memory of man can become the complete memory of God, the repository of the original soul blueprint; and in this possibility is the hope of salvation in the Light, the Christ who lighteth (illumines by his Mind) every man who comes into the world. Those who willingly open the door to this Mind/memory bank, containing the original patterns of things perfect in the heavens of one's Higher Consciousness,[3] admit the inflow of every good and perfect influence of the Holy Spirit.

The soul (sole) requirement of every hour is complete release from the sin of harmful manifestations and the acceptance by each lifestream of the directing Christ-intelligence of his own Mighty I AM Presence. The merciful violet fire of freedom's love is the means whereby this may be accomplished permanently—unless the individual chooses by his own free will to re-create those very conditions which he has already eliminated.

Beloved Jesus warned of this probability when he said, "Go and sin no more, lest a worse thing come unto thee."[4] Thus, "Stop sinning!" is the surest command of the Christ Self for the breaking of the self-perpetuating formulas of thy sinfulness.

Our students who are so accustomed to the ready unguent of the violet fire to soothe life's hurts ought to remember that the majority of mankind have never even heard of the violet fire. Although the knowledge of the violet fire and its application are presently limited to the few, its service on behalf of earth's evolutions remains the active principle of the mercy of God. However, the uses of the violet fire are not entirely understood by many who do use it.

Of note to all users and potential users is the statement made a number of years ago by the beloved Elohim Arcturus, who declared the violet fire to be the divine memory of God:

> Let me tell you that one of the greatest services of the violet transmuting flame lies in the truth that the sacred memory of

God's perfection is held within this violet
fire! When permitted so to do, this violet
flame simply raises the vibrations of all it
contacts until divine order is brought into
manifestation through its merciful, forgiving and transmuting power of Divine Love.

This violet fire is itself the memory
of the perfection of what should be—in
everyone, everything, every place and in
every instance. Wherever and whenever
this violet fire is called forth, it always
leaves a residue of its substance, nature
and feeling in every person, place, condition or thing it purifies. [5]

Thus, you can begin to understand that by
its inherent quality of divine mercy, the violet fire
automatically transmutes, or changes, all else
into the harmony of the Mind and Will of God.

Theologically speaking, the sacrificial aspects of Christian propitiation have strengthened both sin and schism, creating confusion in
man's understanding of God, his will, and the
plan of Life. We would wipe away all that by
teaching you that the use of the violet fire, when
combined with the ritual of the sacred labor in
daily service to Life, is the sole atonement Life
requires.

For those engaged in the ongoing service
to Life, community, and family—who also love
and forgive—the violet fire completely frees from
sin: cause, effect, record, and memory. The cup
which every son must drink is communion with
the Godhead through the science of words and

works in affirmation of his Presence—and the elimination thereby of all imperfection.

Preceding the symbolic and actual Last Supper, beloved Jesus admonished the apostles, saying, "Ye shall drink of it."[6] I am declaring to all that to the present day this cup shall not pass from you[7] until you have been a partaker of its purification.

This royal liquid violet fire, symbolized in the purple nectar of the grape, recalls the ever-newness of the eternal kingdom and the wonders of divine grace which wipe away all human sorrow, mistaken ideas, and confusion, replacing them with the glorious likeness of the Father's own image. Thus, the divine memory retains the pure perfection of the soul when the soul's image is stripped by the violet flame of all overlays of the human consciousness.

You see, not only does the violet fire 'destroy' what is unreal, but it perfectly preserves what is real—even as it re-creates the whole man. Truly, the violet fire is the Trinity of God in action as the eternal Creator, Preserver, and 'Destroyer'.[8]

Beloved ones, we have reached the apex of our current transmission concerning sin. We declare to you that by transmutation—by the love of the sacred fire which is God and by that obedience which is greater than sacrifice[9]—all shall come to the place in life where, in joyously freeing all others from the stigma and the sting of condemnation, they shall accept the mercy of God and draw forth enough violet fire to achieve complete victory and the fullness of Christ-accomplishment in their lives.

In this manner, the Father's will, confirmed by the Son, shall overcome by the sacred fires of the Holy Ghost all so-called venial and mortal sins, increasing each one's sense of identification with the memory of God. This unity with the universal Mind is a pearl of great purity and great price, affording solace, harmony, and restoration to the soul. In this lovely consciousness every child of God shall find his heaven, his peace, his victory. Christ-absolution and every good and perfect thing shall be his in Jesus' name.

I admonish you to forsake sin and its attendant suffering, to be gracious and childlike, failing not to warn the brethren of the wiles of devilish minds seeking to bind the redeemed (who have been washed clean by the blood of the Lamb[10]) to former states—of sins long since forgiven, forsaken, and canceled out by the law of mercy and compassion.

Fully clothed with hope for the new day, I commend you to the ever-new consciousness of the Christ and the words of my beloved brother Jesus which follow.

I AM ever your humble brother,

Kuthumi

Mercy

"Our God Is a Consuming Fire"

To All Who Will Dissolve the Sins of Past Lives
by the Violet Fire of Transmutation—
Concerning the parable of the rich man and
Lazarus[11] which I gave as a lesson on karma,
I would call to your attention that many have
misread into it glaring and terrible doctrinal
errors which have caused great fear and suffering to the faithful. I am issuing this instruction
to amend the contrived concept of everlasting
punishment which is so far removed from the
blessing which I had intended my own to have in
the underlying message of this parable.

Beloved ones, the dependency of mankind
upon the elements, as well as their inability to
control them, especially fire, has caused them to
stand somewhat in awe and fear of Nature. The
idea of eternal condemnation has appealed to
some of the more zealous evangelists, whose
concern for the souls of my Father's flock has led
them to take a forceful and compelling stand (at
times even violating free will) in order to save the
flock from both ignorance and backsliding, and
from entering a state which they perceive to be
one of eternal torment.

I am certain that no loving father on earth
would ever create for his children so dire a situation as one from which there would be no
escape from perpetual pain. Dear ones, the very

fact that Life is so lovingly given to man speaks of the mercy of God in affording his children the opportunity to come to their rightful place of eternal happiness.

The fact that millions have lived many lifetimes in error, solely by the mercy of God, in order that they might have opportunity upon opportunity to be God-taught and return to the fold of absolute Truth, would also prove that the Father, who would leave the ninety and nine to find the one lost sheep,[12] would upon his return never forsake the rest of the flock. Therefore know, blessed ones, that reembodiment *is fact*. It is the manifest mercy of God which eventually provides for each lifestream the certainty of escape from every record of sin and error.

It is not enough to tire of the husks; you must develop a taste for the reality of heaven! You have lived long in human vanity and the vexation of your spirits.[13] Though you have sustained the sense of struggle, to God your life is a life of hope; for he has vested the entire creation, including *you*, with the energy and consciousness of his being. I am confident, then, that patience will show you how to climb graciously, without backtracking.

Beloved ones, I now reveal to you a mystery. God has been spoken of as a consuming fire and indeed he is. The sacred fire is the being of God. The flames of God are all flames of freedom; for God is Truth, and the power of Truth does make all free through the fiery baptism of the Holy Spirit. Therefore, fear not, little ones, any man-made doctrine which purports that God desires aught but what is best for you! He does not desire to see you suffer perpetually or "forever and ever" but longs to see you become perfect and complete in him.

The lake of fire, referred to in beloved John's recording, into which "the fearful and unbelieving, and the abominable, and murderers, and whoremongers, and sorcerers, and idolaters, and all liars" are cast,[14] is a place of transmutation and change where the perpetually self-burning, all-consuming sacred fire, itself embodying the qualities of the masterful Divinity, does set all Life free from the painful memory of both the sinner and the cause, effect, record, and memory of sin. Sin is temporal and undignified. God is eternal and full of grace.

Remember that my beloved apostle John declared in the Revelation he received on Patmos that the sea gave up its dead and that death and hell were then cast into the lake of fire—which burneth for ever and ever.[15]

First let me say that the sea which gave up the dead is the astral plane, the lowest vibrating octave of planet earth, referred to as Gehenna or Hades. Those whose misuse of free will in the misqualification of divine energy has resulted in an unusually heavy karma take their lessons (at the conclusion of earthly life and prior to reembodiment) at this level of earth's schoolroom. Here, according to the merciful law of karma, they experience the effects of their wrongdoing, or "sin," that they might repent from their evil ways in the next round of opportunity afforded by reincarnation.

Such was the plight of the rich man who cried out for mercy from the 'Ascended Master' Abraham, who from the higher level of vibration and consciousness known as the etheric plane (referred to as paradise—which indeed it is, as compared to all other octaves of earth) was instructing him in the Law in preparation for his soul's next incarnation.

The "great gulf fixed" between these two octaves, forbidding any interchange between Lazarus and the rich man, is the sealing of the place where evil dwells, confining the disobedient to the causes they have set in motion in order that they may learn, by directly experiencing the effects of their actions, what suffering they have brought upon Life—this, mind you, never to punish but to instruct and to inculcate the desire to love and be loved. Thus, their own karma becomes their teacher (for they would listen to no other) that they might relent and turn bane to blessing in their next life (physical embodiment).

The denial by Abraham of the rich man's petition for mercy teaches that debts incurred in the physical octave must be balanced there. Reincarnation, then, becomes his only hope for salvation—i.e., *self-elevation* to the higher planes of consciousness. This he achieves through acceptance of the path of forgiveness, transmutation and love, worked out daily as he takes responsibility for past mistakes and misdeeds—born again to enjoy the blue sky and the stars at night and the verdant Mother Earth, happy to receive her prodigal son in new garments of opportunity.

Thus, those assigned to the astral plane may not graduate from this schoolroom until the required lesson is learned and the karma (debts incurred) balanced. Even in their succeeding embodiments, they will bear the physical burden of the astral plane until they elect to avail themselves of the wondrous opportunity of casting their sins and sinful sense into the lake of violet fire.

Though God forgives sin, man must enter into the Spirit of forgiveness. Forgiving himself and all whom he has wronged or who have wronged him, he must yet go and sin no more and perform good works of mercy until the Law is satisfied and those previously afflicted by his neglect or malice are healed. This is the true joy of the ongoing process of re-creating oneself in the image of Christ.

This accountability of the Law, together with the violet fire, enables all who will, to escape the false doctrine of eternal torment—'eternal' only in the sense that the weight of karma seems endless until it is consumed by the sacred fire. The lessons of Life, impartial to all, decree that the individual must consciously engage in this process if he is to receive the LORD's promise of transmutation of karma:

"Though your sins be as scarlet, they shall be as white as snow; though they be red like crimson, they shall be as wool. . . . For I will forgive their iniquity, and I will remember their sin no more." [16]

These dispensations are given to the children of Light who were lost in the wages of sin and are found again because they have found themselves in Christ (the best mediator) and accepted the reality of their own I AM Presence.

What, then, is the second death "reserved for the devil and his angels" and those whose names are not found written in the Book of Life?[17] This, too, is the mercy of God to deliver the world from the consciousness of sin.

You will find, blessed hearts, written in the Epistle of Jude and the books of our Father Enoch as well as in my Revelation to John a record of certain angels "which kept not their first estate but left their own habitation."[18]

For their ungodly deeds, these fallen angels were consigned to physical embodiment by the decree of my Father—thus to be convicted by their own words and deeds, once uttered as blasphemy in the higher octaves whence they were cast out, now continuing in their mockery of my Word in these latter days.[19]

Thus the mockers of my Church walk after their own ungodly lusts—these who separate themselves, "sensual," from my Mystical Body, "having not the Spirit."[20] Thus it is reserved unto the Last Judgment that these who have not and would not repent of their deeds cannot receive forgiveness—for they dash its cup, even when I myself offer it to them directly from my hand. Likewise, they reject the living witness, desiring not communion with the saints but only revenge against me and my own.

Because they have desired not to be in God, taking my light from the innocent by subterfuge to consume it on their lusts[21] and only to prolong their evil ways, the great mercy of the Law fulfills the mandate of their nonbeing—their nonidentification in God—and the sacred fire cancels out the consciousness of sin, including the non-self of those who have completely identified with it. This is the second death: it is the canceling of further opportunity for repentance unto the wicked who desire no remission of sin and no reintegration with the Father through the Son or the Holy Ghost.

Their experiment in free will has failed. They will not dwell forevermore in God's kingdom, neither will they suffer forever and ever in the lake of fire. Their end is swift and sweet, for they, too, have come to the end of their desire for struggle. They have been committing spiritual suicide for aeons and if Life itself would not mercifully 'pull the plug', they would, in the end of their evolutionary spiral, do it themselves.

Try to understand, precious hearts, that the Father has already provided for the resolution of the dilemma of the unremitting evil of the fallen angels. Thus, when death and hell are cast into the lake of fire, it means that the end of the consciousness of death and hell is come—and all who embody that state by free will, all who occupy that lowest vibrational level of Hades, are judged according to the karmic record of their unrelenting works of infamy.

Once they are judged and the plane which they occupy is cast into the lake of fire, they and their karmic condition are entirely transmuted (canceled out) in the sacred fires. Those "not found written in the Book of Life" are the ones who long ago lost (let go of) the divine spark through their abuse of the Light. These became the nameless ones, nonentities without identity in God. Their lost image (soul pattern)— lost because willingly forsaken by themselves— is likewise canceled out by the sacred fire of Alpha and Omega.

When this takes place, the worlds in all octaves will be seen as a "new heaven and a new earth"[22] and there will be no more astral plane (sea) or dwellers of that plane, for the choices of all lifestreams will have been made and the golden age will be the reality of universal Life for all who have chosen to make it their own. About this, beloved, we will speak in another chapter of our ongoing work. For now, simply accept that these conditions of death and sorrow and crying and pain shall themselves be dissolved in the divine fire of living Mercy!

For I am declaring to you today that in the perfection of God, the sea of human souls who are my own *will* give up its dead by surrendering its consciousness of death. And these souls quickened will express that Life eternal which is to be found in the sacred fire by all who accept this gift of God's transmutation in Love. I am also declaring the great truth that the elements of death and hell that have tainted the minds of my little ones are themselves cast into the lake of fire and are forever transmuted, leaving only the pristine perfection of the Mind of God as the true and original soul pattern of the children of the Light.

Into the violet-fire lake of divine memory are cast all lesser human memories. The children of God, then, who were gone astray, have repented and returned to the Father's heart. These come forth in the holy name of God, charged with the mercy which Life offers to all who seek until they find.[23]

Accept my enlightenment and study these lessons with care. Thus you, too, shall be free from every delusion concerning sin, free also from the power of discord yet generated in your "feasts of charity"[24] by the fallen angels. And as faithful children you shall apply yourselves more diligently to expressing those qualities which no being, ascended or unascended, can express for you or in your stead.

One by one, you *shall* assist the Ascended Masters to bring the evolutions of earth Home and to make possible that God-peace among the seed of Christ which I am confident shall eventually enfold my children in light, love, and living beauty.

May the Christ consciousness of the Eternal Mind dwelling within you—uniting with the Christ Light of every Ascended Master and cosmic being—express the fullness of God now and forevermore!

Lo, I AM the Resurrection and the Life of your complete acceptance of the great light of the Divine Majesty within—

Jesus the Christ

Responsibility

"Work Out Your Own Salvation"

To the Identifiers with God
        in the Messianic Sense—
    The Holy Christ Self of each lifestream holds an immaculate and therefore sinless concept for the soul, regardless of whether or not the outer self desires or manifests it. Great assistance from on high can be given the individual through his recognition of this fact.

    The divine nature never has and never can be subject in any way to human control through discordant energies. It is true that the energy which man directs into discordant and therefore sinful thoughtforms is originally from the divine power source; hence, it is the misqualification by the human will which charges (*changes* the vibration of) such energy so as to sustain an overlay of impurity—the form itself sullied and appearing so unlike its former state as to be unrecognizable.

The Keeper of the Records for each one's life automatically refers such actions to the Karmic Board, by whose hand the Law itself determines just how and where the *re-action* of karma shall afford the best possible lesson for each lifestream—by divine decree. The observation that divine justice is slow but sure was phrased by Longfellow in his "Though the mills of God grind slowly, yet they grind exceeding small; though with patience he is waiting, with exactness grinds he all." [1] But the suddenness of the descent of the Law is also seen as the mills act with the swiftness of a courier of light, hastening the redemption of mankind's mis-used energies.

Ecclesiastes described the operational law of karma in this wise:

> I know that whatsoever God doeth, it shall be for ever. Nothing can be put to it, nor any thing taken from it; and God doeth it, that men should fear before him.
>
> That which hath been is now; and that which is to be hath already been; and God requireth that which is past.
>
> And moreover I saw under the sun the place of judgment, that wickedness was there; and the place of righteousness, that iniquity was there.
>
> I said in mine heart, God shall judge the righteous and the wicked; for there is a time there for every purpose and for every work. [2]

The valiant, the victorious, are ever the ones who retain in consciousness the divine idea — the original image of God patterned for the perfect man, or *man*ifestation of Himself. The formless Light directed into the 'thoughtform' of creative expression manifests the winged image of each soul's own victory.

To forget God who is only Good, to prefer the imperfect pattern to that perfect pattern imaged forth by this magnificent Good, is to remain in a rut of chaos and confusion that is the product of the unprincipled, unordered mind. To sustain the image of God in mind is to sustain a powerful magnet — verily the inner blueprint of the divine will, which automatically sweeps out imperfection and draws more of the divine leaven (Christ consciousness) into the human loaf of egocentric existence where it raises every facet of expression.[3]

The conclusion of the process must be the sinless state — which is the estate of Christhood — and the nurturing of that God-design which thrills the being of man with the full measure of his own divinity.

Soon after realization blossoms, the reward of all endeavors of Love comes to fruition and the paradise of God is perceived to be alive within man at the central altar of his being. Not mere words but the essence of eternal reality — "The kingdom of God *is* within you"[4] — becomes the law and the key to the realization of Life's perfection.

So glorious is the Christ-manifestation of every child of God that all efforts made to contact it, however long or arduous, are acclaimed "worth it all!" as one beholds the magnificent outpouring of Christ's living radiance face to face.

If man continues to allow sin to have dominion over him, he must function in the realm of illusion and the willful separation of his identity from the God Presence. The *carnal sense* of the fabricated personality which is separate from God[5] is itself unreal and can never satisfy the true longings of the soul; therefore it is vague, vapory, and self-terminating.

Spiritual continuity is the deathless portion of the lifestream who enters the sinless realm by accepting the dominion of his Holy Christ Self as central to all being and existence. The tiny babe of Bethlehem swiftly expands his light and limbs from infancy to the unspeakable grandeur of a living Christ. The accompanying God-success made known by the power to heal, the wisdom to heal, and the love to heal (as karmically and divinely intended) makes such a one a dominant figure on the world scene, whether recognized or not by mankind.

In reality, the sinless Christ comes to the portal of each one's being to manifest Love's service without limit. The divine seed, represented in the Christ of each one, must wholly bruise the mere human intellect of serpent's head.[6]

When by free will the soul allows this

displacement of antichrist by Christ within consciousness, the figure of the historical Jesus becomes personally relevant as the archetype of the Messiah (deliverer, anointed one) who is the Holy Christ Self of each individual. Every lifestream who has been identified with the physical manifestation of God in the Adamic sense is now become completely God-identified in the Messianic sense.

The vicarious atonement, as salvation through this One Sent, is perceived as the universal ideal to be fulfilled every day on the ongoing path of personal Christhood. All disciples contribute to this "at-one-ment" whenever they amplify the Light shining as the divine unity of the beloved of Christ, illumining the Way in the temporary obscurity of humanly divisive darkness.

The star of the east is the Light of the I AM Presence within which guides each soul to the state where, in loving adoration, he is able to humble himself as an individual manifestation of God and perceive the universal Messiah in eternal, living nativity within himself and others. This Light sheds its beams across the span of time and space to exalt each man, woman, and child beyond the stations of the cross to the heavenly state where all dross and density of the human nature are transmuted in the ecstasy of the ascension.

In the Father's plan, no favoritism is bestowed, no escape from responsibility is possible. Rather does His full measure of grace illumine and raise each successful aspirant into full-orbed Sunship, erasing every sorrow and shadow, each blight of recessed sin.

Truly His grace is the full power of God unto salvation for everyone who believes in divine justice in perfect balance and determines to hold to the love of his own God Presence without fail until complete and final freedom is achieved.

This is working out your own salvation, not with fear and trembling[7] but in Wisdom's immortal way!

I AM your cosmic teacher,

Kuthumi

Discipleship

¹dis·ci·ple \ də'sīpəl \ *n* -s [ME, fr. OE *discipul* & OF *deciple, desciple*, fr. LL *discipulus* personal follower of Jesus Christ in his lifetime (fr. L) & L *discipulus* pupil, perh. fr. (assumed) L *discipere* to grasp, comprehend, fr. L *dis-* **¹dis-** + *-cipere* (fr. *capere* to seize) — more at HEAVE] **1 :** one who receives instruction from another **:** one who accepts the doctrines of another and assists in spreading or implementing them **:** FOLLOWER: as **a :** a professed follower of Christ in his lifetime; *esp* **:** one of the twelve apostles **b :** a convinced adherent of a school (as in philosophy, art, or politics) ⟨a ~ of Kant⟩ ⟨a~ of Rubens⟩ ⟨a ~ of Jefferson⟩
²disciple \ " \ *vt* -ED/-ING/-S **1** *obs* **:** TEACH, TRAIN **2** *obs* **:** PUNISH, DISCIPLINE **3** *archaic* **:** to make a disciple of **:** CONVERT
discipleship *n* [fr. *disciple* + *-ship*]: the state or function of a disciple, or follower of a master ⟨[He] dyd it not onely to allure them to hys discipleshippe, but also for our commoditye —Latimer⟩ ⟨Such as is a mans disciple-ship, such is his Christianity —Hieron⟩ ⟨Wisdom...invites us to come into her Discipleship —Norris⟩ ⟨The old reverent feeling of Discipleship... had passed utterly away —Carlyle⟩ ⟨No Lydgate or Lytton was ever more obsequious in his discipleship —Swinburne⟩

Corona Class Lesson 25

Requirement

"Here I AM, Send Me!"

To Guardians of the Eternal Truths—
Kuthumi and I shall now speak on discipleship.

Kings and princes may dwell in marble halls and sleep well-guarded throughout this mortal life, but the true disciple lives not so much to be protected as to guard the eternal truths of the heavenly Father from any and all desecrations.

Let the words "Watch and pray!"[1] be remembered today—for peril in the form of karma, individual and worldwide, still stalks the earth and will remain until the last victory is won. By daily service to the Light, much transmutation occurs and the business of serving God moves forward. To advance the cause of freedom for love of God and man is the definite aim of many sincere people, but few there be who can attain true discipleship.

Our purpose in this series of Corona Class instruction on discipleship is to address those who would learn to teach others the Way and find thereby greater illumination and avenues of service for their own mission. We now desire to bring the brilliance of God-illumination into play upon the sacred pages of the lives of the devotees so that the bread that comes down from heaven[2] may be on earth the living Word.

First and foremost, the would-be disciple must learn to forget the importance of his own personality and to remember that God's thought about him is greatly to be esteemed. How wasteful is the daily dissipation of energies expended in defense of the personal self with all its whimsical characterizations. Beloved Saint Germain in his embodiment as Francis Bacon wrote, "All the world's a stage, and all the men and women merely players: They have their exits and their entrances; and one man in his time plays many parts."[3]

Let my words to Martha concerning Mary be recalled: "And Mary hath chosen that good part"[4]—and let my disciples of today also learn to choose the better part on the stage of life that they may play it well. Dedicate yourself to outpicturing nobler ideals in more Godly characterizations, thus following the path that leads to the Life victorious—your ascension in the Light attained through the overcoming of every discordant manifestation on the Emmaus walk of dedicated discipleship.[5]

It is understandable that to the man or

woman accustomed to ordinary ways of living, the road of discipleship leading to personal Christhood should at first seem strange or difficult. Those whose hearts have burned within them to know the nearness of God will find the road less difficult and certainly less cumbersome than the broad way of materialism. If they stick with it, I guarantee all will find the reward at journey's end to be beyond compare.

My statement "Man shall not live by bread alone, but by every word that proceedeth out of the mouth of God"[6] must be applied to the understanding of God's laws in living as a son of God. Living by material standards, no matter how high, cannot possibly connect our disciples with the pure vibration of spiritual compassion which so reveres the Word of God that every moment is perceived as an opportunity to stand forth as a living example—a living revelator of God, interpreting God unto man not through the vanity of earthly ideas or even the grandeur of cultured prose, but through living successfully as a divine embodiment here and now.

The concept of man as a son of God and a divine manifestation is a part of the high calling extended to every soul who cometh into the world—but few there be that have found it.[7] And so, each disciple must esteem himself to be worthy of God in order that he might anchor himself in the Great Law which will then walk the earth through him in the pure Person of his own beloved Christ Self. Through realizing that

man made in God's image is not a sinful crea-
ture but a divine being, he is able to discern the
LORD's Body.

My words to Peter, "Simon, son of Jonas,
lovest thou me more than these [the net full of
great fishes]?"[8] were designed to teach my apostles, and the many other disciples that should
follow in their footsteps, that learning to love
God first and more than all else is a prerequisite
to discipleship.

Summarizing early requirements, let me
say: Put aside the desires of self-importance and
cultivate the thoughtform that will allow your
own God Presence to exalt you in due time.
Avoid discharging your energy in fruitless self-
defense; rather commit your entire protection to
the great Masters and cosmic beings while exercising common sense by courageously walking
wisdom's way before men.

Choose the better part—the burning heart of
a seeker. Learn to live to outpicture the words
of God daily by discerning his Body (the Spirit
of grace and glory), and then follow that love
wherever it may lead you, knowing that you
were not created to serve the loaves of materiality but the living bread which came down from
heaven, who is the Word within you testifying to
your spiritual origin as a son of God.

Countless dedicated people exist, but they
often tie their energies to wrong premises. Many
believe that if their motives are good, they will
still attain—even if their precepts should be
proven wrong. Let them recall the perception of

Saint Paul, who, long after his illumination by me on the Damascus road, [9] declared: "The fire shall try every man's work of what sort it is. . . . If any man's work shall be burned, he shall suffer loss: but he himself shall be saved; yet so as by fire." [10] Thus, in his teaching on karma [11] Paul also saw the great necessity for the ongoing refinement of one's spiritual understanding as the foundation for a correct doctrine and for deeds deserving of divine merit—even after the direct encounter with my Presence.

Blessed ones, good motives are better than bad ones, of course; but the refining action of the sacred fire must and shall preserve the Good (Godlike) qualities and restore (transmute) all else to its original perfection, returning the currents thereof to the God Source whence they came.

As you seek the responsibility of the ministering servant which comes with advanced discipleship, you should be aware that the energy misused by man's free will and released in discord is a permanent loss to his lifestream; whereas, rightly qualified, it could have accrued to his record of good works in the storehouse of the causal body. Once having been misqualified, it is returned to God without the stamp of personal positive qualification—an opportunity missed to expand God's kingdom and, correspondingly, His consciousness within oneself.

Truth and Love abide forever: therefore, whatsoever ye shall build that is not built upon the rock of Christ Truth [12] shall indeed be washed away in the torrent of Divine Love which carries back to the Source all energy that demands purification. The impure momentums of the human consciousness cannot move the bedrock of Divinity gainst which the gates of hell shall not prevail![13]

Verily, verily I say unto you, my words shall not pass away,[14] and each disciple who shall anchor himself within the heart of the Word of God's eternal Truth shall likewise abide forever.

Do you see, blessed ones, that true discipleship can never be false? It must go deeper[15] than the surface mind and retain solid quality to the very core of one's being. You can never fool your True Self, and the genuine disciple will not try. Of this you may be certain—that disciples are still being born and made and are sorely needed in this hour to carry my word and radiation and the power of the sacred fire to God's children.

Heaven will not spurn you! Remember my parable of the lost sheep.[16] Let this opportunity for discipleship—learning to teach men the Way—be regarded as the highest and noblest of endeavors, exalting every facet of God's consciousness in your being. It is never impractical to be a disciple of the great Masters, a student of the disciplines of the Great White Brotherhood. Truly, all lesser callings must pale into insignificance before the Truth of the Call of thy Christ.

To those of you who would be my disciples today, we say, let this word from our hearts initiate a resurgence of your spiritual aspirations. Know that with God all things are possible, and that you can and shall be called that which in reality you are—Children of the Most High.

Initially, you must establish a hallowed sense of the reality and the tangibility of the blessing you can obtain and bestow on others as a true disciple of God's great Brotherhood of Light. Let your hearts be humble yet unafraid, desiring to perceive your errors only enough to correct them and your virtues only enough to express gratitude for them. Then I am certain you will find the grossness of the human condition giving way to the refinement of eternal values within you—and as your views change to those of heaven, the reality of the kingdom shall enfold you as a mantle of power.

A disciple is one who is disciplined and whose course is parallel to my own. Each such a one I lovingly call brother—sister. Welcome into the family of those who consciously present themselves to the eternal Will and Purpose, saying with Isaiah, "Here I AM, send me!" [17]

May the light of heaven bestow its shining reality upon all the earth through you, thereby blessing every heart each day.

I AM lovingly offering the mantle of my own Christ-perfection to lives as much beloved by God as my own.

I AM your brother of the Resurrection Flame and your World Teacher—

Jesus the Christ

Consecration

"I Have Given You an Example . . ."

To Living Disciples—

There is a Christ-radiance that surrounds a true disciple of the Ascended Masters, and it is a most hallowed vibratory action. It should be borne in mind, blessed ones, that everyone on earth has this radiance streaming forth from his causal body and that it is most lovely.

The difference between the disciple and the ordinary lifestream is one of consecration and conservation. The disciple is consecrated to the Mighty I AM Presence and the great Ascended Masters and he is dedicated to the conservation of his pure Christ-energy which he draws in allotted portion from the Godhead. He knows that by storing each precious feeling of love, each tender memory of those hallowed moments when the Divine comes very near, he will one day possess a most wonderful momentum of God's pure energy, which will rise up at the precise instant when he is required to manifest the healing Christ.

I am looking back on the years when this knowledge was not a part of the disciple's storehouse of spiritual treasures. I well recall the days when, as Francis of Assisi, I wandered midst the confusions and conflicts of the social community without truly understanding the delicate leadings from the Godhead which were calling me to come apart and serve the Christ (Light) of my own being. From time to time, I was fraught with elements of despair—it was the sometime hopelessness of a shepherd boy learning to pipe his first notes and sensing his pitiful inadequacy.

The long pathway from one's first responses to the call of the Most High to the consummate attainment of the embodiment of the Christ flame is a saga of soul-stirring magnitude. One marvelous example is that of the little boy Samuel hearing God's voice and crying in response, "Speak, LORD, for thy servant heareth!"[1] Today he is the glorious Ascended Master you know as your own beloved Saint Germain.

His great love for freedom is typified in the figure of "Uncle Sam," popularized as the prophetic spirit of America. This blessed land which he discovered as Christopher Columbus became the great home of the free he had envisioned as Francis Bacon in his writing *The New Atlantis*.

Who can know but your own God Self what you shall one day be when, by reason of your obedient response to God's voice, you, too, shall follow in the footsteps of the Aquarian Master who long ago responded to the call of the Ancient of Days. The call of your Mighty I AM Presence is a blessing equal to the descent of the Paraclete,[2] and it is your loving response to God's call that will vest you with the fullness of the Holy Spirit. This investiture of God's radiance is intended to be used to fulfill your divine plan and not to be consumed by human vanity!

Discipleship, precious prelude to the ascension!—how shall I make popular that which is still a long and lonely way amongst the rocks and crannies of the summit heights? Beloved God Ling in his embodiment as Moses struggled with his own soul in the heights of Horeb, the holy mountain, and so each lifestream must win his own victory over the temporary delusions of the senses.

It would be far simpler for you to attain your freedom and victory as a disciple of the Ascended Masters if you would pursue spiritual graces as easily as you are able to cull earthly favor. It is for want of vision that the people perish,[3] and it is for want of spiritual sight that the disciple suffers in his discipleship.

You know and believe that separation does not exist in God, but because of mortal conflicts and blinded spiritual senses, most chelas are not able to perceive in its entirety the heavenly grace that always surrounds them or to know when the Ascended Masters are blessing them. If they did, inasmuch as blessings are constantly being poured out, the disciples would never sense anything except the beauty and love of God flooding through them as an ocean of cosmic mercy; and their Christ-image of immortality would soon quicken them above every subdivine stratification.

The essence of one of my prayers well-known today, taken up by a modern disciple, contains the phrase "O Divine Master, grant that I may not so much seek to be understood as to understand."[4] Therefore, I point the way of discipleship as one of gratitude for divine opportunity wherein you lovingly seek to understand others, making them happy by first sensing their struggles and then bestowing compassion, offering your prayers and petitions to God on their behalf.

Think, dear ones, how Christlike this quality of the ministering servant is. Try to realize why the outpouring of loving concern to another is essential in maturing the soul and developing the heart chakra of the disciple. "Verily I say unto you, Inasmuch as ye have done it unto one of the least of these my brethren, ye have done it unto me."[5]

The grace of God is sufficient for everyone.[6] Your understanding of this reality will help you to overcome any apathy you might feel toward certain types of discordant manifestations that parade before you. To cleanse the spiritual lepers encrusted with material sense-density and call them brother is a part of the service of a Christ.[7] It must be borne in mind always that the chief goal of every disciple is to take upon himself the disciplines of a Christ so that he may become a bearer of men's burdens (karmic load)[8] and a carrier to them of the vibratory action of God's own love and light.

By meditating on the luminous aura of a saint, an Ascended Master, or a cosmic being, and visualizing that light around you with focused concentration, you may draw forth the intensity of your own Christ-radiance stored in your causal body. Like the finest silver, your radiance may at first appear tarnished by karmic doubts and fears, until your faith attains the brilliant polish of works in the form of deeds of love.[9] For perfect love in action casts out (transmutes) all self-conscious fear and self-doubt.

All deeds of love are not made known to everyone, for some remain entirely unperceived by men but are held in the purity of the blessed disciple's living aura. It is the prerogative of cosmic experts to judge in the light of their pure knowledge the degree of the disciple's devotion through the life record and auric reading, which are true and exact.

Let every disciple realize that each response to the call of Divine Love—whether bestowed upon angel, man, or beast—if lovingly and sincerely given, can only magnify the power of that dear one to render a greater service. Thus the kingdom (the consciousness of God) expands on acts of grace.

Now, acts of grace are the deeds of disciples. These always intensify Love's I AM Presence with the disciple and are most assuredly karma balancing. Of course, it is the (questionable) prerogative of anyone's free will to avoid expressing God's compassion when the opportunity is presented.

Blessed ones, you may not always realize it at the time but Life regularly and repeatedly gives you the chance to show your light, your love, and your grace. And the final tally on Life's scoreboard reveals the winners to be those loving souls who do not miss the chance when Life calls!

Beloved Jesus, in his embodiment as Joseph (son of Jacob by Rachel), was regarded by his brothers as an idle dreamer; [10] yet in his lifetime he was able to assist a pharaoh to govern an empire! [11] The cup placed in his brother's sack [12] is symbolical of the one he later offered to the reincarnated sons of Jacob when he called them from their nets to take up their true vocation as "fishers of men." [13]

During the Last Supper they did drink of that cup in a very real and spiritual sense. Thus they beheld once again the Love that had captivated the "idle dreamer." Now before their very eyes their own brother, born again to his true Sonship, was demonstrating the victory of the I AM THAT I AM over the world and death itself. They witnessed his resurrection and ascension brought about by the same power which had given life-substance to the people during the seven-year famine in Egypt. [14] How beautiful is the Christ-life weaving the seamless robe of immortality through the centuries of the soul's incarnations!

Living as a disciple is the only way of assuring one's spiritual attainments. The Great Cosmic Law can never be fooled by anyone, neither will it ever deceive those who trust in it. Webs of human stress and strain are woven solely of each one's own life-substance which once entered form as God's pure energy but, alas, became gray and hardened by the condition of depressed (concave) chakras.

It is this same energy which, when humanly misqualified, composes the astral nets of binding karma in which people are enmeshed and that create every downward spiral of human error from which they must be cut free by the Christed One.

The idea of living your life as an example to the brothers and sisters of Light as they go about their various activities should be considered. Human accuracy in measuring the sincerity of another may be rightfully challenged, but who can question a perfect example? People watch the life of every disciple, and this makes every day your opportunity to be a living proof of Ascended Master love in action.

Blessed people, while God has "winked" [15] at human error in many poor examples who had sincere hearts, lifting some into their ascension because by cosmic law they merited it, I wish to emphasize that these are not quite the inspirational souls we can use as exemplars to the tired and confused masses who long to behold one they can justly idealize as the Christ.

Other sheep I have which are not of this fold: them also I must bring, and they shall hear my voice through my own; and by the example of my disciples there shall be one fold and one Shepherd—the universal Christ who is the Real Self of every child of God. [16]

Now, if you will give these topics which I have raised a good deal of your thought, you will realize that your Mighty I AM Presence is able to answer your every call made in order that you might fulfill my calling and my teaching. No matter how many mistakes you have made in the past, your Presence is standing with outstretched arms, waiting for the moment when your hungry heart will reach up and demand the chalice of your own perfection.

The Life which will be poured into the cup of your being shall be everlasting and the illustrious nature of your own God Self shall shine forth as the sun illumining the city set on an hill of discipleship (a pyramid of spiritual attainment) which cannot be hid! [17] Thus, ultimately the path of the disciple presents to the world and to the Ascended Masters another candidate for the glories of the sacred ascension in the unfailing Light of God.

A cloud of glory received the Christ, beloved Jesus, out of the realm of human sight, but as every ascended being knows, "this same Jesus, which is taken up from you into heaven, shall so come in like manner as ye have seen him go into heaven."[18]

Look, therefore, for the glorious appearing of the Christ in your own being. He, as your own Holy Christ Self, will guide you into all Truth. As your eternal Preceptor, your Holy Christ Self will continually beckon you on the way of living discipleship.

I AM your friend and cosmic teacher,

Kuthumi

Corona Class Lesson 27

Vision

". . . Senses Exercised to Discern Good and Evil"

To the God-Victorious Disciples
　　　Who Pursue the Master's Eternally
　　　Perfect Vision of Beauty and Love—
　　　The disciple in imitation of the Master[1] is expected to assimilate an intense feeling of oneness with his Great God Source. "I AM in the Father and the Father is in me"[2] was the statement which I used often in order to anchor the affirmation of true being within my thinking and feeling worlds. Unlimited good will come to all who faithfully use this statement as a divine decree (mantra) and acknowledge this blessed concept of their cosmic unity with God.

　　　Whatever the appearance, blessed ones, through affirming your unlimited attunement with God, you are able to rise above it! It ought to be known that merely thinking upon God is a tangible link connecting the world of the disciple directly with the Father of all.

Intellectualism, pride of person, and pride of accomplishment are deterrents to the unfoldment of that loving Christ consciousness which can be developed through realizing that it is God within you who is permanently acting *through you* to fulfill your highest good and to express the allness (beingness) of his nature.

Your physical senses ought not to be desecrated by your holding in mind the idea that, because they are physical and 'outer' in nature, they are necessarily sensuous. Such old-fashioned ideas only give power to evil! Quite the reverse, your senses, as instruments of your Christ nature, have the inherent power to discern both Good and Evil and therefore to protect you by foreknowledge from the wiles of the 'Evil One'.[3] This discernment serves as a protection to your vision of God as the All-Good, that it might not be marred.

I am declaring that in order to drink of the cup of discipleship, you must be constantly aware that all things that come from Above (from your Higher Consciousness) are good and pure so long as they are immaculately sustained as divine ideas or chalices therefor.[4] Hence, the instruments of seeing, hearing, smelling, tasting, and feeling are hallowed when you use them to take delight in the Great Cosmic Law.

By the power of Truth, affirm your perfect sight to be the vision of God, an activity of the formless Law, expressing the geometrical perfection of that Law in flawless form—and train yourself to screen out what has no part with that perfect vision.

The voice of God, referred to as both the "still small voice"[5] and the "voice of many waters,"[6] must be understood to be the vibratory action of the Great Law which can be heard by a disciple (who is attuned with his inner Self) as the living Word of God. The taste of the divine nectar is the sweetness of the Law of the LORD in which the sincere of every race and creed will take conscious delight.[7]

The prayers of the saints were referred to as a sweet incense unto the LORD by my beloved disciple John, as he wrote down my Revelation.[8] I am certain that these prayers resemble the calls of the sincere disciples of the present for the perfection of themselves and the world to be made manifest.

Purity of heart creates a vehicle through which the radiance of divine love manifests as a floral perfume to the outer self and as a blessing to the inner man. Your feelings, blessed ones, especially the sense of touch, are your means of communication with the outer Matter density, preparing you for contact with Spirit's intensity.

It should always be realized that all substance is divine and has a core of pure light. This fact will enable you to bless all that you touch with the God-radiance which shines forth from within your developing heart flame. The realization that you already possess spiritual senses and that these manifest through the physical senses is the key to raising the physical senses into their divinely intended functions.

The notion that the corporeal senses of mankind are of themselves evil must be denied, whereas putting these wonderful channels to use in acquiring knowledge concerning the soul's environment and karmic circumstance should be pursued. Exalt all vision, hearing, tasting, smelling, and feeling as an adjunct to victorious discipleship!

The students of this Light which we transmit herewith should determine to acknowledge the perfection of these faculties of perception, no matter what the appearance. The affirmation "I AM the Resurrection and the Life of my perfect seeing, hearing, feeling, tasting, and smelling now made manifest!" should be repeated often in order to raise the senses to their natural and spiritual perfection—sharper than a two-edged sword when probing the physical dimensions.

The purified consciousness when put to its best use is ever so effective in quickly changing the thought from the shadows of error-inducing unhappiness to pure Christ-vision. Thus cleansed, the student observes the Great Law producing eternal joy within his members[9] whenever that Law is called into action.

I have given the foregoing commentary in order to correct the mistaken idea that the world is evil or that the body of man is vile, imperfect, or impure. The idea that a person, place, or condition is inherently bad—when held in mind—can actually result in a manifestation of imperfection. Only by recognizing the perfection of the God Source can the students of the Light externalize the Father's perfect world—in themselves and in all others.

Certain of the early Christian writers have been greatly misunderstood and, in some cases —although they were truly seekers and endowed with great spiritual blessings—they did not always apprehend every divine principle as clearly as they might have. They continued to "see through a glass darkly," but through subsequent embodiments and since their ascension, they have been able to see "face to face." [10]

Quite naturally, when such a disciple ascends and realizes, to his dismay, that he is responsible for setting forth or even codifying error in his writings and teaching, he does his best from inner levels to correct his mistakes by attempting to open the way for his followers to manifest a more perfect understanding.

Unfortunately, many who have been influenced by the best of men and women who set such devout examples as to be considered almost infallible have gotten stuck in doctrinal error. Out of a false sense of loyalty to the saints and the Holy Church (for one's true loyalty ought to remain tethered to Truth as to the water of Life—uncircumscribed by the vessel), these students have not kept up with the spiritual strides of their teachers. Alas, the only recourse of the ascended saint to correct that error has been through channels outside the confines of established orthodoxy.

When a church or a world religion no longer admits to that progressive revelation which truly is forthcoming, it blocks the direct interaction of the faithful with the ascended founder. The open-minded and forward-moving disciples ought to be free to forgive the past errors of their teachers while still exalting the Light these teachers did indeed bring forth while in embodiment, albeit circumscribed by the then-established interpretations of Holy Writ.

One example of a major loss which occurred through just such a refusal of the clergy to move forward with Holy Truth is the present denial of or utter silence on the doctrine of reincarnation and the preexistence of the soul, taught both by me and my disciples and by Origen of Alexandria, which has been confirmed many times over in the direct experiences of the saints and just ordinary people.

If the embodied disciples of a living Ascended Master do not allow that Master to progress beyond his attainment at the conclusion of his final embodiment, then how can the disciples expect to move forward in the expanding Light of cosmos! Progress as progressive revelation is the law of spiritual evolution. For with each new level of attainment, even after the ascension, vistas of knowledge transcending the old open before the soul. And some of this knowledge will even seem to contradict one's former understanding or prophetic insights, even as a child grows into new truths and discards the outworn mode of expression.

Thus, I admonish patience with the Word, with its exponents, and with oneself. My disciples through the ages have done the best they knew how at their level of perception; and when they knew better, having transcended a few veils, they brought forth from the next level of their comprehension revelations which exalted all who were moving up the mountain with them.

Thus, do not shun the prophet in your midst, nor judge him too harshly. For he is willing to improve, even to shuffle off this mortal coil entirely, if you will allow it. Give him the freedom to be who he is—as God gives to you the same—and in so doing you will find that the Great Law will also impel you to "Come up higher!"

One of the main reasons for being a disciple is to become more like the Master, who has an eternally perfect vision. Either one's own blessed God Presence and Holy Christ Self or the perfection of the Ascended Masters should be emulated at all times. Mimicry of human ideas and figureheads has brought about untold distress, while imitation of the ascended beings does just the opposite and therefore should be all the more encouraged by sincere seekers.

Unfortunately, would-be disciples frequently become so involved in the utter importance of their own ideas that they lose sight of the Father's plan—which, after all, is but the organization of God's ideas! In order for you to be a genuine disciple, many outworn concepts must be cast aside. Often the way turns out to be not as it was thought at the beginning, but is found to rise sharply at one point so as to almost leave the human totally behind.

This break with the patterns of human identity is frightening to some who do not realize that a disciple's inner contract with God includes renouncing the works of the mass mind to the point of not even looking back (nevertheless retaining that heart discrimination that chooses the right and rejects the wrong).

When this happens before heaven is in view or the spiritual visions and perceptions have been focused and opened, it sometimes (at least in his imagination) leaves the student almost mortified with the sense of a spiritual vacuum. Confusion and a wish to escape have caused some of these to be "turned into pillars of salt" by reason of their continuing to look backward on their once rejected and renounced human way of living and seeing.

For this reason, in this Pearl of Wisdom I am releasing the idea of perceiving in the immediate octave the beauty and love of God in manifestation. Searching diligently, find out how much natural beauty you can perceive all around you each day. Draw forth the divine perfection inherent within all Life you contact and thus magnify the kingdom of God.

Behold the fresh pages of each day as a scroll of opportunity to express the law of discipleship. You are by the grace of God becoming more like the Master as you imitate his actions.

The Ascended Masters are examples of perfection and they invite you to be like them. Reconsecrate yourself daily to the path of renewing the beauty within persons, places, conditions, and things all ways. Determine to raise your thought of the world above the battleground of Good and Evil to the place of holy communion.

Blessed ones, it is true that the acceptance of evil has created hideous and frightening appearances—but as disciples, you must exercise great care that you do not further amplify human difficulty. To you it is given to clearly know the mysteries and to take constructive dominion over each imperfect manifestation by blazing the violet fire of freedom's forgiving love into every condition you sense requires it.

I am certain that as you glimpse the inward vision of my thought, it will work miracle-producing wonders of happiness for you. It is my mission to serve my brothers and sisters continually by giving my energy to exalt the world into the purity of the ascension.

I AM your brother of Light,

Jesus the Christ

Corona Class Lesson 28

Will

"... Made Known to Us the Mystery of His Will"

To Sons of God

I Extend the Cup of God-Identity—

Beloved Jesus has significantly conveyed our joint thoughts to you concerning human and divine ideas about Life. We strongly advise shunning the wrong idea that Life is formidable or austere and advocate replacing it with the right idea that Life is a marvelous divine opportunity.

Blessed ones, Life is full of perfect hope, glorious love, and an ultimate destiny which transcends all mortal dreams. It is essential that the true disciple master the means of transmuting whatever outer condition seeks to corrupt the Life principle. The idea that each life is a manifestation of God must become permanent in the heart of every disciple.

Now, the son of God is expected to be like his Father as he asserts control over the natural elements of the earth. All of the elements of physical matter which the ancient alchemists categorized under the headings of fire, air, water, and earth are under the custodianship of the Nature spirits, called *elementals.* Salamanders, sylphs, undines, and gnomes are subservient to their hierarchs who direct natural forces as servants of the Father and his sons.

As such, the elementals have no innate rights or bestowal of authority for self-government. Acting on the command of Elohim and the Four Cosmic Forces, they also respond by nature to varying stimuli, both human and divine. Under the extreme burden of mankind's imposed discord, the elementals, like children out-of-sorts, do not always obey the hierarchs of their respective domains. Conflicting planetary forces, inharmony among their numbers, and overbearing planetary karma results in natural cataclysms which bring on untold human suffering.

This is unnecessary, and for that reason beloved Nada, Chohan of the Sixth Ray, advocates in the name of divine love and devotion that every sincere disciple ponder the example of beloved Jesus' control of the elements and their obedience to him.[1] Each chela can learn to direct natural forces, as greater and more significant spiritual achievement becomes a fait accompli in his life.

My brothers and sisters—it cannot be overstated that peace and harmony are the key to your God-control whereby you gain entrée and take dominion in all octaves of natural life. Thus, with all your heart, still the tempestuous emotions, cast anger, revenge, and hatred into the sacred fire forever, and wage the warfare of the Spirit against the ego with its pride, ambition, and cunning. A word to the wise is sufficient unto the victory.

Because ideas and concepts are so important, and further because thought is so far-reaching, we have advocated that the disciple emulate the Master by first giving obedience to his own God Self. A real disciple acts as an extension of the divine will, an arm of his I AM Presence, and reaches out to command in order that Life may obey the same divine will which has become the conscious controlling factor in his world and mind. "Not my will but Thine be done!"[2] is the perpetual prayer of disciples who would subdue the wind and the wave of the physical as well as the astral sea.

Some have thought God's will to be entirely contrary to human will, and this, too, is a part of man's unfortunate heritage of error. God desires man to be eternally happy and to live here and now in abundance.[3] The Father desires the best gifts for his beloved son and knows that any privation experienced by the prodigal is self-imposed by his own wrong thoughts, which by cosmic law *must* return to him for redemption.

Human will is often destructive, but not always—for in many areas man's will has become imbued with enough sense of cosmic righteousness that he actively seeks cooperation with God. Such unity between the divine and human will is brought about as you surrender (even as you subdue) the carnal will, invoking the power of Archangel Michael to bind the force of the anti-will, and the alchemy of the violet flame angels to clear the way for your soul's expression of the pristine purity of the divine image which is the hope of your world.

I am strongly advocating that every disciple take seriously his responsibility to be an example of the Father's love and to accept the wonders of each day as a segment of eternity given into his keeping and trust. To embellish Life by correctly using your talents is never a matter of gilding the lily, blessed ones. Do not fear to do your part as God wants you to. Accept the rigors of karmic conditions only as a temporary necessity, and realize that you have within your grasp the power of Light to change every wrong condition into Christ-victorious accomplishment!

Many people are frustrated by religious doctrine and scriptural interpretations which have been imposed upon them by those who honestly believe they are doing God's will. Blessed ones, the time has come when these weary prisoners (both the spiritually blind and their blinded followers) shall go free. "Verily, verily, I say unto you, The hour is coming, and now is, when the dead [the dead in sin and ignorance, soon to be quickened by Christ's forgiveness] shall hear the voice of the Son of God: and they that hear shall live."[4]

Verily, verily we declare unto you, Life is God, Life is glory, Life is just, hopeful, merciful, and wonderful! And Life will be the crown of your Christ-accomplishment when at last you realize and accept within your soul that these statements are indeed Truth!

The Taj Mahal is a dream in marble, but Life is more splendid still. For it is God's living artistry—more wonderful than the greatest examples of human love ever externalized.

"Let not your heart be troubled. Ye believe in God, believe also in me."[5] With these words, beloved Jesus explained the intimate contact between the evolving soul personality and the Holy Christ Self. He admonished that the student should not let his heart be troubled by outer conditions, for as he believes in God as omniscient, so he must believe that such omniscience is in direct touch with him through the Great Mediator, who is Christ.

It is the Father's good pleasure to give you the kingdom.[6] Therefore, when the mirrored reflection becomes one with the immortality of the Architect's design, the gift is at last received.

The servant is not greater than his lord.[7] Truly, humility is valuable if it be neither false nor servile; but greater still is the realization that if man is made in the divine image, it is right that he should be as great as his LORD intends, which intent is nothing less than the complete identification of the servant with his LORD—his Mighty "I AM" Presence.

The cup of God-identity is offered to each disciple, and drinking all of it[8] means immortal gain; for his partaking of the divine essence, by free will, is the natural means of escape from human bondage.

Fear keeps men bound, for they fear to believe lest they be found gullible and they fear to doubt lest heaven spurn them. Teach them to pay homage neither to belief nor doubt but, in being true to themselves, to remember the words of Descartes, who declared, "I think, therefore I am." [9] Let men perceive by logic that inasmuch as they live and affirm "I am," therefore God lives to create and affirm "I AM THAT I AM" and to sustain his creation!

Saint Augustine in his *City of God* draws worded images of the heavenly hierarchy, but these magnificent passages are limited by comparison to the actual glories themselves when perceived by the full-orbed vision of the expanding soul.

Remember, blessed ones, sectarian teachers who would proselyte the souls of men are usually not content to let them tarry in indecision but seek to force acceptance of that which they believe to be true. Teachers of Truth, arise to the Law of Love! Divine Justice sends forth to each lifestream the immortal call to his own immortal destiny. To every son of God the highest goal is made plain.

No one should make a decision based on the emotional pressures of fear. It is the Ascended Masters' intent that in the golden age all people on earth should dwell in harmony. If teachers of spiritual principles compel their neighbors to don their dogma and wear it precisely as they

do, they will alienate souls and prevent the tender sprouts of Truth (which ought to be offered
graciously in the name of freedom) from taking
root and growing in the fertile field of consciousness. Let our teachers hearken to the golden
words: "Love thy neighbor as thyself,"[10] and
give Truth as they themselves would like to
receive it—freely, simply, and not too much at
a time.

Try to realize that the power of conversion is
the gift of the Holy Spirit alone; hence, man is
compelled by his own spirit to accept the idea of
his own immortal existence (which only fools or
the godless deny). Out of this initiatic idea of
one's immortality—the eternality of self, spanning past, present, and future ages—each day
unfolds from within a greater understanding of
divine Law.

Do not try to rush your own or your neighbor's comprehension, blessed children of the
Light. Let patience have her perfect work[11] as
you realize that your diligence in pursuing the
Path according to the best within you is God's
way of encouraging self-disciplined action in
others.

Free from human oppression, each lifestream that issues from the Sun Source will
ultimately come forward joyfully to the altar of
Truth, seeking to be illumined by his own Great
God Self, the omnipresent I AM of Being!

The Ascended Masters' guidance is invaluable to all who are striving to increase the scope
of their understanding of the self (psyche) in

God. We release a continuous stream of divine wisdom to augment the interpretive ability of every seeker that he may cherish the deep things of God. We make the entire concept of Life more beautiful for all children of the Light, simply because its premise is God!

Because Life is God, reverence for it will make it more wonderful. Gratitude will expand its blessings and victory will crown its achievements.

Disciples, remember: glorious opportunities await your discovery daily!

I AM your brother following the Christ—

Kuthumi

The Calling

"Come, and I Will Make You Fishers of Men"

To the Quick
    Who Respond without Reservation—
    The prelude to the calling to be a disciple of
the Ascended Masters may be sensed by the
outer consciousness, but often the only indica-
tion is the still small voice in the depths of the
soul of which the outer self is scarcely aware.

    If you are engaged in mending your nets
when the call comes, as some of my disciples
were, you will forsake all and follow me.[1] Blessed
ones, unless your response to the voice of God be
quick and without reservation, you will be left
as the rich young ruler who sorrowed because
he had great possessions which he could not
forsake to find the eternal kingdom.[2]

    In every such case it is fear, blessed children
of the Light, which rules the heart and crystal-
lizes the consciousness in human brittleness
and frailty. Alas, men do not derive the joy they
thought they would from clutching their pitiful

possessions. Did they not first receive all these gifts from God, the Father, and are they not called to be stewards of his graces?

Behold, then, the Father's love and let go of vain human imaginings which have not brought you to the gate of happiness and the Life everlasting. Enter in at the strait gate[3] which admits only divine love—and find power, amplification, hope, and expansion in the realms of that eternally creative Love who is God.

Our dear students have often lamented the fact that so few sincerely seek the spiritual path and yearn to know God. You are a part of our band of Light's children; therefore, blessed ones, remember this: only the few have found, whereas the many are still seeking but know it not. We rejoice that you have opened the door of your heart to the fullness of the Ascended Masters' love and thus are learning to help change world conditions in order that the many may also find the narrow way (spectrum) which leadeth unto Life.

O how glorious it will be when every blot and stain of sin is removed—cause, effect, record, and memory—from the minds and hearts of men! What a holy communion there will be on that day when the last child of earth accepts the fullness of his own Mighty I AM Presence! It will be a great day indeed.

I urge you, dear ones, to accept this possibility and be not affrighted by present appearances. The jagged peaks you behold on the steepest climb, whose towering heights are beheld at close range only by the wild animals and yourselves, are but sentinels of accomplishment guarding the path to the summit you shall attain prior to your ascension.

I am confident that every sincere child of Light, when God-taught in the science of the spoken Word, will rejoice in removing and transmuting every galling memory from the realm of the four lower bodies and will likewise welcome the fullness of God's loving plan manifest in his life. My precious ones, how often humanity find that their delights have turned to ashes and that the pleasures they have sought in worldly ignorance have ended in bitter disappointment. How can warfare and vanity compare with the lovely plans of God for his creation?

There is no need to struggle, blessed ones—the fullness of creation is yours for the asking. "Ask, and it shall be given you; seek, and ye shall find; knock, and it shall be opened unto you"[4] was my declaration to my disciples, and it remains as eternal Truth to the present. If you do not hear my answer to your every call, if you do not see the soul progress you are making, however slight, do not challenge the Law by self-doubt or misgivings, but rather seek and find the error in your application of the Law.

"Seek ye first the kingdom of God and his righteousness, and all these things shall be added unto you."[5] This admonition contains the formula of man's eternal covenant with his Maker. It is your first "test question" on your self-examination checklist, if your current results are not all you expect them to be. Ask

yourself: "Am I really seeking God's consciousness *first*—each morning and before every decision—before I get involved in my own human
reasoning?" If your answer is not an unqualified
"Yes!" then I say, "Mend the nets of your consciousness! Come up higher!"

Call unto me, blessed ones, and know that
I AM always with you to assist you in unfolding
the radiance of your seamless garment of light
and the benediction and comfort of the Holy
Spirit which shall lead and guide you into all
Truth. Not everyone who says, "I am the Lord,"
is speaking Truth;[6] but they who do the will of
the Father shall retain his holy vibration forever. (Only those who acknowledge, "The 'I AM'
in me is the LORD," embody the real Truth of
being and manifest his will.)

I am joining the entire Great White Brotherhood in confirming the law that "the last shall
be first, and the first last";[7] for all have been
called but few have chosen to answer the call.[8]
I await the renewal of ancient pledges.

The blush of the disciple's first love for his
Master, like the roseate dawn of the golden age,
will open the windows of heaven to flood the
earth with so much love that the kingdoms of
this world[9] will become the domain of those
Christened ones who have made their own calling and election secure.[10]

I AM compassionately extending to all the
mercy and love of our Father, today and always.

Jesus the Christ

The Opportunity

"Give Ye Them to Eat"

Protectors of the Sacred Fire
    in the Citadel of Consciousness —
    So exalted is this calling of discipleship that each one must enter into the anointed Presence of his Great God Self in order to receive the fullness of its outpouring and the opportunity to distribute its blessings to all. The disciple of God's wisdom must strive to enter into the heart of God to commune with that central Source and then to outpicture (precipitate) each day in the physical octave the manna (daily bread) which the Father freely gives to all his children who ask that they may receive.

Beloved Jesus and the great Masters who have made their ascension studied and practiced this fundamental law of universal creativity, or precipitation. By drawing forth the eternal substance from the mighty storehouse of God's pure energy, they were able to feed the multitudes the spiritual leaven of the Christ consciousness as well as supply their mundane needs — whether bread, coin, or wine.[11]

Control of the elements, mentioned in our last dictation, is achieved through learning the daily ritual of gathering spiritual substance from the cosmic altar (by dynamic decrees and the meditation of the sacred fire breath [12]) and protecting it within the lower strata of one's being, ready for immediate release (through the sacred centers, i.e., chakras) whenever the need should arise.

Also, beloved ones, the instantaneous healing of every discordant condition can be had by those disciples who will discipline their thought and feeling worlds and govern the total outflow of their energies even as the rhythmic intake of light is put under the control of the God flame.

As you absorb the radiance of our dictations, whether spoken or through the written page, guard well the citadel of your consciousness, that the tramp thoughts of the carnal mind and human riptides of feeling do not rush in to steal the harvest of light which you have so diligently garnered and increased by the Father's love. One of the primary functions of our dictations is to release to you that living, pulsating sacred fire which is absolutely essential for your achievement of the works of a Master in physical embodiment.

The goal of life and the Father's purpose for your present embodiment as a chela of the Ascended Masters is to be a Christ, having authority and dominion over every outer condition. It is not enough to sit at the Master's table; today there is a great need for vigilance and service among the students in order for these teachings to be made known far and wide "as the waters cover the sea." [13] This is a prerequisite to your ascension.

Take to heart, dear ones who must exceed all past performances of the hearers of the Word, the Pauline passage:

> How shall we escape, if we neglect so great salvation; which at the first began to be spoken by the Lord and was confirmed unto us by them that heard him;
>
> God also bearing them witness, both with signs and wonders and with divers miracles and gifts of the Holy Ghost, according to his own will?[14]

We urge the student on the Path to be alert to the opportunities of discipleship, to demonstrate cosmic law in his daily affairs and to maintain the equanimity of the Christ consciousness, no matter what subtle argument might seem to compel him to descend into the depths of mortal vanities. In order for the students to move forward, it is necessary for all to make a covenant of peace and harmony with their Mighty I AM Presence this very hour, asking the beloved Presence to charge their minds and worlds with such a powerful action of the sacred fire that its very holiness transforms their lives and makes the slightest disturbance of that precious flame unthinkable.

It is absolutely essential for the students to realize that to misuse the energies so lovingly bestowed by the hierarchy upon their beings will not only rob them of the blessings at hand but also prevent further progress until they consecrate anew their lifestreams as chalices of God's purity and perfection.

The Mighty I AM God Presence intends every abundant grace to be enjoyed by his beloved children, and so we stand ready to help each disciple on the pathway. Hear the calling, precious hearts, and expand the flame of Truth throughout your four lower bodies by resurrecting every divine hope dormant in the quiescent streams of your soul (i.e., solar) consciousness!

Let there be vigilance, vision, and victory for every chela until every vestige of mortal limitation is transformed into a vestment of God's shining glory and you stand once again before the altar of your Mighty I AM Presence in the glory of your ascension.

I AM your constant companion on the road of discipleship.

Kuthumi

Mastership

"If Ye Continue in My Word . . ."

Good Stewards of the Essence of All Goodness—

The way of discipleship never ends. The absorption of this idea is imperative if you would advance to the heights to which the very soul of God inspires you! Explore the idea of the unceasing Wisdom, the ever-flowing River of Life, and the infinite Mind, and you will discover why this is so.

Blessed ones, are not all things relative? Your relation to your Mighty I AM Presence is so intimate and lovely, and yet it is relative to your capacity to absorb and retain the beauty of God. Now, if you increase your capacity to assimilate Light, as the Christ consciousness, will not your relationship to the Master also change?

You see, it is your power to comprehend, your wisdom to comprehend, your love to comprehend (i.e., take in) God that defines the nature of your ongoing discipleship "worlds without end" as you espouse the path of unceasing discipleship under each succeeding representative of the Master of Life.

How quickly a sponge absorbs water as long as it is not already wet or clogged with dirt. Yet, all sponges do not have the same absorptive quality and therefore some retain considerably more water than others. Now consider the levels of individual capacity to absorb Light. Some take in a great deal of the divine radiance but do not long retain it; others have less power to take in but are able to hold on to each blessing substantially longer.

To "eat" and "drink" the spiritual body and life-essence of the Christ—to enter into, to put on, and to become the Master's consciousness is the true way of discipleship. And this Way ye know, for the Beloved said to his disciples, "Except ye eat the flesh of the Son of man, and drink his blood, ye have no Life [God] in you."[1]

There is an ideal situation to which all should aspire, and that is the highly spiritual, ecstatic state wherein identification with your Mighty I AM Presence is the high prize to which your total being aspires.[2] This aspiration to Light's ecstasy elevates the inner vision to the point where the white fire core of matter comes under one's conscious control, according the devotee the privilege of increasing his own capacity and power to internalize the sacred fire. Thus, the ultimate Way is approached and the disciple is led step by step through the gates to the Infinite, ever higher on the upward spiral of Being.

Mastership is the goal but it is always a conferred title and an assumed grace. I shall clarify this a little by stating that all advancement comes to each lifestream through the hands and heart of his own God Presence, and it is this lovely God Presence that confers upon the victorious disciple the title of "Master," either through the Maha Chohan or the Lord of the World.

In order to attain mastership (self-mastery over the four lower bodies, the chakras, and the elements of one's psyche—*by Love*), it is necessary for the sincere disciple to assume the role and posture of master of the fohatic fire and to invest his consciousness with grace by attuning with the Ascended Masters' Electronic Presence, which we will superimpose over the disciple's aura in answer to his call.

A final word is in order. The greatest Masters consider themselves to be eternal disciples because they perceive that in a universe where only God is the ultimate, realized completely only by Himself and only partially by the individualized parts, there exists a series of octaves of light which expand endlessly as an eternal echo, or reflection, of the Infinite. These extend ad infinitum as universal hands of receptivity outstretched to receive the ideations and conceptions released momentarily from the Mind and Heart of God.

In accepting this creativity of the Father, a loving, spiritual rapport is needed. The disciple's mind is best suited to this purpose because it is a receiving mind. The Master's mind is a transmitting mind, revealing the way that has already been attained as "footsteps of light." But beyond this, the disciple's mind obtains directly from the Father a perennial ecstasy in the flow of knowledge, power, and love and transcends itself in the orderly, everlasting consciousness of God.

Countless would-be instructors in God's laws either have not understood their role first and last to be the eternal chela of the Great Guru or have been reluctant to explain to their pupils the facts pertaining to the law of mastership.

I doubt not that human ego and human ignorance have both been responsible for this sin of omission on the part of many who have sought sincerely to teach men the Way. Therefore we must state for the freedom and enlightenment of all seekers for Truth that the soul moving Godward, no matter how advanced the degree of his adeptship, always remains God's servant, a follower on the path of discipleship in Christ, the only Light of the world. Therefore, it is well to remember that a student of cosmic law is never the possession of any earthly teacher—who is no teacher at all if he attempts to control or hold back his students.

The motto of the true Master is "Lead me to the Rock that is higher than I."[3] The true Teacher advises his students that he speaks the word of the One who has sent him,[4] thus directing the aspiring ones toward the summit that rises beyond his own level of attainment. The true Shepherd rejoices to see his flock climb the mountain before him, grateful that he may stay awhile and hold the balance of Love for their safe and masterful ascent—even if it mean the fore-going for a season of the crown of achievement, or that another may receive it before him.

It is well to note that the Great White Brotherhood, under their own sacred code, have demanded that true initiates never reveal their advancement to one another. To do so would hinder or stop one's spiritual progress, and surely this would in turn defeat the purpose of the Great Law, which conducts each true disciple through successive states of illumined glory to the throne of permanent initiation.

Initiatic degrees are conferred as a perma-nent estate by the Great Law in much the same manner that a doctorate is bestowed from a university. Once given, the degree is never with-drawn unless through malpractice the life-stream deliberately violates the code of the Brotherhood and sends forth harmful vibrations to another. In such cases, the degree with its commensurate authority (i.e., attainment) may be suspended until the needed correction is humbly sought and the Path once again adored and pursued.

To be a disciple of the great Master Jesus is the goal of many who desire to follow him in the regeneration.[5] Let me remind you that every Cosmic and Ascended Master is one with all others. To be assigned to a specific Master, or even to be temporarily transferred for training purposes to another, is the accepted means whereby Life gives you a unique and blessed opportunity for greater learning.

Welcome each opportunity to increase your spiritual self-mastery in all planes, and realize that the eternal student is a walking question mark, leaning upon the shepherd's crook of the seeker-adept but anchored in the symbolical dot below the mark—namely, that consciousness which focuses the white fire core of knowledge, power, and true divine love. Such students keep on asking questions and seeking answers to Life's mysteries, recognizing that they, too, have been given a torch of illumination for the steadfast journey as disciples of the Christ.

All are not given the identical experience pattern, for some do not require what others do. One day we shall reveal to the Lightbearers of earth a greater understanding of their origins than they have previously known. Until certain facets of the Christ consciousness are mastered by the people of this planet, such treasure might serve only to confuse many.

What is vital and of immediate consequence to the happiness and well-being of the general populace, and our disciples in particular, is that they learn to govern their energies. Emotional excesses generate humanly qualified, downward-pulling vortices that tend to swallow up the undisciplined in old and new momentums of karma.

A disciple is one who practices the disciplines of the God Self, ruling over and disciplining the outer personality and his own ideational patterns, having the God-awareness of himself as an individualized manifestation of the I AM THAT I AM. Those so fortunate as to have chosen discipleship as a way of life have thereby chosen to serve the Light. By always placing the Light first, these will find that one day the Light will place them first—at the very center of God's will. Then nothing will be impossible to the disciple, for it is not difficult for the Master.

Through every moment of the day, God is releasing to everyone on earth the same pure energy of his own nature—the essence of all Goodness. Yet the end result of this release, impartially given, is that one receives and amplifies it as a good steward while another wastes it by spilling it on the ground.[6]

The final point to keep constantly in mind is that living vigilance must countermand every human impulse which does not have the approval of one's own Christ nature. Hour by hour, every human impulse must be replaced by the ever-watchful direction of the Christ Self's heavenly intent.

Do this, beloved, and see how the fullness of the seamless garment of Christ-perfection will descend and abide with you, waking or sleeping, conscious or unconscious. I tell you truly, this garment of your Christ-image will magnify without limit that God-plan which invokes for you, the disciple, the fullness of the Master's image.

Valiantly in Christ Truth, I AM

Kuthumi

Habit

¹**hab·it** \ 'habət, *usu* -əd·+V \ *n* -s
[ME *habit, abit,* fr. OF, fr. L *habitus* condition,
appearance, attire, character, disposition,
habit, fr. *habēre* to have, hold — more at GIVE]
1 *archaic* **a :** CLOTHING, APPAREL ⟨costly thy ~ as
thy purse can buy —Shak.⟩ **:** mode of dress
⟨in the vile ~ of a village slave —Alexander Pope⟩
b : a garment or a suit of clothes : OUTFIT
2 a : a costume indicative or characteristic of a
calling, rank, or function ⟨monk's ~⟩
b : RIDING HABIT **3 :** BEARING, CONDUCT, BEHAVIOR
— used esp. in Scots law in the phrase
habit and repute ⟨marriage by ~ and repute⟩
4 a : bodily appearance or makeup **:**
physical type **:** PHYSIQUE ⟨his corpulent ~ of body,
natural both to the vigor of his type and to a
sedentary way of life —Osbert Sitwell⟩
b *obs* **:** the body as a physiological organism **:**
the system of bodily processes **c** *obs*
: the body's surface **5 :** the prevailing disposition
or character of a person's thoughts and feelings
: mental makeup ⟨where he has gone to indulge
a contemplative ~ —L.J.Halle⟩ ⟨a whole ~ of
sensibility —F.R.Leavis⟩ **6 a** *of a person* **:** a
settled tendency of behavior or normal manner of
procedure **:** CUSTOM, PRACTICE, WAY ⟨contributed
letters to the newspapers—a ~ that became a life-
long one —B.J.Hendrick⟩ ⟨the local ~ of building
in perishable materials —Bernard Newman⟩ **b** *of
a thing* **:** a usual manner of occurrence or behavior **:** TENDENCY ⟨black clouds there have a ~
of sitting right on the water —Ira Wolfert⟩ ⟨paste
has a ~ of going hard and lumpy once opened⟩
7 a : a behavior pattern acquired by frequent repetition or developed as a physiologic function and
showing itself in regularity ⟨the daily bowel ~⟩ or
increased facility of performance or in a decreased
power of resistance ⟨a cocaine ~⟩ **b :** an acquired
or developed mode of behavior or function that
has become nearly or completely involuntary ⟨put

the keys back in his pocket through force of ~⟩
8 *of an organism* : characteristic mode of growth
or occurrence ⟨elms have a spreading ~⟩ ⟨a grass
ubiquitous in its ~⟩ **9** : the characteristic crystal-
line size and form of a substance **10** *archaic* :
close acquaintance : FAMILIARITY ⟨he inclines to a
sort of disgust . . . with the system and he has
few . . . ~s with any of its professors —Edmund
Burke⟩ **11** : a generic entity occurring as an external or supernatural reality or force constitutive of
or acting on an individual **12** : ADDICTION 2a ⟨was
forced to steal to feed his drug ~⟩
syn HABITUDE, PRACTICE, USAGE, CUSTOM, USE, WONT:
these all have in common the sense of a way of
behaving that has become more or less fixed;
in most cases they have the sense of such a way
considered collectively or in the abstract. HABIT,
usu. applying to individuals, signifies a way of
acting or thinking done frequently enough to have
become unconscious or unpremeditated in each
repetition or to have become compulsive
⟨the *habit* of dawdling on the way to school⟩
⟨a persistent *habit* of coughing⟩ ⟨*habits* of mind⟩
⟨speech *habits*⟩ HABITUDE usu. suggests
habitual or usual state of mind or attitude ⟨you
who are so sincere with me are never quite sincere
with others. You have contracted this bad
habitude from your custom of addressing the
people —W.S.Landor⟩ PRACTICE suggests an act,
often habitual, repeated with regularity and usu.
by choice ⟨the team made a *practice* of leaving
their scenarios unfinished until actual
production —*Current Biog.*⟩ ⟨promised the people
that he would establish democratic *practices*
—*Collier's Yr. Bk.*⟩ ⟨the *practice* of self-
examination —Anne Fremantle⟩
²habit \ " \ *vt* -ED/-ING/-S : CLOTHE, DRESS ⟨the nature of such pedantry to ~ itself in a harsh
and crabbed style —R.M.Weaver⟩
³habit \ " \ *vb* -ED/-ING/-S [ME *habiten* to dwell,
reside, fr. MF *habiter*, fr. L *habitare* to have possession of, inhabit, dwell, abide, fr. *habitus*, past
part. of *habēre* to have, hold — more at GIVE] *vi*,
obs : LIVE, ABIDE ~ *vt* **1** *archaic* : INHABIT
2 *archaic* : ACCUSTOM, HABITUATE

Corona Class Lesson 31

Illumination

"Great Is Your Reward in Heaven"

Pioneers of the Universal Intelligence of God—

Thought, in all its wonder, must be governed—just as men harness the tide and the winds. First, it must be recognized that man is not thought but that the power to think is ever a faculty of mind. Man is not mind, but solely a manifestation of God.

The frailty of human reason is ever in its identification with the finite self. A sense of being entangled in the processes of identification with objects and experiences hinders the revelation of man's true spiritual nature.

The idea of God as the creator of the universe easily evolves to the idea of equating God with the universe, but this is ever a mistake known as "pantheism." For the universe could not contain Him; neither is He limited by the finite borders of material substance.

However, it is definitely true, beloved ones, that God is in substance and in form and that the life-elements which compose them emanate from the Godhead. Nevertheless, it simply cannot be said that the identity of God is circumscribed or confined by that substance which composes the universal body of creation called the cosmos.

God is not the matter universe, neither is the universe God. It is, however, the vessel into which he pours his Life; and the only Life there is in matter is God. Furthermore, without the Divine Being extending a portion of Himself into substance—spiritual or material—the inner structure of that substance would collapse. Likewise, should Elohim withdraw their God consciousness from the embrace and the vision of the physical universes—these, too, and all therein would cease to be.

Beloved, God is not the mind that comprehends and knows in part.[1] But the mind of man that potentially senses the things of the Spirit is connected with and utilizes the one universal intelligence of God. This spiritual intelligence whispers to life, and life obeys the impetus of Love's mandates, hastening joyously to observe the ritual of Life's (God's) perfect plan, amplifying the divine intent to the fullness of its power.

The mind is a tool of wonderful flexibility. When it is set free by the power of imagination (operating through the 'third eye'—the spiritual center located at the brow of the forehead), it can envision a multitude of glorious concepts which range from mere fancy to creative sublimity.

Chief among the attributes of Divinity as

expressed by an illumined mind is the power to govern itself. An ungoverned intellect, like unbridled emotion, can result only in disgrace for the erring manifestation. Error cannot affect the pure and holy purposes of universal Love, which are in complete unity with the perfect Mind of God and cannot be divided by the chicanery of the carnal mind.

The forthright statement of the Christ, "Father, forgive them, for they know not what they do," indicates that ignorance is the first sin upon which the Babylonian tower of error, reaching for the skies, is constructed.[2] If, then, it be ignorance which is the first habit to conquer, it can be recognized that by the golden flame of Christ-illumination the realm of shadow is pushed back.

Upon the hearth fires of expanding illumination, the horizons of men expand to pioneer a new frontier of spiritual knowledge and experience. And the rocky abyss of ignorance is transformed thereby into a universal highway of light whose roads, like ribbons of glory, lead to the city of God-happiness and peace (Shamballa).

Ignorance is a habit based on sluggishness of mind and an unwillingness to sharpen and use the tool of thought. Lack of knowledge must be countered by joyful seeking after the glory of God, both below among the learnings of men and above in the lofty hills of sacred knowledge and spiritual experience.

When the process whereby habits are formed is understood in its entirety, a most useful faculty is forged. In order to understand how habits are formed, it is helpful to observe the cycles of life operational in daily experience.

The cycle of the hours, as "day unto day uttereth speech, and night unto night sheweth knowledge,"[3] is derived from the diurnal rotation of the earth on its axis as the hemispheres are alternately exposed to and concealed from the solar radiance. The cycles of the years occur by reason of the revolution of the earth in its elliptic orbit around the sun.

The cycles of civilization respond to the cosmic tides of stellar influence outplayed in the configurations of the hierarchies of the zodiac as these interact upon the bodies of the solar system. So many solar systems comprising a galaxy, so many galaxies in procession around the Great Central Sun present a staggering eye view of what, for want of another word, we call The Immensity. Yet this is not all.

Concentric rings (elongated as ellipses) are the best way of graphically illustrating eternity as distinguished from time and space, which are depicted as a straight line or a geometric angle segmenting the inner sections of the circle of Life into separate parts.

Now, this we consider in order to understand that the same law of energy-in-motion operative in planetary bodies governs the orderly process which occurs each time you create (i.e., set in motion, launch into orbit) a habit in your world. Whether or not men are conscious of this, the law follows its cycle of completion and establishes a habit as a duly recognized result of the law of the circle in action.

Electricity and magnetism play their part in establishing and sustaining the action of habit and the power of habit. Using the example of an electromagnet, I am desirous of imparting to the students an awareness of the circles used in winding wire into a magnetic coil; these are indicative of a repetition of the law of the circle—which circle, in this case, becomes a spiral gathering momentum with each turn, even as a habit is strengthened by its recurrence. The more turns of wire about the magnetic core, the greater the induction and accompanying magnetism that is created in the electromagnet as the electricity flows through the coil. [4]

As we compare the natural laws of physics to the metaphysics of human psychology, we ask the student to pause for a moment to equate for himself this reinforcement of desired or undesired action (as though each act, a thing in itself, gathered unto itself a momentum of energy forming a spiral around the spinal altar) and to consider how this magnetizing of the core of self (one's energy and consciousness) happens each time he mentally or physically goes over (repeats) such repetitious cycles (turns of the wire) as he habitually releases his energy (electricity) into the same habit pattern, or coil. It will be seen that the power of any habit, good or bad—or a collection of habits—is actually a dominant (electromagnetic, if you will) force, a veritable momentum attracting Good or Evil in both the human and the divine personality of man.

These facts are not intended to frighten but to free by soul illumination all who would take control of their daily lives. However, the average student will require more than the armor of this beginning knowledge to bind the power of old and entrenched habits unwanted, unfruitful. Like the barren fig tree,[5] these habits—though they lock a great deal of man's energy in a magnetic coil of repetitive desires and deeds— bear no fruit of Higher Consciousness (much less, positive human achievement for social good, which is to be anticipated of every chela on the Path). Therefore, they must be "cursed" (judged) by the Christ, "withered" by the withdrawal of all energy invested therein—their spirals arrested by a fiat of the will, and their consciousness and momentum cast into the sacred fires of transmutation invoked steadfastly in dynamic violet flame decrees.

We have provided this foundation to our study of the law of habit and habit formation in this first discourse on our subject in order that you, our blessed disciples, might, in the spirit and tradition of Jeremiah, "root out and pull down and destroy" all negative spirals and self-destructive habit and "build and plant" all positive spirals and constructive habit necessary for your self-realization in God.[6]

We shall follow with an ordered outline of study whereby the formation of habits will be seen to be tied to the setting in motion of temporal cycles governed by the law of the spiral which each one sometime, somewhere has established for himself. The law of habit dictates that the one who has created a habit is the only one who can uncreate it—simply because it is *his* energy, *his* free will, and *his* self-creation on the path of self-mastery that are involved. If one does decide to uncreate a habit, that one must then adjust the cycles of the energy thereby freed so as to divert it into constructive channels.

It ought to be understood that when good habits are established and erroneous ones transmuted, a more Godlike nature is evolved whereby the living Christ once again appears and is honored "in the flesh." The cause of heaven is served best by making man the master of his own household (his four lower bodies as well as the members of his immediate family), thus enabling him to take his rightful God-intended dominion over the citadels of his domain, as ever-widening spirals (good habits) of responsibility make him the logical steward of the Good on behalf of communities and nations.

It is the right of every spiritual teacher to understand how to give practical advice to those lesser-illumined seekers who may from time to time come to him for knowledge. Bearing in mind that these seekers are God-sent and belong to Him alone, the teacher should show his pupils how they may combat the elements of materiality, the grossness of mortal concepts, and the density of human thought patterns. The teacher must carefully illustrate how human thought patterns radiate into the world, creating and sustaining centers (vortices) of a negative influence which are destructive and unhealthy to the evolving spiritual bodies (and souls!) of the children of Light.

The veil of Kashmir, woven by ethereal hands of loveliness, conceals the intense beauty of Christ-radiance which shines forth from the Holy of Holies within man, passing through calcified matter concepts and irradiating all with the penetrating Mind of God. As decadent habits are *dismantled* or done away with entirely, there is a gradual parting of the veil and a tangible manifestation of the Holy Grail is revealed before the errant eyes of the knight-seeker for the nobility of heaven.

I AM lovingly enfolding all in a *mantle* of God-illumination, a garment from out the sun of splendor shining unto a more perfect day.

Kuthumi

Corona Class Lesson 32

Thought

"No Man Can Serve Two Masters"

Engravers of Self-Luminous
        Intelligent Substance—
    Immortal energy patterns are being woven
continuously by the children of God, both
ascended and unascended. Whether they are
formed carelessly or lovingly, these engravings
are cast in the die of self-luminous intelligent
substance, ever flowing from the heart of the
Presence of God. Once established, they become
like tablets of law—commandments which, from
the level of the subconscious, exercise authority
in the world of the creator and sustainer of the
original pattern.
    Today is the accepted day of grace (salva-
tion)[1] when the wondrous power of the Spirit of
God must be allowed to prevail if men are to
become and remain free from each and every
snare, whether self-woven or the unwanted
handiwork of another.

Earnestly and lovingly, all heaven yearns to set free from imprisonment in egocentric ideas all captive minds and hearts and souls. How we long to see the auric forcefield of every child of God charged with the pure and radiant energies of our spheres!

Would that your benign aspirations themselves could set you free! But your yearnings cannot perpetually exalt you; even your intense wishes are powerless unless you implement your seeking with the action of finding and emulating the Good Shepherd (your Holy Christ Self) by gathering the restless sheep of your diversified and dissipated life's energy into the sheepfold of unified and everlasting peace.

So often it is but a mere thread of contact that connects individuals with their mighty God-identity, yet even this is enough if the opportunities Life presents be seized at the right moment. Salvation is a gift of God,[2] beloved ones, but each one must stretch forth the hand of his longings and accept that precious gift.

While many wait for me to save them and to give them the fullness of my comfort—which I long to do—the Great Law of Life, reflected in the law of each one's being, demands that the disciple of Christ prove himself willing to work out his own salvation with reverence (fear, awe) and the tingling joy (trembling) of the Holy Spirit.[3] This Holy One of God floods the children of God with light and bathes their four lower bodies with a mighty tinge of angelic and cosmic glory. Expanding at last into the fullness of divine comfort, the soul communes with the Father/Mother Source of his own blessed life.

Long ago, as I expanded my soul into the essence of communion with the Holy Christ Self of all through the universal Christ, I sent forth the call on wings of light to the eternal Father, to his heart of creation and being, to flood the essence and consciousness of himself into the hearts of his children so that all who did hunger and thirst after righteousness might drink of the water of Life freely.

Blessed ones, the water of Life flows freely from your I AM Presence charged with the feeling of the unlimited and unmeasured current of God's being, imparted unto each son and daughter of immortal Life in accordance with his capacity to receive. It is this full quality and power of God's immortality and intelligence in the very 'water' (energy) of Life which quickens in every son and daughter of Life the sense of the soul's eternal mission.

This unifying, intelligent current from the heart of the Creator flows into the hearts of his offspring, enabling the alert and perceptive to imbibe the fullness of their inherent potential, regardless of how far short of the mark of Christhood they may be. The Father is ever a fount of hope!

Were it possible at this very moment for every seeker of oneness with God to outpicture the fullness of the divine nature, there would be no continuing need for greater effort; for the reality of Life would have dawned. Alas, such is not the case, for lesser aims have consumed men. Therefore, they must retrace their steps, realign their energies to more sublime goals, and sit at the feet of the Master Presence of their own God Self once again to renew their vows and to accept the aid of heaven without fear or mental reservation.

I am standing with beloved Kuthumi for the purpose of illumining every teacher and every student with the beautiful simplicity of that God-understanding which will enable all to fathom just how they have been brought under the power of habit and how they can best escape from every negative, binding, and unwanted condition for the sake of their soul's eternal unfoldment of the heart's rose of light.

Habit and thought are akin and the products, somewhat, of each other. Habit, of course, stems from the conscious election to think and carry out a thought and from permitting one's life energies to run in appointed channels, whether by design or haphazardly.

Thought is a product of the habit of reflection. It may be described as the agitation (cogitation) of ideas, or ideation, resulting from the ray of illumination focused from the Divine Mind commingling with human reason—and unfortunately diluted by error and misqualified energy. Thought is capable of logic, as in the inductive and deductive reasoning processes exercised by man in his analysis of the substance and circumstance of his world of cause and effect.

In higher octaves, the thought process may

be replaced by a direct apprehension or sudden, a priori awareness through contact with the all-knowing (omniscient) Source of universal wisdom. Stored in the Great Causal Body of cosmos, the fruits of the cogitation of the saints are employed to bless all Life as the collective thought/property of all manifestations (extensions) of the one Mind.

Inasmuch as Truth is one in those realms of light to which we are accustomed, the recall (or memory) processes do not err. Therefore, the oneness and invariability of Truth remains the same yesterday and today and forever.[4] This is the state of the Christ Mind, which is solely under the power of God and is never controlled by the unbridled habits of the human mind.

Humanly developed habits, nonreflective of the divine habits and habitats of Be-ness, are a mischievous assembly of pernicious practices, transmitted from man to man by the contagion of devilish concepts and fallen examples. There are many good habits which should be further developed and retained. Good habits are conducive to amplifying the power of the higher octaves and harnessing the light of higher dimensions to do the bidding of the seeker for the Christ consciousness here below in the physical plane.

The very process of breathing is itself a habit resulting from the inward impulse and will to live. This involuntary process functions automatically twenty-four hours a day, serving to fan the flame of Life within each lifestream.

Now, there is a shift of consciousness which occurs periodically within individuals whereby voluntary habits established by the mind and free will of man become involuntary processes through the internal consent of the body elemental. This is usually accomplished when actions are indicated as desirable by the outer self through frequency of repetition.

It is just as easy as not for men to establish unwanted attitudes and conditions of consciousness whereby the spur of an emotional episode — such as the reaction to another's glance, driving habits, or tone of voice — can cause powerful vortices of tornadic anger to charge from the emotional body like a thunderstorm unleashed without warning.

This is a decidedly wrong action, and the God-guard of an altar of sweetened consciousness should be held in the face of each such trial, if balance is to be kept by the individual and a lesson in God-control mastered. It is far better to prevent the stain of sin before it becomes etched in the memory than to permit it unbridled entrance into the thoughts and feelings.

The repetitiveness of the indulgence and the intensity of the feelings determine the depth of the imprint made upon the recorded memory of man. At times, even resistance to evil can intensify rather than diminish the action or reaction of evil — unless that resistance is accompanied by the serious use of the violet transmuting flame.

The ministering servant must understand my words of old "Resist not evil"[5] and balance them with the scriptural admonishment "Resist the devil, and he will flee from you."[6] In rightly dividing the word of Truth[7] in daily living, it must be perceived that there is a time to resist and a time not to resist—whether the enemy be bad habit or the Evil One.

Undesirable habits can best be overcome by a nonresistant state wherein the soul of man is literally flooded with such intense goodness from God that discordant, even deathlike appearances are swallowed up in the harmony of heaven. Thus, Good overcomes Evil by being its own directing law and intelligence in action.

However, militant evil directly attacking an individual through the mental projection of the malevolent thought of another—because of its very subtlety and unseen nature—must be dealt with by the firm denial of its power and the affirmation of the all-power (omnipotence) of Good to overcome and annihilate all negative thought or unwanted conditions.

Therefore, resist this type of an attack of evil until it flees from you and returns like a boomerang to the one sending it out. The result is that the inrush of misqualified energy, turned back upon itself, is self-destroyed.

Care must ever be exercised, in dealing with such aggressive mental suggestion, to practice Christ-discrimination and to keep a sincere heart. Those whose nature is not yet fully illumined are sometimes incensed in ignorance or influenced by limited knowledge to direct wrongly qualified energy against their own brethren, thinking they do God a service.[8]

This ignorant yet malicious practice can manifest as militant evil or even in psychic murder. The resultant misqualified energy is thus made available to the sinister force, which uses it to tempt the devout in diverse ways by means of intense, almost hypnotic thought projections of fear and of hate and hate creation and its counterpart, insanity.

The light energy used to sustain such malignant and malefic error, even by well-meaning individuals, becomes nevertheless perverted and inverted into darkness within them. Thus, I warned the abusers of God's power with the words: If the Light that is in thee be (misqualified) darkness, *how great is that darkness!*[9]

This grave darkness covering the spiritual senses and densifying the chakras prevents the individual so engaged in misqualifying the light from seeing the mote in his own eye and the need to remove it.[10] And this clouded state of unknowing begets the wider sin of projecting one's subconscious criticism, condemnation, and judgment upon the unsuspecting.

The disciple mounting the path of Love through the Law of the One utterly refuses to be brought under the power of entrenched evil projected against him from any source known or unknown. He cleaves unto the Father and his beloved I AM Presence as his supreme shield against all unrighteousness.

Blessed ones, the temple of God is Life, and the moneychangers who would make of Life a den of thieves must be cast out of one's consciousness *and Life*.[11] Allegiance to the honor of God demands that this be done in order to keep the Father's house a place of prayer and communion with him.

Little children, I have warned you that anti-christ should come.[12] Now learn that bad habit is his entrance to your world. Therefore, form good habits of strong, positive thought centered in God's love and you will not be led astray to enter into the worst of all habits I know: criticism, condemnation, and judgment of thy fellowservant striving, and ofttimes struggling, to also reach my heart.

The treasured concepts of immortality re-quire the chela's complete dedication. And *you are* being tested daily. To go on and to finish the course, you need a mind pure and strong that will not succumb to the wiles of gossip.

While I am aware that many admire me as Jesus the Christ, I consider that the highest honor anyone can pay me is to give his alle-giance to the source of the all-power of God and its foundation in my life: obedience to the pre-cepts of God — a mind dwelling in the constancy of his love and dedicated first and foremost to him, and thence directed as a beam of light to all creation. Do thou likewise and attain within thine own being the victory of Love. This is true worship and perfect adoration of the Father.

Remember always: To establish heavenly habits enables the disciple to evolve to a higher state of Christ-illumination — a state which overcomes the world, casts out every unwanted thought (or feeling) of human creation, and attains its cherished victory.

We unite our consciousness with every sincere follower of Truth and offer here and now our most powerful assistance in overcoming undesirable habits and replacing them by a mighty fountain of Christ-virtue.

I AM blessing you now with the full power of Illumination's Flame.

Your teacher and friend,

Jesus the Christ

Corona Class Lesson 33

Character

"Mark the Perfect Man and Behold the Upright"

Blessed Seekers of the Great God-Design—
   "When the fullness of time was come..."[1] is a statement symbolizing different things to different people. Every lifestream has a matrix, or God-design, which he ought to outpicture each day. Unless this is made known to the outer self of the seeker, it is difficult for him to cooperate with the mighty plan of the inner life.
   It is most helpful, when, either through prayer or invocation, by decree or earnest effort, students determine to find out everything they can about their great God-design—and then begin to experience elements of that design day by day through a practical plan of action.
   It is essential for all who would bring the power of negative conditions under the submission of the Real Self to realize that they have a listening ear in heavenly places awaiting their call for the secrets of their own beings to be revealed—especially the spiritual means to change

what must be changed. When you know the method whereby your energies can be aligned, you can swim with the current of your I AM Presence instead of struggling against the mighty tide of Life.

Many people retain the dim memory of the internal magnificence of their own God plan, and this serves to spur them on to an externalization of some facet of that wondrous purpose. For others not yet awakened to the same degree, a void seems to exist and they remain in a rut of unknowing and insensitivity to the vibrations of the Higher Self. Those in such a state find it difficult to understand how the true spirit of genius works, and they often gaze spellbound at the spiritual progress of others without understanding how it all came about.

Recognizing the differences in soul advancement between people, all should tread softly the path of self-discovery and magnetize more faith in the glory of God shining just behind the outer appearance, giving luster, when invoked, to every man's accomplishments. As faith in one's Real Self mounts up, it will draw to each lifestream many of the qualities he or she may lack.

Sometimes this "fullness of time" seems to tarry unduly long and it appears as though the tender shoot of the soul's progress will never burst through the earth into the light of the day's appearing. Therefore, we direct that it is the responsibility of every student to wait upon the Presence by actively building into consciousness those qualities which are representative of the Godhead.

As one of the World Teachers, I am urging the gentle students to abide in the cleansing shower of the fountain of wisdom, knowing that the correct use of spiritual power does garner results which will be self-evident in due course. Frequently it is the very depth of the stain, builded layer upon layer in consciousness, which seems unyielding to the application of God's will by the faithful. It is this "layer upon layer" which must be erased by persistent application of the violet fire and not the mere dabbing of the sponge of sporadic attention.

Beloved Jesus and I are particularly concerned that the seeker understand that he is not rejected by God merely for his temporary immersion in inequity or so-called sin. Nevertheless, it should be stated that all of one's human virtue could not cancel out one sentence of human discord unless the action of the Law of Love through the sacred heart (developed heart chakra) were to balance the wisdom-power outpouring.

It should also be understood that man is not a vacuum, neither is he a void: twenty-four hours a day, energy is released from the Presence and directed by him either to the good of himself and his fellowmen or in an idling mode whereby the superimposition of tramp thoughts and feelings of others—incarnate or discarnate— may engage the lever of the mind and produce the temporary manifestation of error sowing.

Habits of negative thought and feeling have been fed by human attention for millenniums, and it is this constant repetition—of channeling the flow into the same old troughs—which must be counteracted by the indomitable love of God. Now, the love of God is so mighty that when you also love mightily—and love Him more than your outworn habits—Love as God can and does cancel out in rapid order generations of wrongdoing.

When casting out the demons of negative habit, it must be remembered that the house swept clean needs protection from the invasion of the mass habit-consciousness of mankind. Did He not say to the one healed of the thirty-eight-year 'habit' of infirmity: "Go and sin no more, lest a worse thing come unto thee"?[2] He knew that the re-creation of the thoughtform of illness or the condemnation by forces of antichrist of the healing performed by the Son could open the door of consciousness to this mass habit-consciousness which daily enslaves and *re-enslaves* millions in a round of vain repetition.

Those whom Christ commands to take up their 'bed of habit' and walk, realigned with the will of God, must bear a flood of regret in the event of their return to the human habit of mediocrity; but, nevertheless, some do go for (prefer) the questionable comfortability of familiarity!

Powerfully good habits are the best assurance any lifestream can have that the power of unwanted habits will speedily disappear. The filling of the spaces of consciousness with the

Mind of Christ, with the Love of Christ, and with the Power of God builds enormous reserves of spiritual treasure which must by divine right accrue to the depositor's credit. The infallibility of karmic law is too frequently overlooked by the impatient chela who in a moment of despair casts discretion to the winds and behaves as if he were not forever God's creation.

Human creation may be transitory, but, in the guise of permanence, it has for too long bound those who should be free and should have freed themselves by poking holes in its repetitive illusion. I am joining with beloved Jesus in proclaiming liberty to the captives and in opening the prison doors to them that are self-bound[3] by the God-power they have wrongly invested in wrong habit.

Not fear but a sense of awe, as respect for the perfection of the Law, is the quality we would develop in all our students. When respect, founded upon love for the World Teachers and the One whom we represent, lives in the disciple's consciousness, it serves as an ever-present rein and reminder that if he does well, he will be accepted; and if not, he will find, as the LORD told Cain, that sin (one's karma instead of grace) lieth at the door.[4]

Nevertheless, heaven expects a return: "For unto whomsoever much is given, of him shall be much required. And to whom men have committed much, of him they will ask the more."[5]

There are so many good habits which can be developed, that we advise the alert chela who wishes to overcome so-called bad habits to direct his attention to those most readily attainable. Each good habit is a stepping-stone to the next and more difficult 'stone' which the Law requires child-man to master ere he become the joint-heir[6] of the full Christ consciousness.

The establishment of right thought multiplied by the repetition of right action cannot fail to crowd out the banal influences (duplicated ad nauseam) and set the student on the path of self-perfection by the Law of the One: one God plus one universal Christ in singular manifestation in the disciple as one consistent habit equals Love in action!

Far too much attention has been paid to self-analysis, faultfinding, and the old shoes of error; far too little has been offered the Ascended Masters by their chelas as useful raw material whereby the Brotherhood may assist the individual to build in his world the essential Christly character traits. When faithfully exercised, such traits evolve to become the composite of living masterful personalities patterned after Ascended Master law and destined to win for all time the victory of the ascension.

All who are determined to enter the era of the eternal Now and to manifest today the salvation of God must bid welcome to the corrective influences of heaven—ever pure, constant, loving, instructive, and eternally useful—transmitted by angels who are thy teachers and the guardians of thy victory. (Sent from our retreats, they know exactly your need, if you will only listen—and develop the habit of good listening.)

Every chela must be forewarned that the initiates and would-be masters of the Light must be tested! The battle-tested armor should be worn. Invulnerability must be attained! We laud the effort and stand with you—

Kuthumi

Corona Class Lesson 34

Call

"Builded Together for an Habitation of God"

Sojourners of Earth Seeking
  Inter-Soul Relationships and Dimensions—

Foremost among the problems men need to solve for themselves is that of the power of habits of negative action.

Let no one's heart be troubled because he has long endured banal habits; let none feel a sense of absolute frustration or loneliness concerning the overcoming of these unwanted conditions. I AM the compassionate Christ anchored above each lifestream, longing to pour the full momentum of my assistance into every waiting consciousness chaliced in the attitude of receptivity.

Beloved ones, you do not walk alone. It is ever foolhardy to insist upon solving your own problems without calling to us for aid. It is equally unwise to feel that once the call for assistance is sincerely offered, heaven will deny the earnest petitioner any pure desire of the soul for more light and grace to manifest the God-intended designs of immortal Life!

You are my disciples in the Word when you daily demonstrate the Law of the Word. The circle of your oneness—two of you or more united in prayer—establishes the polarity of Alpha and Omega necessary for the precipitation of the light and will of God in the physical octave. Thus, the oft-quoted verses from Matthew, which I did indeed speak to my own, are a scientific formula of the Paraclete for disciples of the universal Christ in all planes of Matter and all systems of worlds:

". . . If two of you shall agree on earth [in the Matter universe] as touching any thing [person, place, condition, circumstance, problem, or plan—past, present, or future] that they shall ask, it shall be done for them of my Father [the Mighty I AM Presence] which is in heaven [in the Spirit universe]. For where two or three are gathered together in my name—I AM THAT I AM Jesus the Christ—there am I [there is the I AM Presence of me] in the midst of them."[1]

Remember: The call *does* compel the answer. If you ask the Father for bread, he will not give you a stone[2]—for the alchemy of the Holy Spirit is precise. But if you ask and receive not, search your soul and seek the good habit of God's will, that the kingdom without fulfill the blueprint (will) of the kingdom within.[3]

You have heard it said that one day is with the LORD as a thousand years, and a thousand years as one day.[4] Blessed ones, so is the consciousness of the Almighty Creator and Father of all: his consciousness is yours if you will but drink in the fullness of all that it represents.

I am eternally grateful for the counsel and love given me so generously by my blessed mother, Mary. I am grateful for the love of the angelic hosts and the dear Maha Chohan, for the allegiance and devotion of Lord Maitreya and all of the brothers in white whose consciousness of the purity of God was given to me long ago in answer to my call.

Enhanced by the loveliness of inter-soul relationships and dimensions, my mission two thousand years ago belonged to the fulfillment of the universal Christ consciousness in the heart's love of many who assembled around me, drawn by the magnetism of the Holy Spirit and the sweet yearning to see the perfection of God manifest upon earth.

Today, when the hearts of many are disturbed by seemingly imponderable problems and unbearable weights of world and individual karma, I urge that habits of hopelessness and depression be forsaken and that momentums of thought and feeling which generate despair and feed the alliance of animalistic magnetism be shunned.

Look upward instead to the starry field of heaven and enter into a calm spirit of knowing that in the awesome expanse of God there is the ever-present watchfulness of eternal Love! That blessed Presence (whose will is implemented by myriad angel hearts) waits to serve the needs of earth and each brother or sister seeker who would find his way among the shadows of the night, among the densities of all sorts of contrived oppositions to Truth, among the vain and unruly conversations of men which brutally waste the eternal energy without ever so much as freeing or blessing one solitary precious life-stream!

"I AM the immortal consciousness of Truth. I AM that Christ Truth which affirms the power of Light and Light's intelligent energy to establish in my world, mind, and affairs the perfection of permanent Good!"

Hold this consciousness. Decree and determine in your heart that all discordant and base habits shall come under the power of Christ-domination. Thus shall the Light continue to expand in the citadel of your being, raising you up and healing you from all unwanted conditions that have ever troubled your heart!

Beloved Kuthumi and I have noted current trends among the youth to become subject to the nefarious influences of dope and licentiousness. In their search for soul freedom and in their ignorance of spiritual law, they do despite to their souls. The devils have piped their tune and the children of this generation, throwing caution to the winds, are engaging in most dangerous practices without moral restraint or respect either for their bodies or for the sacred energies of their chakras which they do violate by these unbridled activities.

We are well aware that the many are not inclined to observe the sanctity of holy orders. This we have not asked. But we do offer our hand to every child of God seeking freedom from unwanted conditions of sensual habit and addictions of the flesh which corrupt the spirit. Know they not that the temple of God is holy, which temple they are, and must not be defiled?[5] Well, "Tell them!" for thereby peace and joy shall abound in your daily living as God intends, and many shall be freed—by my Spirit working through you—from the terrible guilt, the condemnation of self and brother, and the arrogant demons of alienation (from God, from family, from society) currently indulged.

The human habit of censure—after the party is over and the death of a friend or idol by an overdose of drugs sobers the carefree—is not the cure for a malaise of the soul nor for the desire to escape from the responsibilities of karma. It will take more than a moment of remorse to free the soul from the power of enslaving habits reinforced by denizens of the underworld. (Make no mistake, I kid you not!) Yet those who are bound while claiming they are free assume a form of self-righteousness which is powerless to transform them or to cut them free from the real problems of emotional and mental control which they must face sooner or later, though this, too, they deny.

To return to the fold of infinite Love is to find the ready hand of divine assistance which will enable the chela not only to rise above unwanted conditions to their complete transmutation, but also to put to good use God's energy formerly dissipated in a round of senseless self-indulgence. Leaving off the insidious practice of condemning society, parents, or an inequitable materialistic civilization, the revolutionaries of the Spirit express God's unlimited freedom in the building of a new world and a new age based on the Higher Consciousness of the Christ of each individual.

Let the *habitual habit* of positive affirmation of the Good, and the effective denial of the works of the iniquitous, generate a momentum of God's power within the soul to overcome all self-induced bondage. Let praise of the Holy One of God—your own beloved Christ Self—in an exalted and wonderful manner to the glory of the Almighty and the blessing of this generation be the key to necessary change in man and society!

Beloved ones, there is much that needs to be developed among the ministering servants of the nature and habit of the Good Samaritan.[6] It is the building into character of charitable qualities that strengthens our trained teachers to hold such attention upon the Great God Source as to draw down the universal intelligence of the I AM that will enlighten and enliven them with a charge of the Father's great love. Then effortless victory shall be theirs solely because they are saturated with the eternal joy and radiance of knowing that the light of God dispels the darkness and shadows of all human ignorance with the greater purity of Himself.

How futile it is to let a lack of grace deter you from outpicturing the fullness of the light already given you. Grace is a quality of the heart of Christ containing all mercy and forgiveness, love and light. Contrary to the accepted doctrine that grace comes only from myself, you yourself can increase the grace flowing through your heart center (chakra) from your Holy Christ Self. This you accomplish by various loving means, including the multiplication (expansion and refinement) of talents given into your hand instead of burying them in the napkin of despair.

These talents are, in fact, your past momentums of good habit built up in previous lives of service to the God of Truth. Each talent is a developed genius acquired by hard work and diligence to the duty of unfolding the soul's inner potential.

Your talents, presently in your hands, are the fruits of former striving and accomplishment plucked from your Tree of Life by your I AM Presence and released from your causal body for your further good use and increase as you shepherd my own flock in this life. Talents exercised produce tangible grace which you may share with all friends of light. Do this with a magnanimous heart and the habit of goodwill and you will find your freedom from all grief and mourning, despondency and a sense of littleness or fearfulness.

You are beloved, whether fully aware of it or not, and I am certain that each one of you who will read these words and look up at me right now and call for my light will feel me standing within your room in my Electronic Presence radiating my light and blessing you with the precious anointing of spiritual assistance and my Christ-victory which overcomes the world.

Beloved ones, be of good cheer! Because I have overcome the world, you can hope to do so, too. For you also are one with the Father and myself as you embrace the Life within you which is God, the Mighty I AM Presence, in obedient action everywhere toward all hearts.

Your expansion of your faith in the Divine Being where you are will prove of inestimable value in attaining your victory. If you believe that you can draw forth from God the desired qualities of Life, I tell you they are yours already. It is doubt that dilutes the essence of manifestation until it is so dim as to be unrecognizable.

You need to (1) Shut out unwanted thoughts and conditions from your world firmly, (2) Call forth the protection of your tube of light faithfully, (3) Use the violet fire of freedom daily, and (4) Call for the protection of heaven, the radiance and the power of the Archangels and Ascended Masters constantly—without fail. No matter what men may declare to the contrary, without the assistance of many of these wonderful beings of Light, I would never have been successful in my own mission!

Surely, then, if it was needful for me to have cosmic assistance from the Great Ones—with all the previous training and assistance I had been given at inner levels of life (for I came forth from

God and descended from heavenly places)—you, too, should feel the need to call it forth.

Some have continued to call forth love and light without seeing any tangible results or very little fruits for their labors. Let them look within motive, heart, and akashic records for fortitude. If motive be pure and heart be pure, then they will see in the records that the answer has been given, for the call always compels the answer!

Never in the annals of heaven's contacts with earth has any reasonable or lawful request, sincerely made, been denied. Those occasions when it has seemed so have always been governed by inner laws and heavenly reasons known to the Karmic Board. No cause for alarm exists in this universe. It is fearfully and divinely made;[7] its form, dimension, and guiding intelligence are God's love in action.

With the coming dawn, I am certain you will find that the vain shadows of the night of human reason shall have passed away. All things shall be made new under the power of habitual good established within the seeking heart as the kingdom of heaven, which is even now within you!

Ask what thou wilt and my Father will give it thee. Call to me, and I *will* answer you.

Lovingly, I AM

Jesus the Christ

Corona Class Lesson 35

Spirituality

"Be the Children of Your Father in Heaven"

To Hands and Hearts Outstretched
    We Offer Our Own—
    Naught else but eternal Life can water the soul with the refreshing rain from heaven. The vanishing material concepts will never be missed by the pilgrim who pursues the way of peace.

How mighty is the power of eternal habits. Is it not customary for men to refer to a monk's "habit" when speaking of his garments? Let the habit of spirituality clothe the sincere follower of the Ascended Masters with the greatest gifts— with the incomparable magnificence of the very best gifts heaven can bestow.

"I AM the all-enfolding garment of Light charged with the life, truth, and radiance of God, Good! Naught of the human can distress me, for I AM the victorious, all-powerful consciousness of God in action—blessing, guarding, guiding, and directing me in all that I do!"

Blessed ones, the chariot driver of days gone by held in his hands the reins to control the charging horses which conveyed him hither and yon. The reign of Ascended Master God-control which nothing can dismay (whereby the Christ of you holds the reins which control the 'four horsemen' of the four lower bodies) ought to keep you in perfect control of every situation.

Can the raging (astral) sea, the raging heathen [1] energies (of the mass consciousness), or the die of the human thought matrix stay or destroy the perfect beauty of the eternal concepts God has about you? Of course not! But the thoughts God holds for you as an individual i-den-ti-fied with Life (I AM densified, or co-alesced, in form) *must* hold sway in your world, and the priceless treasures of heaven *must* become a daily habit *before* you can be vested with the power of all Good.

Blessed ones, the story attributed to my life as Saint Francis, of the image of the Christ Child appearing in the crèche one Christmas,[2] holds this meaning: the image of the Mighty I AM Presence activated in man by purity and love does indeed give life to the immaculate God-concept of the Christ, the Son of God, in every child of Light who will accept the gift.

Within the manger scene surrounded by the adoring angels and related ones who understand that the Christ of Nazareth is the Christ of every man, the perfect habit and gift of Christ-mas lives and is made alive for all the years in each receptive heart. And the power of God, the

Divine One, clothes all with the habit of thought-perfection like unto himself.

How lovingly the ones who have gone before in steps of spiritual progress leading to the ascension offer hearts and hands of light to strengthen the bonds between the unascended chelas and those already blessed with the completeness of Light's bond of ascended perfection.

Hold fast the hands of Love that have borne you thus far; for he who fashioned thee of old, fashioned also the Christ! The Light that shines beyond the years overcomes all fear and clothes thee now with the auric radiance of God's own love—the magic circle of Christ's family unity. Let them *try* to shut thee out—*God has taken thee in!*

Be filled with God and all else shall be overcome, for the Most High shall overcome all imperfections in thee by his gift of Light, Love, and Life, which remain to this day unbroken by any or all patterns less than perfection!

Lovingly, I AM

Kuthumi

Vision

Hearts Burdened by the Shadowed Image,
> I AM Come!

Let none tarry overlong in the densities of human stagnation. The clear, calm pool of immortal Love waits to bathe the world, the soul, and all that breathes the essence of eternal Life, with the concepts of God himself. How can the shadowed image long remain when heaven's wondrous face is bending o'er the soul to see reflected there the glory of Eternity?

I AM come to bring peace to the troubled heart and calm repose to the soul in the dignity of life, sustained by the wisdom of iridescent spheres. Let each one know the Christlike power of dynamic vision, the power within the concept of God's truth in action here.

Beloved ones, we won our freedom by the power of Light. Can Light do less for thee? A million concepts of error are as chaff before the winds of God's exalted vision in action.

What is the threshing floor of Life? Is it not the seat of thine own person? And does not the hand of Life serve thee there? Does not the flail and the skill of the harvester divest thee of the husks until the golden grain stands ready for milling—for the transmutation and the raising unto the LORD's table?

You are not intended merely to be guests, but sons and joint-heirs with the unfailing Light of God, clothed with the wedding garment of immortality, the joy of angels, and the all-knowing peace of the inner heart of God's Presence.

In the present-day turmoil, I am confident that the sincere student will perceive the disciplines of the Spirit as the sure means of keeping the soul expanding into its mighty matrix of perfection.

In the littleness of error-habits, men sow seeds of imperfect stature. In the cultivation of the perfection of God's thought, in the harmonizing of the consciousness with the all-knowing wisdom of God, in the supreme oneness of spiritual unity, all else is swept away. All human error and disappointment are forever inundated by a flood of loving purpose, whose end is but a door ajar into the eternal cycles of the rolling spheres, visible and invisible.

As thy Daystar shines more perfect still,
    Keep ever conscious of Good Will
For peace on earth can come to all
    Who, openhearted, heed the Call
And live in faith and grace and love
    Toward God who watches from Above,
And to mankind extend the plan
    Of Love in action, Light I AM!

Fraternally,

Jesus the Christ

Corona Class Lesson 36

Seed

"The Son of Man Soweth the Good Seed"

Scientists of the Spirit,

Apply the Law of Cycles and Be Free!

Nothing is so vital to man's steady progress toward his ascension as the establishment of good habits. These serve to sustain the power of righteousness within the orbit of each one's personal world.

In Nature, the power of habit is the innate quality of each specific manifestation. In man and society, the power of habit sustains either a benign or an unhappy status.

I am wholly persuaded by the direct vision of divine reality that the Godhead sustains the quality of perfection everywhere and that the immaculate concept is a direct extension of the fullness of immortal Love expanding itself into all manifestation.

The diversification of Love in Nature manifests as a multitude of different trees and shrubs, flowers and grasses whose variety is pleasing to the eye and inner sensitivities. By a like token, the unique quality of an individual mission (though in some ways similar to others) is the gift of the Spirit to each lifestream. This he learns to develop by the power of good habits and by the wisdom of those inner realizations which constitute a revelation from the heart of the I AM Presence.

The scientific factor which governs the establishment of habits is as plain and simple as the sand and the sky. Consent and repetition are prime factors in establishing both negative and positive habits. Denial and abstention are the means of breaking negative habits.

The attention must not be placed on the unwanted condition and no battle must be engaged. Such attention stirs up the dust of emotional energies which tend to strengthen negation while opposing it, rather than successfully eliminating and transmuting the undesirable habit. With the consent of free will, reducing the frequency of indulgence in bad habits, when accomplished by an orderly and painless withdrawal, weakens the conditioned responses of the subconscious mind. Thus, self-restraint is of real assistance in thwarting the perpetuation of wrong living.

The rejection of unwanted habits must come about as the result of the soul's expansion into the divine sense of being God in action, and not as a militancy which drives the untoward desires of man into subterranean catacombs of consciousness, one day to crop out as illness or festering frustration. The best way to reject human qualities is to simply forget them through the substitution of Christlike opposites. Such a method is spiritually scientific, for it flows with the rising currents of divinity expanding from the heart of man and drawing him upward to the universal Christ consciousness.

It is invaluable for the chela to pause and consider some of the wonderful yet basic seed ideas of Truth. These you will prove with ease to be God-ideas that can be expanded until the whole self, rising with them, is exalted into the all-knowing, comfortable Mind of Christ.

I know of no more blessed experience that can come to anyone during the Christmas season (or at any time of the individual rebirth of the Christ consciousness throughout the year) than the spirit's awakening to the realization that the universe, like a sheltering mother, holds in contemplative wonder his own blessed being. Her boundless love desires to see the living Christ stretch his tiny limbs within the manger crib of limited human consciousness and expand to reach for the skies at last, beaming as the star of Bethlehem with peace and good will to every divine manifestation, saying with the angelic hosts in tones of purest love: "Glory to God in the highest, and on earth peace, good will toward men!"

The Christ, as the infant Messiah within men's hearts, cannot long remain a babe but must expand and rise to fulfill the divine destiny and mission Life demands. The sin-sick world of social disorder with its accompanying poverty, pestilence, war, and plundering energies—the personal world with its psychic and emotional illnesses, its fears and frustrations—must yield to the idea of God embodied in the Manchild. For He shall rule the nations with a rod of iron [1] and dash in pieces [2] the limited and limiting human creations which have never brought freedom or peace to the waiting hearts of men.

How shall the kingdoms of this world become the kingdoms of our LORD and of his Christ,[3] blessed ones? It is the powerful precept of heaven that only by the *personal* acceptance of each individual—his believing in the Christ-reality of himself ("Man, *know* thy Self" [4])—can salvation (Self-elevation, i.e., the elevation of the Divine Self) occur.

When out from the masses the Great Light brings many sons and daughters to the stature of Christhood, the social order will give way to peace and abundance on earth. God cannot fail to produce that peace and plenty wherever his law and love are called into action by the Christed (anointed) ones.

Men cannot expect, if they sink back into lethargy and unconcern, that they will automatically find grace. Grace is given to the meek who seek first the kingdom (consciousness) of God and His righteousness (scientific application of the Law), which they know the all-loving Father has put into action for their use and usefulness unto Him.

Such as these do not bury their one or many talents in a napkin of disservice or discouragement. Rather, they daily gird their energies around them (concentrate their light in the chakras) as a belt of chastity (sacred power) and victory. Centered in the Christ Self, their own High Priest, in the place of the Holy of Holies, they call for their soul's purification by the essence of God's heart. They count on the answer of immortal Life to the call of their lifestream. And they go forth victoriously with the tread of mighty conquerors, lords of life and victors over human destiny, putting death and hell beneath their feet through the omnipotence of divine Love.

Consider the beautiful flame of Life in the ever-green trees whose lightness and verdure are perennially lovely! Think upon the wonderful angel devas and elemental spirits guarding and blessing God's precious children upon the highways and byways of Nature. Revel in Godly happiness in the cloud shapes drifting effortlessly through the skies above the treetops.

Love the aureole of the dawn becoming the radiance of the solar path, announcing the journey of the Sun of man out of the East unto the West.[5] Let the hours of dawn and noonday speak to your heart of hope and prayer activating all Good. Move with the gold of the western sky hushing into even as an Angelus of Christ-peace, resting like a mantle of deeds well done (accomplished in God's name I AM) upon the villages, the hamlets, the spires of city and country as upon the aspirations of the tender hearts of men everywhere.

Go forth daily in the name of God as a sower of good seed, saturated anew with the bounties of heaven. Let love prevail by the power of new habits of thought and feeling which make it easy for you to forget the rugged past. Gaze with childlike eyes into the mighty accumulation of Good without limit that is the universe in action.

Of all this, say to yourself: I AM apart from manifestation, for I AM the all of God—the allness of God, the wholeness of God. The I AM is my Father, and the I AM and I are one!*

So do thou establish the habit of Christhood, of the divinely Good Samaritan, of the Great Shepherd of the sheep, the victorious Son of God.

In Love's victory, I AM

Kuthumi

---

*Each time you affirm I AM you are actually witnessing: "The Great I AM within me is . . ." Replace the I AM in any decree with these seven words and see how this phrase lends new meaning and power in the sacred name through your complete identification with it.

Immortality

¹**im·mortal** \ (')i(m)¦mȯ(r)d³l,ə + \ *adj* [ME,
fr. L *immortalis,* fr. *in-* ¹in- + *mortalis* mortal]
1 : not mortal **:** exempt from liability to die
⟨the ~ gods⟩ **2 :** connected with or relating
to immortality ⟨I have ~ longings in me —Shak.⟩
3 : destined to persist through the ages **:**
exempt from oblivion **:** IMPERISHABLE, ABIDING
⟨those ~ words⟩ ⟨his fame ~⟩
²**immortal** \ " \ *n* **1 a :** an immortal being **:** one
exempt from death **b immortals** *pl, often cap* **:**
the gods of the Greek and Roman pantheon
2 a immortals *pl, often cap* **:** a body of troops
immortal in some way: as **(1) :** the royal body-
guard of ancient Persia whose number was
always kept full **(2) :** troops famous for gallant
behavior in war **(3) :** troops that never see war
b : a person (as an author) whose fame is lasting
c *usu cap* **:** any of the 40 members of the
Académie française **3 a** *in Confucianism* **:**
an ideal human being of antiquity **b** *in Taoism* **:**
one that has reached a divine state that is the
highest to which man can attain
c : a Chinese saint **d :** Ascended Masters
im·mortalism \ " + \ *n* **:** a doctrine of or belief
in the soul's immortality **im·mortalist**
im·mor·tal·i·ty \ ¦i(m),mȯ(r)¦taləd·ē, -lətē, -i \ *n*
[ME *immortalite,* fr. MF *immortalité,* fr. L *immor-
talitat-*] **:** the quality or state of being immortal:
as **a :** exemption from death or annihilation **:**
unending existence **:** everlasting life
⟨the ~ of the soul⟩ ⟨human ~⟩ **b :** exemption
from oblivion **:** lasting fame ⟨the ~ of these
stirring words⟩ ⟨his deeds have earned him ~
in the hearts of men⟩
im·mor·tal·ize \ i(m)'mȯ(r)d·³l,īz \ *vt* -ED/-ING/-S
[fr. L *immortalis* + *-iser* -ize] **:** to make
immortal: **a :** to cause to live or exist forever **:**
endow with everlasting life **b :** to exempt from
oblivion **:** perpetuate in fame **c :** to cause
to ascend ⟨God *immortalizes* the soul through
the ascension flame —ECP⟩

Corona Class Lesson 37

Perfection

"Be Ye Therefore Perfect..."

To Those Who Would Return
        to the Eden of Conscious Immortality—
    The rite of immortality, the goal of every man who retains the great truth of illumination's golden flame within his heart, is a ceremony of eternal purpose released into a time-spacial dimension by the Light of God that never, never fails!

    Entrusted to the children of God are many mysteries wearing the disguise of simplicity, yet these stand as pillars of Truth to reveal the most profound laws governing immortal manifestation. When ignored by men, these great laws nevertheless continue to act, for they are living Truth. The penalty for unbelief or inattention to the laws of God is a false sense of existence, entertaining drudgery, mortality, oppression, and darkness—quite the reverse of the God-intent of the soul's exaltation unto the glory of eternal Life!

Let divine knowledge be increased concerning the heart and intent of spiritual mastership.
At the same time let gratitude be expressed by
all who are the conscious recipients of each petal
of loving Truth which forms a carpet of fragrant
reality beneath the feet of man's own real identity. The passions of restless minds are best
stilled in the rapture of Godliness; therefore, the
eternal search must go on and none must ever
turn back from pursuing the wonders of God's
love for man.

Mighty spiritual power may be expressed in
a childlike way with sweetness and uncomplicated simplicity, but in the eternal Christ man it
is always expressed through the wholeness and
maturity of immortal concepts.

Thousands of years ago, in ages dimly recorded in the archives of men and all but forgotten in their subconscious memory, events were
forged in iniquity which drove men from the
Eden of conscious immortality into the thralldom of the senses and the thorny pangs of death,
sorrow, and parting. Never, no never in all the
chronicles of heaven has one iota of divine intent
ever predestined the sons and daughters of God
to the fearful events precipitated upon the screen
of life by mortal disobedience and doubt.

The events preceding the descent of the
sons of God from their abode in the etheric
octave to dense bodies of flesh were directly
related to the betrayal of the Great God by the
fallen angels and their corruption of the race of
Homo sapiens which populated the earth. This

led to mankind's misuse of the power of free will, their discovery of the misuses of the sacred fire in sorceries and miscreations, and an evil imagination[1] working all manner of vileness, untethered to the mighty power of divine Truth.

Is it any wonder that the blessings of immortality are so intimately related today to the golden flame of illumination—to the use of that flame (through the reopening of the crown chakra—the spiritual center focusing the all-knowing Mind of God) and to the recognition by man that he is a son of God descended from on high, a pilgrim in a darkened world?

When faith grew dim in the hearts of mortals (mechanization man), they kept a pseudo-faith, a cult of superstition according to their changing needs of the moment. They knew not the one God but only the relative good and evil of their supergods (Nephilim). They identified with the shifting sands of time, place, and season without realizing that their attention upon error was being transmitted and absorbed even by Nature.

Imperfect concepts, rooted in the subtle logic of Serpent and his seed (a pseudonym given to a band of fallen angels who on Lemuria and Atlantis became the archdeceivers who rivaled the sons of God and betrayed the children of Light), gradually built up a mounting pressure which finally gave way and was unleashed upon life as the harshness of loveless fear, decay, and terrifying diseases, which wrong thought and feeling always bring into manifestation.

In those long-departed days of perfection,
communion with the wonderful Source of all had
made the happiness of the sons and daughters
of God supreme, enabling earlier root races to
fulfill the purposes of higher octaves uncontami-
nated by human reason. Life unfolded like a
flower of Edenic beauty, and the obedient ones,
children of the Light, basked in the sun of eternal happiness.

Meanwhile, error was taking form in the
depths of the astral plane like a giant squid,
poised to poison the clear waters of the earth
Mother, bedim the truth of being (the Sun
behind the son of *man*ifestation), and destruct
the embryonic civilization and path of individual mastership which was gently blazing in the
temple of an infant lifewave upon this dear
earth.

I AM come today in this Corona Class to
speak to all who yearn to teach and know the
fullness of merciful, transmutative love and to
find their way back to that glorious state of
perfection they once knew.

Life, immortal Life, is within all. It exists as
a tiny flame of perfection, fanning hope into a
bright beacon in the minds of many devotees of
Truth, but bestowing upon the divinely perceptive few the living way to overcome the last
enemy, which is death.[2]

Your dedication, precious hearts of Light,
joined with my own, to destroy this death (and
the hell that is the abode of the godless dead)
does clear the way for immortal Life to take

command, dominion, and control over your life-streams from the threefold flame enthroned on your hearts' altar.

By God-direction and only thereby, man returns to the state of grace whereby heaven is secured in the present rather than postponed by doubt or uncertainty. The laws of man's destined immortality and living grace can never be broken except in the life of the individual who woefully abuses the precious gift of free will. Therefore each obedient one, by cosmic law, does come to a place of comforting inner awareness—the long dark night is past and the dawn floods the soul with peace and the restored hope of return to heavenly grace, attainable here and now.

All who break the law of eternal Truth in outer consciousness, by diverting their attention away from Life (fixing it on the ways of death portrayed in the mass media), do not do so with impunity; and the day-to-day frustrations encountered by men are visible proof of this law. It is so well known in our octave as to be elementary that the Godhead desires only to *deify* man ("to glorify as of supreme worth," i.e., to make man Godlike by his complete soul-identification with the Spirit of Deity) by giving him his full release and freedom from oppressing circumstances (of karmic retribution).

Unfortunately, those who most need the assurance of this comforting knowledge are just the ones who find the divine ideas least comprehensible. The people of earth have absorbed much of the pseudoculture of the Cain civilization, whose standards have far too often been set by men of lesser objectives seeking material success without the Spirit and popularity without Truth, and consequently never making a ripple upon the waters of the Mother's cosmic achievement.

The magnificent backdrop for reestablishing world order, for mending the ills of the body politic, and for reinstating masterful and Godly self-control by every man, woman, and child is so much hidden behind a useless clutter of debris of ageless feuds and vendettas. The view men have of the future often seems too nebulous and far away to be of any consequence, with the exception of the thin slice they claim as their allotted span of days, though they know not from moment to moment their tenure of office in their houses of clay. Still, the hearts of the few have in every age responded mightily to the impetus of divine love, eager to use the many avenues of heavenly service open to them for the blessing of their fellowservants made in the likeness of God!

I am convinced that the hope of the world lies in expanding the victory of those comparatively few God-illumined and God-seeking individuals who in every age have moved ahead spiritually. Fortunately for themselves but not so for the world, many of these do graduate from the earthly scene and obtain their freedom and ascension. This creates a seeming vacuum at the top of the spiral and makes the ratio of the illumined compared to the mass consciousness seem to be a figure of diminishing returns in contrast with the "broad way."[3]

However, the ideals of every Ascended Master and the devotees of Ascended Master love have kept earnest and God-illumined beings anchored to the earth and its atmosphere as an act of grace and mercy whereby from the ascended octave, the Master offers his highly spiritualized endeavors for the freedom of the whole "I AM" Race. These are the lost (marred) sheep of the house of Israel[4] unto whom I am sent and unto whom I send my disciples. These are of the seed of God-Reality—the spiritual descent of the Ancient of Days (Sanat Kumara), also referred to as the seed of the Woman[5] (the Divine Mother).

You see, beloved ones, it is necessary for us to maintain personal representatives as focal points for our Word (Alpha) and our Work (Omega) who will cherish the spiritual energies of heaven and enshrine them in a holy atmosphere on the altar of a consecrated life, disseminating our teaching, love, and light creatively in multifaceted ways. We must have embodied lifestreams willing to publish abroad by love a true understanding of the laws of God and the full complement of instruction for the path of the ascension. (We know only too well that, by definition, this involves some personal sacrifice to accomplish.)

Our outposts thus fulfill the cosmic law which decrees that on earth man is the authority

for his world. Except under extraordinary circumstances or through a life already surren-
dered to God's will, heaven does not intervene
or intercede in mankind's affairs without his
freewill, prayerful request or that of a devout
representative whose upraised chalice of conscious receptivity is constant to contain the divine outpouring.

Thus, our call goes forth for ministering
servants to serve under our jointly held office of
World Teacher. We are in search of disciples
who will teach men the Way while they are still a
light *in* the world.

In no heart is this Truth so well received as
in the heart of the one who is lovingly determined to obtain the state of immortality by
assisting others to win their freedom from the
curse of Edom.

Remember always, I AM the Way.

Lovingly, I AM

Jesus the Christ

Faith

My Brothers and Sisters

Putting on the Breastplate of Faith—

The earnest endeavors of the faithful who seek to obtain their victory over death may not be fully recognized by those who remain after the ascending one is taken up from them, but the skepticism of the mass mind does not affect the illumined who rocket skyward on the power of that divine grace which they have faithfully invoked. However, the impediments of unbelief do attach to unbelievers, acting as a deterrent to their own manifestation of immortality and victory.

To win a state of consciousness charged with vital faith is a major step to obtaining the deathless state. How this is so can be understood by sincere followers of the Light by noting the effect of faith upon the spirit of man.

Lift up personal faith in immortality, and life becomes worthwhile. Life becomes a kingdom of sharing and achievement where the entire family of the Lord's Body finds hope, loomed by love, keeping the flame of eternal comfort blazing in the consciousness of the Community of the Holy Spirit.

I can note in my own spiritual journey the wonderful advent of renewed faith—how like a lodestar it drew me onward and upward, teaching me through the victory of beloved Jesus how God intended me to make his victory my own. It is wise, ever so wise, blessed ones, to relate Truth to one's self. Only by drawing God into manifestation in yourselves can you find renewed hope and the means to overcome human despair by Divine Love.

Questions on the origin of Life are best considered by the finite mind in terms of a round of cycles having neither beginning nor ending. These traverse the Infinite and aim progressively higher in dimension and wonder. A straight line seems to have a beginning and an end, but a set of cycles or spirals goes ever onward and upward as the God-intent decrees, manifesting daily in a blessed unveiling of Infinity to the joyous heart of the child of God.

Beloved Jesus and I intend to bring you in these Corona Class Lessons a greater awareness of immortality and of how you can achieve your personal victory over death. With fond hope we shall inform the students of means to accelerate faith. And faith herself will generate a greater understanding of the science of Being, which when applied will alleviate much distress and fear from the mass consciousness and enable our beloved chelas to be of significant service to restore the earth to the golden Edenic state referred to by beloved Jesus.

We dedicate this series to this purpose and decree that angelic hosts bear limitless blessings of immortal assistance that shall manifest in the world of every sincere student of this Light of God which does not fail.

To the victory of Love
I AM dedicated forever,

Kuthumi

Corona Class Lesson 38

Charity

"Though I Speak with Tongues . . ."

Lovers of the Power of God unto Salvation—

If you could perceive at inner levels, as we do, the deep and almost painful longing within the hearts of God's children to find a greater understanding of life and deliverance from the confusion which is a part of the human experience, your hearts (if at all responsive to your brothers' needs) would swell with great desire and a mounting fervor to increase the tempo of deliverance upon this dear planet!

The wonderful devotion of many of our chelas is marvelous to behold, and we do commend their many benign attitudes and right action. Yet, scurrilous attitudes still permeate the mass consciousness, spilling over by semi-conscious habit into the lives of our chelas, preventing the fullness of their manifestation of immortalizing love in action.

Now, it is true that salvation is a gift of the power and grace of God rather than a matter of men's works [1]; it is also true that the ascension is the fullness of the divine intent for every child of Light (the terms *salvation* and *ascension* are both defined as the soul's reunion with God, the Mighty I AM Presence, through the mediatorship of the Holy Christ Self).

Nevertheless, it is needful that the scriptures be correctly interpreted in order to bring greater understanding on what in Eastern philosophy is referred to as "karma yoga" [2] (union with God attained through the balance of karma by right action). Just so, in his blessed writings James, a disciple of Jesus, stated that if a man had faith, good works should follow as a testimony thereof, concluding that faith without works is dead. And Love is truly the fulfilling of this law.

The symbology of the LORD's "common table" reminds us that the Law of Love is based on the great unity of Life—a love of Love, by Love and for Love! How can God forget man whom he has created, seeing that he, the Creator, is endowed with infinite grace and mercy? Those who are the true followers of the Divine Mind, perceiving his grace and the fullness thereof, must respond in the mode of the Father to the spiritual hungers of his little ones and, in the Master's words, "Feed my lambs!"

There are any number of dedicated lifestreams on this planet who, although they do not fully understand the law of their own being or the universal principle of the individualized Mighty I AM Presence, do understand the needs of mankind and do respond with good works and good causes to the heart calls and crying needs of the multitudes. With consummate skill our devotees, through their heightened understanding, seek to alleviate distress and suffering by direct invocation to the Godhead for a mighty intercession of his hosts on behalf of the many, not neglecting to also pour out their assistance with loving concern, constancy and a practical spirit of grace.

In a very real sense, both groups—the humanitarians and the ministering servants—are showing their faith by good works; and eventually they will find that the karmic record of their lifestreams, which is always accurate, reflects every good work credited to their personal account.

Inasmuch as immortality is the gift of Life intended for all—one which must be apprehended and claimed as a birthright by each individual son of God—those who assist souls in finding their way back to their beloved God Self are likewise, by this act of the Good Samaritan, helping themselves toward their own ascension.

Why do you suppose, blessed ones, that those of us who attuned so valiantly and devotedly to the Deity in past embodiments elected the humble way of service? Why did beloved Jesus lovingly offer his energies for the many who were unable to obtain for themselves that release of spiritual grace which he did? Why did so many of the illustrious, known avatars and servants of God, wrestle with humanity, regardless of expressed inappreciation or ingratitude, even to the point of hostility?

Blessed ones, it may have seemed a selfless act from the human standpoint, but from the divine it was enlightened self-interest. Those blessed ones knew that their return to the heart of God would be greatly accelerated by their full acceptance of the blessed opportunity for service on earth. They also knew that their earthly service would one day be transcended by the opportunity for greater service rendered from the God-victorious ascended state, even as I am now doing.

With the Brothers of the Golden Robe I am serving mankind in countless ways, helping them to obtain greater wisdom from God and the beauty of illumination's flame. As a servant of God in the office of World Teacher, it is my duty (dharma) and steadfast intent to intensify in all our students, as at Crotona[3] long ago, the flame of devotion to Truth.

Now, my beloved heart friends of the ages, I would point out that discouragement is often the lot of the aspiring ones who assess their progress against the scale of the unreliable, untrue human personality. If men and women on the spiritual path will leave all judgment to God through the Mighty I AM Presence, not even judging themselves, turning rather to their Great God Source and the Ascended Masters with a more intense love, they will find a greater power coming into expression in their worlds. It is this power of God unto salvation[4] that we would see expanded (with its commensurate deliverance from the Evil One), not self-degrading thought-forms of one's self-imaged imperfection which only set the soul on a downward spiral.

The body of Light-servers (the Mystical Body of Christ) must be reinforced by men and women who are not afraid of absorption unto the Godhead. How ridiculous it is for man to fear to return to the Great Source whence he came! Do men actually believe that they can be all of God and still remain men? As they manifest more of God, they will yearn for all of God, their only regret the fact that the very quality of self-transcendence prevents the acquisition of Infinity, making the joyous pursuit of Divinity the self-transforming purpose of forever!

Could it be that man wishes to give power to the clay rather than to the Great Potter[5] and to his blessed wheel molding life's experiences? Beloved, the creation of the incoming soul personality of the Son of man within God's heart takes place with so great a devotion that no gentler, no more powerful action of love could be conceived or comprehended by the offspring of the Most High.

Jesus, my beloved co-servant, expressed this love in his compassion for the multitudes as he "took our infirmities and bare our sicknesses,"[6] thereby entering in to the Father's never-ending re-creative love, daily giving new birth and new life to the soul personality of his children. After the buffeting taken by his little ones making their way in the world, I am certain that the majority would more than welcome the reintegrating ministrations of the Holy Spirit given to the prodigal son.

Now, I do not intend to entertain the notion that the Godhead is powerless to interfere in the domain of earth—as some have avowed. O beloved brothers, the power of God is unparalleled anywhere, above or below—for, viewed from any angle, omnipotence is stupendous! Surely all should know that God does temper the wind to the shorn lamb[7] wheresoever upon earth man, by free will, makes the Father's will the directing authority of his actions.

As I speak of lambs, I think of the scripture that declares, "He is brought as a lamb to the slaughter; as a sheep before her shearers is dumb, so he openeth not his mouth."[8] Blessed ones, the service of compassion offered by every ascended being on behalf of earth's evolutions has not been accomplished without some opposition, apparent or not.

The abysmal swamp of human ignorance and the restless sea of delusion inundating the mass consciousness act to oppose the extension of the Light. But we declare, It has no power or permanence! Hitch your attention, blessed ones, to the star of divine power and heavenly permanence, and watch how your desires are fulfilled by the action of the immutable law of love and grace.

By giving comfort to others you cannot help but receive in return, and the world is so full of need. Immortality is best achieved by service, then; for by doing the Father's business,[9] the stream of divine love is channeled through you, and God will not deny his own channel the boon of the divine interchange.

How necessary are instruments of service, in not one but many fields. Let all serve God as the great light of their Divine Self directs. And may all be blessed thereby with the rewards of immortal service so enjoyed by the Ascended Masters!

The many mansions of the Father await unfoldment by devoted lifestreams consciously pursuing the path of immortality, graduating from earth's schoolrooms in order that they may serve either "here" or "there." Truly, "I AM here and I AM there and I AM everywhere in the service of my God!" is a statement of the cosmic order of the day—and the Daystar appearing.[10] The elect need never want for happiness derived from seizing the torch of opportunity (from those who have gone on in cosmic service) to serve here on earth.

The spreading abroad of love is the prerogative of angels. However, man, made a little (while) lower in the hierarchical order, as he attains the fullness of his freedom through self-application to grace and good works, accepts the gift of God and is crowned with even more glory and power![11] Thus is he exalted to the fullness of the honorable state of the Ascended Master octave where "one with God is the majority"— understandable in action through the use of universal power, wisdom, and love.

The personal self is naturally unhappy when confined to a state of stratification with no escape in sight. How well I recall this feeling which came upon me in my embodiment as Francis Bernardone when I was slated to take over my earthly father's business and make my way on the path of worldly glory and honor.

To the consternation of my father and friends, I forsook this cup of earthly inheritance and a prosperous business in order to strive for a better reward[12] from my heavenly Father. I talked to Brother Sun and Sister Mother-Earth as I sought to impress the tenderness of Jesus' love and the love of God upon each grain of sand wherever I walked. I drew forth the flame of God and asked him to let the light within me flow forth to hallow each of my footsteps, that all generations to come might thereby be blessed.

You see, your immortality is attained here and now, blessed ones of the Light. It is won in your joyous use of the shining hours, in your radiant, God-expressed harmony, in paeans of praise released to the heart of God from your own wonderfully charged, beating hearts, swelling with the love-tide of gratitude for Life.

O come now, let us make a joyful noise unto the LORD![13] Let us together praise immortal areas of service, magnetized in the present day of salvation and then left as landmarks for all, that they, too, may find their way Home!

O Love of God, immortal Love,
   Enfold all in thy ray,
Send compassion from Above

To raise them all today!
In the fullness of thy power
Shed thy glorious beams
Upon the earth and all thereon
Where life in shadow seems.
Let the Light of God blaze forth
To cut men free from pain.
Raise them up and clothe them, God,
With thy Mighty I AM Name!

Kuthumi

Body

"Now Ye Are the Body of Christ"

To Students of the Christic Mysteries
    Who Will Learn the Law of Immortality—
Thou radiant perfection of Light, descend into the hearts of men and let them partake of thy Reality, let them become thy Immortality, let them know the fullness of their Being!

I AM come that men might have Life (God), and that more abundantly.[1] How can it be that those who profess to believe in God can fail to understand that the expansion of divine privilege is the will of God for all? Inasmuch as Life is a divinely endowed privilege, it follows in the fullness of God's will that all men should receive more abundant Life as their faith calls into action the intended manifestation of God's blessings.

Timidity, which hides its light under a bushel[2] of neglect and rationalization, can never inherit the kingdom of God. In order to draw forth the required momentum of victorious immortality, a waning faith (faint heart, feeble spirit, hesitation, inaction) must be replaced by confidence in our Father's plan and its certain unfoldment in man.

The contact our students make with God at inner levels of consciousness may not be fully appreciated by the outer mind due to the fact that they are not entirely aware of the inner grace (light) they already possess (through the crystal cord and the threefold flame). If those who yearn to experience the affluence of the Mind of God and his inner guidance will persistently call for the expansion of the flame of divine illumination within their hearts, they will be amply rewarded; for out of the consciousness of this inner grace (transmitted by the Holy Christ Self) comes the understanding of Life and the instruction on how to energize the cells of the physical body and how to control the bodies of thought and feeling.

The memory body of man (called the 'etheric', or fire, body) must likewise be energized by spiritual power until the 'parts' of the Whole which manifest in man become the sum of his inner-level experience. This is accomplished, dear ones, through thy meditation on Light precipitated in thy members through the science of the spoken Word.

Now, there are schools which do not place enough emphasis on the exercise of the faculty of memory; others encourage its abuse through learning by rote without soul comprehension (the education of the heart) or the integration of the mental and spiritual faculties. And this we would warn against—for out of the divine memory of continuous self-conscious awareness throughout all previous existence there is impressed upon the mental body, the desire body, and the physical body the attributes (spiritual 'genes') of the soul personality. These cycle into manifestation not all at once but little by little as the child develops into an adult and throughout life.

Thus, through schooling and the disciplines of the Brotherhood, the outer mind must frequent the spiral stairway to the inner memory, thereby establishing the channel for the descent of higher powers and the release of genius attained in previous lives—also recorded in the blessed memory body, truly the archives of the soul's history.

The blessed vehicle of the memory was created to record the divine pattern for each lifestream as well as the truth of his experiences on the etheric plane and his soul awareness in the higher octaves of being. Throughout man's evolution in human form, there has been impressed upon it, however, those discordant thoughtforms, misqualified energies of the mass consciousness, and everyday trivia which crowd out the crystal purity and simplicity of God's continual self-revelation to man, abundant in variety and rich in blessing.

The need of the hour, then, is the purification of the etheric body from the debris of sense consciousness in order to uncover the original records of the Creator's intent and to make room in the "inn of being" for soul consciousness—the Christ Light of true felicity in the bliss of divine experience. I know of no more efficacious means of accomplishing this purification (presently available to our disciples) than the application of the violet fire through the daily giving of dynamic decrees.

Prayer, fasting, meditation on the Presence —physical exercise, yoga, breathing in fresh air and sunshine, et cetera—and, above all, harmony in the feeling world, high-mindedness, proper rest and a wholesome diet will complement your application of the Word for maximum acceleration of the divine memory of the Mind of God within your etheric body and its anchoring in the physical cells of the brain and central nervous system. Observing the above steps will contribute that needed balance that makes you both peaceful and energetic, confident of your path and person, and a cheerful example spreading joy and enthusiasm to all! Such as these breathe the air of holy purpose and accomplish it!

The God-identity of each disciple is to be found in his acceptance of the power of the I AM Presence to outpicture his blessed divine plan in the physical octave through the four lower bodies, under the guidance and tutelage of the Holy Christ Self. Bearing in mind that we have revealed the memory body as the keystone in the arch of being, connecting the 'Above' and the 'below' of your consciousness, please consider the following:

Since the physical octave is the proving ground for spiritual achievement and the place where the gift of salvation is appropriated by good works, it is here on earth that God-identity must be realized—not in some nirvanic state following a life of inaction, or contemplation and yogic practices without works. The four lower bodies, then (as memory, mind, feelings, and physical form), are the instruments through which the perfection of the I AM must manifest in order that it might be fulfilled: "I AM thy will being done in earth as it is in heaven."[3]

Beloved ones, that which you are outpicturing in your four lower bodies is the index of your present conscious understanding—or your unconscious or subconscious ignorance. What you are and what you think can clearly be seen in what is manifesting in those four lower bodies, both from our vantage and by the spiritually attuned and perceptive unascended teachers.

The vision of God-identity which you have first beheld and then held in the chalice of your consciousness is that which you are outpicturing, however limited that concept might be. The Law states that unless you are outpicturing in your four lower bodies (the four sides of the great pyramid of self) the fullness of the divine image, you have not, in fact, accurately perceived that image: As a man seeth in his heart, so is he in outer expression.[4] Conversely, he cannot be or become that which he has not seen.

Now, it is our fervent desire (*de-sire*) that from the *De*-ity you *sire* that "Sun of Righteousness" which shall bear you up on healing wings of God-Thought and sustain within you the perfect matrix of your immortal Selfhood.[5] Your etheric body is the logical vehicle for this, being, in its pure state, the highest vibrating body of the four lower bodies. In each conscious or unconscious output of energy, you are either molding or marring the divine image within you—the result being a consequent manifestation of that energy pattern, duly consecrated or desecrated, within the three lesser bodies.

The etheric body is a chalice for the sacred fire of your I AM Presence, the vessel of the chakras and the temple of your Christ Self—when purified. The soul who has elevated itself vibrationally to a comfortability in this exalted plane wears the etheric garment as a vehicle for so-called out-of-the-body 'soul travel'. Thus we emphasize that upon your deliberate purification and spiritual exercise of the memory body depends your accomplishment of assignments given to you prior to this life as the set goal of this embodiment.

The key to scientifically accurate precipitation within the walls of your tabernacle—the place where you can learn to be the wise masterbuilder, the place where God is—will be discovered by you, beloved, through your implementation of the knowledge that your four lower bodies are the chaliced focus in this octave for the will, wisdom, love, and power of God.

It must be seen that these bodies are not four horsemen in competition for the prize of individual identity but a team of stallions driven by one charioteer, your True Self, who uses their combined energies for a unified effort to win the cup of balanced action in the thrust for the immortal purpose of Christ-identity.

You see, my blessed disciples, it is the Holy Christ Self who must be given free rein over the energies lowered first into the receptacle of your memory body, thence directed to the mental body, the desire body, and the physical body. These energies are entrusted to your use to glorify God in the physical octave. In surrendering the reins of controlled action to the Mentor who holds the outline (map) of your life's course within his hand, you are thereby declaring your acceptance of the precept embodied in the first commandment of the Law, "Thou shalt have no other gods before me."[6]

By your free will, you thereby deny all power to the idols of the 'kings' of this world[7] and stand in the grace of my mission. Having taken conscious dominion over the wilderness temptations,[8] you will return to the kingdom (the consciousness of the City Foursquare "coming down from God out of heaven"[9]) in the confidence that when the prince of this world cometh, he shall find nothing in you;[10] for you shall have made of your four lower bodies the tabernacle of God, supported by pillars of divine will, illumined by wisdom, and outpictured by the power and love of the Creator.

Indeed, there shall nothing be found within that city which lieth foursquare that taints (defiles[11]) the divine identity, for having once subjected yourselves unto the law of immortality, in unity of purpose to the expression of "Thy kingdom come, Thy will be done," the hypothetical laws of sin and death (mortality) can no longer hold sway over your existence.[12]

Thus your immortality is gained in the here and now through the conscious taking on, day by day and hourly, of that infinite consciousness which includes the universe in its love and regard and can partake only of the completeness of the Christ in both thought and action through the four lower bodies.

Awaken, ye potential saints, to the call of the I AM and of your Holy Christ Self whose clarion voice declares: Arise! Arise! Arise, shine![13] in the acceptance of thy Light and thy immortality through the conscious release of thy four lower bodies into the mainstream of divine direction descending from on high through the crystal cord into the upraised chalice of thy heart flame.

Be still and know that I who made thee will walk with thee alway, for I AM the very core of thy design. I AM thy Light and I AM thy Life and I AM thy soul's identification with immortality now and forever!

In the stillness of the dawn of thy immortality, I AM the resurrection of divinely inspired good works within thee.

Thy brother,

Jesus the Christ

Threefold Flame

"He Maketh His Ministers a Flame of Fire"

To All Who Would Partake
   of the Fruit of the Tree of Life—
   The path of service as a means to finding the
allness of God has been well outlined. Let us,
therefore, study the best method for attaining
conscious immortality as an adjunct to loving
service.
   Blessed ones, the threefold flame, which is
the seat of your life and consciousness, has been
too little understood. This tri-unity of Power,
Wisdom, and Love functions as one: wherever
one quality manifests, the other two must follow
if you are to express and enjoy the fullness of
Christ-good.
   The balancing of these Christly qualities is
the present major goal for our students. This is
accomplished through balancing the threefold
flame, which you may visualize as a single
sacred fire having three 'plumes' resembling a
fleur-de-lis, each plume focusing one of the

primary God-qualities of the Trinity. To increase
the size of the threefold flame remains a second-
ary goal; for unless balance is first achieved, it
would only become more unwieldy.

Power (focused in the blue plume), Wisdom
(focused in the yellow plume), and Love (focused
in the pink plume) are related magnificently to
the angelic radiation of faith, hope, and charity
and to the light of the Father, the life of the Son,
and the love of the Holy Spirit. In fact, these inter-
related flame-symbols of triune action focus the
personification of the Holy Trinity within you.

Now, as Saint Germain has told you, "Light
is the alchemical key." [1] Hence, your comprehension and expansion of the elements of your
Light (which is indeed your Power) is the key
to spiritual magnificence and immortal Life,
guarded by the perfection of immortal Wisdom
and Love.

It so happens that the expansion of divine
Light is a spiritually scientific activity. For this
reason I am going to speak carefully on this
subject (both here and in our classes which you
attend at 'inner levels' on the etheric plane at
the Royal Teton Retreat). It is my desire that all
may benefit from the simplicity of this release
and that its blessing be not confined to scholars
of God's word who love to hear of holy things,
as I do.

Consider for a moment: the core of minute
particles of material substance is composed of
light which emanates from the white-fire nucleus of the atom. This light is directed from the

heart of God in the Great Central Sun to the border kingdom of God in the spherical and peripheral world of so-called matter.

It is important for you to realize that the natural flow of this sustaining power is administered by the Divine Intelligence inherent within creation and directed by specific hierarchical manifestations—such as cosmic beings, Elohim, angelic hosts, Nature devas, elemental spirits as well as exalted man (ascended and unascended adepts)—who have attained by grace various states and stages of control over natural law.

You see, there is a Sun behind the sun. There is a unifying essence behind outer manifestation which is wholly spiritual and an immediate part of God yet contains the formula for the coalescing of matter, molecule by molecule. The great Master Saint Germain has often used the term *Light* to denote this causative aspect of the Deity, as have others of our Brotherhood. However, discrimination is needed, for just as there are people and people, so there is light and there is Light.

Even so, God has retained in his great heart of love, securely locked within the Tree of Life (Causal Body), the mysterious fruit (God consciousness) of that Tree which (when divinely partaken of) does make the Son of man, as the manifestation of God, to live forever.[2] Yet the deepest mysteries of past ages can be understood through a simple explanation if you will give us your undivided attention—for beloved Jesus and I desire you to become as we are by the assimilation of the 'body' and the 'blood' of our teaching.

Divine Love holds the answer to the release of immortality, and anyone who manifests any feeling less than love for all of Life, or any part of Life, is denying himself the secret elixir of immortal Life. Man can no more deceive or thwart the Great Law than he can rise from the earth and ascend bodily into heaven without the assistance of the Almighty and the release of the spiritual energies of his God Self.

The earnest student must believe us when we say that so long as a trace of human feelings—mild dislike, including subtle jealousies or hatreds—remains in his consciousness, he will be unable to summon the great love magnet of the Central Sun to assist him in obtaining reentrance into the paradise of God where the Tree of Life spreads its all-enfolding branches of beneficence. The Law makes no exceptions.

When the necessary purification of consciousness is accomplished through holy service to Life and a concerted decree effort, and the candidate stands purged by the violet flame, stripped by Divine Reality (the Holy Spirit) of every trace of impure thought and feeling, he will be allowed to stretch forth his hand to receive the fruit of the Tree of Life.

This initiation is given by the Great Initiator—our Beloved Teacher—the Buddha Lord Maitreya. This 'first fruit' is the conferment of the power to direct Light's energy (henceforth magnetized by the initiate from his own Sun Source, the I AM THAT I AM) into the atomic structure of his four lower bodies at will.

This Light of God—which is the only light that never fails—then rushes into the original channels where the all-sustaining power formerly flowed. There, through its self-luminous, intelligent quality, the light transmutes, thread by thread, the overlay of the old energy paths and the old garment of the human conscious-ness as it weaves (literally, cell by cell) the tran-scendent perfection of the seamless garment of the living Christ.

By divine grace, some special souls upon earth demonstrate certain phases of Christ-accomplishment without passing through the transfiguring experience of which I am speak-ing. This is because the great Law of Love in its mercy responds to people's hearts, whatever their state of consciousness, releasing them into greater Life, by merit, as a parent would help a child climb a stairway to the stars.

Needless to say, it is the conscious victory of a living Christ in action, scientifically dem-onstrated, which every disciple of beloved Saint Germain, of Mother Mary and Jesus (and of all the Ascended Masters of the Great White Brother-hood) must seek to express in his daily living.

It is beggary and paupery for men to deny the greatness that is within them and to seek without for that Light of God that sustains their very Life. The grace of heaven must be focused within the true domain of one's being and individuality, and here I speak both metaphorically and actually.

The power of the Light behind all light the unfailing Light of God, must be invoked and focused in man ere he can rise in consciousness until he actually ascends into that light realm of freedom which is the heavenly home of everyone who has successfully passed earth's tests and has dared to step beyond the veil of human ignorance. Thus, the glorious flame of illumined obedience to divine Law *must* express the fullness of Love's immortality within man as his thought and aspiration rise toward God.[3]

While the snares of astral and psychic densities continue to pour out a vaporous stream of appeals to human vanity, beloved Saint Germain holds forth, as does every ascended being, the image of the immortal reality of divine Selfhood as the goal of every life. To point the way to the attainment of this goal is the greatest service anyone can render.

Proceeding, then, with the transmutation layer by layer of his human creation (karma), the one who aspires to the office and the divine calling "Ministering Servant" is in the very best posture to concentrate on balancing the integrated action of his threefold flame. This he will do by calling for and affirming in all his affairs a well-rounded manifestation of God's consciousness of Power, Wisdom, and Love—his to command by free will according to his own discriminating intelligence.

First, he will take care that any and all acts, including both words and deeds (which always require energy, power, determination, and will to accomplish), are not compromised by human willfulness, rebellion, pride, anger, aggressiveness, ambition or any such abuses of the First Ray of God's powerful Will.

Second, he will balance all his activities by the necessary application of Wisdom's objectivity and equanimity—preceded by forethought, study, research, analysis, and careful consideration that each thrust for a purpose is constructive, well-organized, and of benefit or gain to some part of Life.

Third, he will test every move, project, or plan by the measure of God's Love, purifying motive and intent with charity and compassion, especially examining it for its practicality—"Will it work?" He will enfold his actions with creativity, devotion, carefulness, unselfishness, and gratitude, giving the glory to God and taking care that the work or word contains the essentials to bear fruit, multiplying grace and increasing the Christ consciousness on earth.

Continuing to use these standards as the guiding principle for right action, he will always weigh his intentions by the simple formula: right reason (Wisdom), right motive (Power), right cause (Love). With consistent striving toward a well thought-out goal and a developed plan of action—realistic and attainable—he may then intensify his mantras to the violet flame, alternating with his prayer to his Holy Christ Self to

"Balance the Threefold Flame in Me!"[4] Lastly and importantly, he will seal his day—his words and his works, every blow struck for the LORD—with the blue flame of protection from Saint Michael (Archangel of the First Ray).

I trust that every sincere student of this Light having Christ-discrimination will recognize his responsibility as a servant of Truth to magnify honor, sincerity, integrity, and transcendence within himself and each individual he contacts, in preference to spectacular psychic phenomena and predictions based on astral readings. A thousand glamorous, glittering snares need have no effect upon you, blessed ones, if you will only hold fast to the forte of your true being and its wondrous reality.

Use, then, the flame of Love to purify your feeling world of mortal sense-consciousness and weave a garment of immortality while abiding temporarily in the vale of human sorrow and tears (*samsara*, the condition of world karma). Thus, as Jesus lived, so shall ye—"in the world, but not of it."[5]

Overcome all outer frustrations by the intensity of your fervent faith and the overcoming strength of that faith. Let no one deny you the power of God unto salvation. Remember, conscious immortality is dependent upon the power of Love in action in your world; and the release of that power into your world is best accomplished after infinite Love has stripped you of all self-limiting human qualities.

Then divine Wisdom can, and she surely

shall, expand her action into the forcefield of your individuality and endow you with such illumination as to make you in truth God-taught. The divine whisper will softly speak your name as God's identification of your Spirit, "I AM," and the meaning thereof will be apparent to you as the soundless Sound, the guiding Light, the presence of Reality manifesting in you, free from the facade of human vice *or* virtue and all pride in self. Then shall you rejoice in the creation of your own immortal consciousness: "The LORD God saw the creation which he had made and, behold, it was very good!"

In the spirit of infinite peace and goodwill, let all amplify the power of Light within the cells of their whole being. Draw and magnetize the Light, but know that this Light is the balanced action of divine Love, Wisdom, and Power—teaching, cherishing, and directing you always into the paths of righteousness for His name's sake, I AM. How else, blessed ones, can man "be still and know that I AM God"?

In his early instruction, Saint Germain advocated the visualization of Light surrounding and enveloping the body for a period of fifteen minutes of intense concentration.[6] Too many people use such valuable spiritual exercises for a while, and then because they begin to "feel so good," they forget the source of their blessings and do not sustain their momentum.

Yet, magnificent beings you are—and immortal beings, too! Remember, the Ascended Masters were once as you are. We are pulling for

344 IMMORTALITY ~ KUTHUMI

you, one and all, to make your ascension and to forever find your eternal freedom in the Light.

The intense action of divine Light released into your use from the heart of your beloved I AM Presence, then freely charged by you with the Wisdom and Love of your developing three-fold flame, is the finest elixir obtainable. From this substance of immortality every potion of a spiritually energizing elixir has been compounded. Take this cup in my name and drink ye all of it. Drink into the kingdom of God.

Beloved ones, there must be a conscious "taking in" of spiritual energy. Every allegory and symbol pertaining to the divine mysteries has pointed to this truth. It is the way of God unto the partaking of his kingdom, it is the communion of the saints, it is the self-chosen Path that imbibes conscious immortality and Life with a sense of holiness equaled only by the Christ.

Behold, I say ye are wholly God's!

Kuthumi

Alpha / Omega

"I AM the Beginning and the Ending"

To the Children of the Light
        of Alpha and Omega—
    Alpha and Omega! What names to stir
the heart and the ancient memories thereof!
Beloved ones, the flame of their Life within you
is immortal! Man, as a manifestation of God
individualized, ought not to be thought of in
terms of finite beginnings and endings—yet men
are prone so to do.

    Never let your hearts be troubled, little ones,
for my statement "I AM the Way" can be applied
to many of life's problems, mysteries, and requirements. God is indeed the way to adjust
every condition, to produce all perfection, and to
provide the power to cope with each situation as
it arises.

    Atomic energy seems so powerful to men,
and yet divine power is infinitely greater, possessing the capacity to roll up the universe as a
curtain[1] and to spread it out again in shining

splendor. "Not by might, nor by power, but by my Spirit, saith the LORD of hosts." [2]

All tests, trials, and initiations, together with everyday karmic experiences, come to the disciples of the Word in order to prepare them for eternal Life. Although the children of Light already have that Life within them, in order for its magnificent power to enter into and then transcend their finite nature, all that is mortal, all that expresses inharmony must first be transmuted so that the full glory of the flame of immortal Life can be safely applied to the mighty God-vested soul of Light's potential in each lifestream.

Would it not be a great pity to infuse eternity with humanly created discord? The God of Love is too firm and too perfect to thus risk the sacred, chaliced treasures of universal Love; hence, by God's great wisdom, the way of the Tree of Life is guarded by "Cherubims and a flaming sword" from him who yet profanes his spirit by sinful and unholy acts and would, if allowed, "put forth his hand, and take also of the flame of immortality from the Tree of Life, and eat, and live forever. . . " [3]

As we have so often told you, it is not a sense of sin that we would develop in the sincere seeker for Godliness, but rather a sense of holiness which like a vein of gold is hidden in the heart of the earth. The spiritual alchemy of Life will raise the sincere who, in purity, are willing to press toward the mark of Christhood for the prize of victory until all that is of the human is changed by the glorious golden fire-ring of heaven into Christlike qualities. So long as the mind is steeped in a sense of sin and error, it is difficult to transfer to the soul the immortal sense.

Beloved, my statements are actually Life, and Life-giving, although they may appear to be simple; for they embody the law of eternal Life which is able to heal you as you drink it in. Unless you are willing to become as a little child and enter into the kingdom of heaven through the doorway of simplicity, you may never find the Way, though you pass through a range of many embodiments.

Many continue to search the scriptures because they think, as they have been led to believe, that in them they will find eternal Life; [4] yet it is the very scriptures that testify of me as the messenger of the universal Christ consciousness.[5] This consciousness is the illumination of the Holy Spirit in which all must personally share! [6]

The depths of God's love and wisdom are to the present hour conveyed to hearts of goodwill who make consecrated application to the heart of heaven. The door of communion is never shut, for I AM the door that opens in response to the quiet supplication of the loving heart for more Light, until at last each living soul stands face to face with his own God-identity.

Heavenly light can be drawn forth or, as we say, 'magnetized' through the power of illumined, God-directed vision. Those who are willing to purify others as well as themselves and approach thereby the throne of grace with loving petitions for all children of Light will find a greater outpouring of forgiveness manifesting for themselves ("Forgive us our debts in the same manner and by the same measure with which we forgive our debtors"[7]) and a further amplification of divine opportunity for service which will prove of great assistance to their spiritual progress.

In order to properly magnetize Light, men must be pure in heart. Remember, the pure in heart are blessed with the vision of God.[8] With purity and consecration of spirit, then, hold the vision of your being (visualize yourself stead-fastly) surrounded with immortal Light.

Such imaging can provide an immediate quickening of God's light through your physical form or at least start the process (spiral) at inner levels (in the etheric body). In any case, the call *will* compel the answer into eventual manifestation, if the student of heaven's law will believe in full faith in the power of the Word and persist in maintaining continuous attunement with the divine purpose of his life—which is to realize the immortality of the Great I AM within his soul.

Men must desire immortality more than all else and cherish their own mighty birthright if they are to attain conscious immortality in the here and now. Although the silent flame of identity blazes on the hearts' altars of all children of God, the soul must assume this flame unto itself by the sacred ritual of internalization.

The difference between the ascended Sons of God and his unascended children is precisely the difference in degree of internalization (assimilation) of the threefold flame by the soul. For all who are of God are endowed from the beginning with the flame of conscious immortality and actually retain the nascent Power, Wisdom, and Love of ascended beings within the mighty flame of Life that beats their hearts.

When Nicodemus came to me by night long ago, I spake unto him, saying, "Except a man be born again, he cannot see the kingdom of God."[9] He, supposing my words applied to a physical reentering of the womb, remained puzzled by his literal interpretation of this concept.

But I spake of purification through the rebirth of water (Mother) and through the quickening of the spirit by the sacred fire (Father) as being necessary for the soul to reenter the consciousness of Alpha and Omega (Divine Principles of the 'beginning' and the 'ending' personified in the 'Father/Mother Elohim') whence he is come and into whose kingdom he shall go.[10] This rebirth by purification through the 'waters' and the 'fires' of Life is the means to enter in to the Holy of Holies of thy I AM Presence. A progressive understanding of the Word and spiritual revelation in subsequent embodiments has since revealed to this blessed soul the truth of my statement.

Spiritual men and women of today recognize that their God-identity is a mighty rushing wind[11] of Power dominated by glowing, infinite

Wisdom and saturated with radiant, holy Love without limit. Souls of vision are universally coming to realize the significance in their lives of the mysteries I taught to my apostles and disciples in secret and in parable.

It remains for the individual to acknowledge that God is in him and that in truth his identity includes—in the totality and oneness of Being and in the externalization of the flame of immortality—both the Son of God (his Holy Christ Self) and the God of very Gods (his I AM Presence). The words *I AM* embody this concept; for even when man declares, "I am," he is affirming below the very nature of his divine being Above. Thus, in the daily use of the verb "to be" he is declaring his existence and his reason for being—to integrate with the Be-ness of God and to know the bliss of the "I AM" consciousness.

It is, therefore, blasphemous to deny the power of God by using the various tenses of the verb "to be" in order to lay claim, by the power of his name, I AM, to lesser human qualities. When you say, "I am sick, I am weary, I am bored, I am angry, I am afraid," you empower these conditions of relativity with the light/energy/consciousness of the One whose name is I AM THAT I AM.

Why not affirm, instead, the immortal truth of Being? "Lo, I AM God in manifestation everywhere!" is a far more accurate statement of your true divine Selfhood. This statement alone, repeated many times a day as a flowing mantra and a song of the heart, will swallow up the petty negatives that tear down your spirituality.

The immortal sense works wonders: It is magic, it is spiritual alchemy, it is divine Truth, and it assists the multitudes in entering the kingdom of God. When this wondrous sense of well-being, in reality a manifestation of the Father/Mother consciousness of Being, takes dominion in you (by the power of the Holy Spirit in both form and formless wonder), the Sun of Righteousness (your beloved Holy Christ Self) will come into your temple with a holy light in concentrated, consecrated radiance, blazing with the full intensity of the Godhead all around you.

And lo, a universe is born! Man is "born again" in the rebirth of Truth. And the LORD God once again beholds in man the creation of that Good which He made because it is Himself.

The weaving of the garment of conscious immortality must be achieved here and now while you are yet in human form, else the plan of heaven for which your soul took embodiment long ago cannot be fulfilled. Therefore, adore your God Presence daily. Give thanks for all that you have and are. Praise and bless Life for its permanent gifts, and in so doing, find release from all the sense dogma of the ages which has surreptitiously established opposition to Truth and filled the spirit of man with an oppressive fear.

Lift up your eyes to the reality of the Light of God which is everywhere and feel the radiance of the Light enfold you. Feel that Light penetrate your being as immortal Love reaching into the very core of your being—physical, emotional, mental, and etheric.

This blessing shall manifest to quicken the vibratory action of these four lower bodies until the power of the three-times-three descends from the tri-angle of tri-une Be-ness: the Father (the Mighty I AM Presence), the Son (the Holy Christ Self), and the Holy Spirit (focused in the three-fold flame, which establishes the unity of the soul with God). Truly, the Light of God conveys the Power, Wisdom, and Love of the Trinity into the outer dimensions of selfhood, and the victory of that Light overcomes the world.

The unity of the Holy City, the New Jerusalem which lieth foursquare, and the holy tri-unity is a consummation of the seven holy lights blazing in the temple of being.[12] Thus, the infinite cycles of expression are fulfilled in the blessing of Alpha and Omega, who represent thy going out from and thy return to the heart of God. "I AM Alpha and Omega, the beginning and the end, the first and the last."[13]

You are a child of the Light. As a son of God, and enveloped in that consciousness of "thy Christ, my Christ,"[14] you are not subject to outer conditions. If you will only fix this firmly in heart and mind, your blessed four lower bodies as receptacles of your thought and feeling vibrations will fulfill the Hermetic axiom "as Above, so below" I AM THAT I AM. So, by the Great Law outpictured in you "foursquare," you shall know the meaning of these words: "Thou art my beloved Son, this day have I begotten thee!"

O immortal Love, seal them within the folds of Thy heart until they, too, are free, returning with me to that sacred altar of Light exalted where all joy is e'er in fulfilling Thy holy Will.

I AM thy life in consecration,

Jesus the Christ

Corona Class Lesson 42

Alchemy

"Friend, Go Up Higher. . ."

To Earnest, Forging Hearts
  Who Would Know God Within—
  Weary pilgrims, throw aside your languor
and plunge into the healing fountain of God-
identity! Declare with the LORD of the whole
earth, "I AM Good," and fulfill the fiat of the
Creator's observation of the creation![1]

  The soul that sinneth may die, but the just
man shall surely live forever.[2] The sinful consciousness and the record of sin must be cast
into the consuming fire of God in order that the
good which man has wrought, and he himself,
may live forever. Therefore, O House of Israel,
come apart from your iniquities and walk up-
rightly with your I AM Presence![3]

  It must be understood that immortality is an
endowment synonymous and concurrent with
Life—a birthright, not a usurpation. The overlay of wrong thought and feeling has too long
veiled by an energy veil (a shroud of humanly

misqualified substance) the Light that is the Life-giving essence of freedom for every atom in manifestation.

Now, the quality of earnestness has its place in the fulfillment of your spiritual search and, together with the quality of forgiveness expressed toward self and others, goes hand in hand with that integrity of being which cannot be corrupted by the distortions of the mass mind. You deal directly with God within yourself; therefore, only through intensifying the oneness of your identity with him—so that you are constantly aware of God living in you as naturally as in the universe—can you obtain permanent reality and thus immortality.

The guise of human creation is full of deceptions and runs so contrary to Truth that it would seem a simple matter for the children of the Light to uncover its lies. The reverse is true, for often self-deception is based on the seeker's own rightful longings for Good to manifest in his world as happiness. When the great spiritual realities of Life do not appear, many feel compelled to synthesize them and they compromise the divine plan, forcing it with their human concepts of how they think things ought to be. Or they sojourn for a while in a wilderness of deceptive self-rule where the very fact of their self-created illusion is cleverly concealed from their own perception.

The mighty gift of immortality is not far from anyone in whom the flame of Life is manifest, for it is the bequest of God to each one made in his image. Mankind dwelling in the beauty of the forest often do not see it for their absorption in the trees. It is not our intention to destroy aught else but illusion itself through the conception (and reception) in man of self-governed perfection and holiness. Only thus is the curtain of mayic mist drawn back and the bright reality of Truth seen to be shining in pristine purity.

When you perceive the truth concerning your own life, it cannot help but quicken your spiritual pulse. Mounting hope leads to enthusiasm for the divine plan. And the inrushing power of the Holy Spirit as a joyous anticipation calms and claims the heart in the noble interest of exalting the whole consciousness into a more radiant, divine manifestation.

The "here and now" of spiritual experiences progressively illumines the tapestry of Reality that is carefully woven within the soul memory. This Reality is inherently a part of the God-identity (the Sun behind the sun) of each life-stream who is blessed by the power and grace of heaven. Your self-chosen yet God-appointed mission unfolds as an ongoing service of the ages; the purpose of your life is no longer isolated in a finite segment of experience called a lifetime. Expansion of Spirit's expression and an infinite self-awareness occurs; immortality is understood and magnetized in the unity of your own God flame.

The magnetization of the life-force through the seven chakras is one of the functions of the flame of Life within you. Only by the invocation of the light of Alpha and Omega through application to the blessed threefold flame can the genuine wedding garment[4] of immortal love be safely woven. Adorned in the mantle of purity, the soul is escorted gently to the altar of consecration where the Great Initiator effects the union of the bride in Christ, anointed for the sake of cosmic progression on the road of immortality which leads to the Holy of Holies, the I AM THAT I AM.

Your discovery of the flame of your immortality is not the revelation of a moment or even a lifetime. Yet, under the guidance of your Mighty I AM Presence and with the assistance of the Ascended Masters, you can hourly hasten the day when, because you are already sealed forevermore in Christ, having experienced the alchemical marriage, you are able to draw forth and magnetize the full power of God unto salvation.

Then, through the ritual of the ascension shall you be permanently charged, not only with the golden flame of the crown of Christ-achievement, but also with your pure Christ-intelligence, the discriminating quality of the Godhead. Thy Father shall surround thee with his all-pervading love of the cosmos which he has made and placed in miniature expression in the threefold flame of your heart.

Holding this goal for you in highest mind, I am commending you to the care of the Good Shepherd, your Holy Christ Self, offering you my assistance—together with that of my beloved and supremely faithful Jesus—poured out in limitless love and sealed in the heart of Wisdom's flame.

To the wise immortality of divine Love, I commit the safekeeping of your being.

I AM graciously your loving teacher,

Kuthumi

Being

¹**be·ing** \ 'bēiŋ, 'bē·ēŋ, *rap.* 'bēŋ \ *n* -s
[ME, fr. gerund of *been, beon* to be — more at BE]
1 a : the quality or state of existing :
material or immaterial existence ⟨artistic form
comes into ~ only when two elements are
successfully fused —Carlos Lynes⟩
b (1) **:** something that is more abstract and
has less intension than existence, nonexistence,
or any other predicate ⟨pure ~ is the empty absolute —W.T.Harris⟩ —used esp. by Hegelians
(2) **:** something that is logically conceivable
and hence capable of existence :
something that has or may have reality
(3) **:** something that exists as an actuality or
entity in time or space or in idea or matter
(4) **:** the totality comprising the possible
and the actual : something that is common to
the objects within a class and to the objects
not included in the same class   **c :** conscious or
mortal existence : LIFE ⟨the mother who gave
him his ~⟩   **2 :** the complex of physical and
spiritual qualities that constitute an individual
⟨it thus enlarges our ~ and gives us strength
—M.R.Cohen⟩ **:** PERSONALITY ⟨one of history's
most enigmatic ~s⟩   **3 a** *now dial Eng*
(1) **:** LIVELIHOOD, LIVING (2) **:** dwelling place :
HOME **b** *archaic* **:** station in life : STANDING
4 : ESSENCE ⟨an analysis that probes the very ~
of religion⟩ **5 a :** HUMAN, PERSON ⟨always a well-
dressed ~⟩ **b :** INDIVIDUAL ⟨a human ~⟩
⟨the incredible ~s you see in the circus⟩
²**being** \ " \ *pres part of* BE
³**being** \ " \ *adj* [ME, fr. pres. part. of *been,
beon* to be] **:** PRESENT — used postpositively
with *time* ⟨enough for the time ~⟩
⁴**being** \ "*or more often* 'bēᵊn *or* 'bēn; "being
as" *is often* 'bēᵊnz *or* 'bēnz \ *conj, now dial* **:**
SINCE, BECAUSE ⟨~ I'm late already⟩
— often used with *as* or *that* ⟨~ that he's your
cousin⟩ ⟨~ as it's you⟩

Corona Class Lesson 43

Man

"I AM the Door"

To Those Desiring to Know God
      in Manifestation as Man—
    The statement "What is man, that thou art mindful of him? and the son of man, that thou visitest him?"[1] spoken of old from the supplicant's heart, still engenders in men the tendency toward self-depreciation.
    Just as pride goeth before a fall,[2] so false humility is an unbalanced expression which our students dare not manifest. A wider understanding of the human ego and of what man is and is to be will enable each child of the Father to enter more fully into the abundant Life.
    Gratitude for the many blessings of Life would rise in wondrous spirals of attainment and God consciousness if people were able to understand more concerning the spiritual realities of themselves and less concerning the mask of mortal imperfection with which they cloak one another through calumny, deceit, and gossip.

In the interest of our continuing service and instruction to those who would teach men the Way, it is my pleasure, together with beloved Kuthumi, to unfold in the consciousness of each aspirant a greater knowledge concerning his coming forth into being from the Father's wonderful heart of universal creativity.

Will ye give ear, then, in his precious name, I AM, to this mighty message of Being, finding mirrored within it and within yourself a more abundant grace that will assist you in doing as I did: to mount up with wings as eagles[3] into that trackless continent of the air where virtue replaces error and understanding replaces ignorance.

Remember, beloved ones, it is not the Father's will that one of these little ones should perish,[4] but that all should come to the marvelous knowledge of their True Self—face to face—even as He knows each one to be in truth. Paul said, "Now I know in part; but then shall I know even as also I am known."[5] John said, "We know that when he shall appear, we shall be like him; for we shall see him as he is."[6]

The question may therefore be asked by every disciple, "How can man know?" And this is a valid question for every serious student on the path of Christhood. In directing ourselves to the question of Being, we must first of all ask each individual to voluntarily silence the carnal mind, with all of its stored-up error, pent-up pride, and resistance to the unfoldment of divine

Truth. And here we speak of the human mentality devoid of Higher Consciousness that is always enmity against God and his Self-knowledge[7] precisely because it has no Christ Self-awareness.

For when that Truth shall fully appear to the soul, the soul shall be set free from the domination of the carnal mind—and that mind, having no more reason for being, displaced by the Mind of God which was in Christ Jesus,[8] ceases to be! For it simply cannot be where Christ is—and is the Christ/Truth in you.

God's truth is the still small voice of his con-*science* (voicing the science of Being) within you. When you still the turmoil of the 'outer mind' in your world, that voice, more powerful still, will be heard in all of its tones of wondrous clarity and its mighty winged messages of love.

It is this love of your Holy Christ Self that will exalt you into the fullness of the divine understanding about yourself. It is this love whose pinions will carry you into the rarefied atmosphere of the kingdom of heaven,[9] and it is this love which must express through you its tangible messages of hope to all God's children, remaining unqualified by human thought and feeling.

So long as you allow the ups and downs of tyrannical human thoughts and feelings to take their toll, you will remain bound by the race thoughts (mortal laws) of disease, old age, decay, death—not to mention the fascination and gripping entrapment that will bind you to the maya of endless psychic thralldom.

The tools employed in the building of faith are as essential as the tool of faith itself. Wise men, handling the building blocks of form, perceive the need for the rule, the compass, and the square. Are tools of mind and heart of less import or reality? I tell you nay.

It is, therefore, essential that those who are agnostics or atheistically inclined be taught the facts concerning the True Self as one would teach these truths to the little children. We recognize the difficulty in this approach. Nevertheless, we admonish you to press on. Do not prejudge your hearer's capacity to comprehend Truth, neither underestimate the power of Truth to communicate itself *through you* by the Holy Spirit.

To men and women who have woven the strands of communion between worlds it is unthinkable to deny our presence. Thus, it is sometimes exceedingly difficult for a spiritual teacher who has contacted the Christ-radiance to realize that there are men and women yet sitting in the shadow of unbelief.

It is essential that a reasonable compassion for such as these be developed, lest in the ivory-towered state there remain no Christ-charity in the heart with which to reach these individuals who may desperately desire help to cross the abyss of their unbelief. Remember the cry of my own, "Lord, I believe, help thou mine unbelief!" [10] and give all the benefit of your faith, as I did, to the temporarily doubtful state of consciousness of the disciple who will later accomplish great works by a faith in my True Self and his—a faith which he will make his own.

We do not propose that you involve your-selves, simply on the basis of human sympathy, with unbelievers in the reality of the Divine Self; but we do advocate a compassionate under-standing of their plight and a willingness, for your own good as well as theirs, to supply a brother's need of faith, that he may take the leap of faith and be where I AM in thee—and thou in me.[11]

Beloved, you are wayshowers even as I am; therefore, in drawing men unto the Father, you yourself must first draw very close to the Father. In approaching the Godhead, men must under-stand that they are not playing a losing game, but that they are winning their own victory.

There is a tendency on the part of the stu-dents to believe too much in the reality of the senses and all that they perceive without paying allegiance to the powers of spiritual sensing which belong to the eyes of the soul. To screen out the nebulous (mistlike, hence mystifying) and vicious thoughts of the serpent mind, to screen out the psychic (astral, mayic) accumula-tions, which like a kaleidoscopic cinema divert the consciousness from the symmetry of the kingdom of God—*is a necessity.* In approaching the spiritual mount, the cosmic Olympus, men must not seek a God made in their image but rather conform themselves to God's image.

The qualities of mortals are all too frequently imputed to the immortals. It seems difficult for men to perceive that the Ascended
Masters are completely free of any imperfect
thoughts and feelings, having ascended into the
perfection of the octaves of universal Christ consciousness.

In teaching people the realities of heaven, let
the waves of aspiration from your heart be
tethered to the stability of cosmic law. For your
soul wed to Christ possesses the capability of
rising through the mirage of human thought
and emotion, through the psychic strata (the
murky astral plane), up to the plane of God
consciousness where all are held in the divine
image.

My statements "I AM the Door. . ." and
"I AM the Way, the Truth, and the Life: no man
cometh unto the Father but by me" imply that
man cannot expect to know or reach God
through the senses but through attunement
with the Christ consciousness, the veritable
image of God, the Sun of the I AM in every man.
By relinquishing sense consciousness and becoming as a little child, "born again," man begins to weave strands of divine sensing whereby
the Infinite is brought down into the chalice of
present reality.

To attain a knowledge of God requires the
faith that He IS. The faith that right where you
are He can declare I AM WHO I AM and unveil to
you, as to Moses, the mystery of Being.

To attain a knowledge of God demands a

willingness to try to sense beyond appearances that Light which is "the true Light which lighteth every man that cometh into the world," though unfortunately to many it is the Light which "shineth in darkness, and the darkness [of material sense] comprehendeth it not." [12]

Faith is the greatest spiritual catalyst to transport the soul into the realities of the octaves of God's consciousness. Quite naturally men will pledge their faith to that with which their reasoning faculties concur; therefore, it is the science of Being which must be communicated to the nonbeliever. Why not begin with the Chart of the Presence as a graphic presentation of the True Self and the true knowledge thereof which is actually transmitted to the soul by eye contact, quickening the inner memory and scientific knowledge of the blessed tie to God.

Grounding your hearers on the Rock of the I AM Law of Being, point out the shifting sands of sudden change present in matter. This will communicate to them the truth that materiality lacks the stability and permanence of the Divine because its basis lies in imperfection and the limitations of the senses.

Teach them that change, alchemical change, in its spiritual context, can be continuous and self-transforming through the creative processes of the Law of Love. This daily putting on of our garments of the LORD's consciousness of your unfolding divinity results in the constancy of newness of life founded on the Rock of universal perfection.

Your beloved Saint Germain in his teaching of the I AM Law has for years communicated the divine stability to you, charging into your worlds the flame of freedom from his own heart. Cosmic freedom is imbued with cosmic stability—with power, with graciousness, with creativity, and with the divine expression. It is a tangible flame all about you which can be contacted to elevate you to our standard of perfection and beauty.

This do and teach, remembering always my words, "Lo, I AM with you alway," even in the very heart of your being!

In the love of Light,
I remain with deepest love,

Jesus

Corona Class Lesson 44

Life

"My Word Shall Live Forever"

Dear Ones Who Would Know
     the Living Master in All Life—
The most gracious gift of God to every life-stream is the totality of Being—not a mere fragment but the *totality* of that blessed Reality. The deceit of the senses has kept men and women from realizing in full potency all that is of the infinite nature within them awaiting holy recognition.

God abides his eternity, peering through the screen of time and manifesting on the stage of life in various phases of his Reality; and yet, this too is Life. From this dream of partial knowledge men must awaken to behold the splendor of themselves in all things.

Each blessed teacher of holy Truth must recognize that it is by the power of example that he can best serve the Great Law, for a good example has the power of ten thousand words and is amplified eternally in the heart of the beholder. If students who desire to teach others concerning the great reality of Life (as God) would determine to know that Reality (as God) and to manifest it themselves, they would by the power of their example bring the kingdom (consciousness) of God far nearer to their neighbors and loved ones than by all other methods of teaching.

Let me make clear that I do not decry the power of words nor the value of holy instruction. But bearing in mind that the Word of God became embodied in form—and that he who was the Word incarnate declared, "Heaven and earth shall pass away, but my words shall not pass away"[1]—I would see you amplify the power of the holy Word in example as the true manifestation of the Christ consciousness. This the Ascended Masters call the *living Word.* And this is the step-by-step process of the Incarnation which Life intends to be as much your own victory as it was that of beloved Jesus.

There are certain teachers in the Far East who, lacking understanding, have declared that only a 'living Master' would suffice to teach them or transfer the essence of Light. These sincere but misinformed devotees have not been taught the meaning of Life, nor do they comprehend who or what is a so-called 'living Master'.

Surely the capacity of God to communicate with his own is not limited to a flesh-and-blood manifestation of himself! Surely the Word was made flesh to accommodate man's comprehension, not God's! Surely a Master who has walked the earth, transmitting the Word to his disciples—performed feats that defy ordinary

physics, with signs following[2] of healings, miracles, and a body of teaching that has withstood
the rigorous tests of time—loses neither his life
nor his mastership by stepping beyond the pale
of temporal life and a body temple ill-equipped
for higher octaves!

It seems that the cherished apostle Paul
covered the controversy quite well: "But some
man will say, How are the dead raised up? and
with what body do they come? . . . There are also
celestial bodies and bodies terrestrial: but the
glory of the celestial is one, and the glory of the
terrestrial is another."[3] Rest assured, beloved,
that the Life of God does not terminate when the
soul of man steps forth from the body temple
and exchanges its earthly garments for one
more ethereal.

As Life is God, it is continuous. The true
Master, whether in the body or out of the body, is
he in whom the Word is embodied as the active
principle for and on behalf of the Almighty's Law
of Life. The power to communicate from the
higher to the lower octaves is possessed by every
Ascended Master and requires but the pole of a
receptive chela to transmit the vibratory action
of spiritual assistance, love, and blessing—
including fresh solutions to stale problems, nifty
ideas and practical inventions that are the gift
from the Master's heart to the chela for the whole
human race.

The Life of God is present in the mineral,
vegetable, and animal kingdoms and throughout the unseen world of Nature spirits—a kingdom teeming with 'elemental' life, the happy

chatter of elves and fairies, gnomes at work (though not always whistling!), sylphs arranging clouds and tumbling in the winds, undines splashing in the waves and salamanders dancing in fiery rings of rainbow rays.

So great a weight of mankind's karma do they bear that the gnomes themselves take on man's ways, becoming grumpy, grouchy until a sweet teacher appears (like the blessed Mother in the guise of Snow White) to lead them gently up the scale of their earthly evolution under their hierarchs, Virgo and Pelleur, the masterful beings who maintain the balance of forces in the earth. The gnomes serve in the physical plane just beyond the veil (spectrum) of ordinary sight. Here they are called the earth elementals. Sometimes you catch sight of them out of the corner of your eye—then think you must have imagined it!

Sylphs service the domain of the skies and the air purification and pressure systems. This all observe in the alchemical changes of weather and cycles of photosynthesis and precipitation. These elementals are masterful creatures who expand and contract their airy 'bodies' from microcosmic to macrocosmic levels, always keeping the flame for the realm of the mind, the mental plane which corresponds to the air element—one of the four elements designated by the ancient alchemists. Hence, sylphs are known as the air elementals. They respond to the command of their hierarchs, Aries and Thor.

The configuration of the earth body and

earth chemistry, reduced to four distinct stages or qualities of substance—fire, air, water, and earth[4]—by the mystical brotherhood of early scientists whose quest to control natural forces included the illusive goal of turning base metals into gold by transmutation—was in fact not far from higher truth.

The four lower bodies of man do relate to the so-called four planes of Matter serviced by cosmic forces focusing through the lesser evolved beings of Nature. In fact, you may be interested to know that the elementals were also created by Elohim to serve the sons and daughters of God as they, too, master the earth sciences and take dominion in space (both inner and outer) and in time. As man seeks to conquer his world in the sea of waters and in the sea of light, in the vibrations of subatomic and supersonic realms by way of proving his God-control of the universe step by step in all facets of the four kingdoms, unbeknownst to his outer awareness he is cooperating with elementals who have kept things under control for millions of years.

The fiery salamanders hold the secrets of the fire element, corresponding with the etheric body. At precisely what point the physical fire, elusive and most difficult to control, becomes the sacred fire is a mystery taught by the Holy Spirit, observed in the sacred heart of the saints, touched upon lightly by nuclear scientists, but held firmly in hand by the fire elementals.

In obedient and loving service to their hierarchs, Oromasis and Diana, their domain stretches from the nucleus of every atom and cell of Life to the core of the earth. They are compassionate and brilliant teachers ready to teach mankind practical ways of harnessing universal energy—from the heart of the electron to the heart of the sun.

The water elementals, portrayed in the elusive but enchanting mermaids, have inspired many a tale of romance between the human and elemental evolutions. 'Crossing over' from the elemental to the human kingdom is a known phenomenon. It is a door that has opened and been shut again to allow, in certain isolated cases, a particularly precious elemental of virtue and attainment to move on in the scale of evolution through the family of humanity, ultimately to acquire the divine spark.

More frequently, elementals cross over to the animal kingdom, accelerating evolution by serving man through the highly intelligent species, such as elephants, whales, porpoises, and even particularly loving and responsive dogs or horses.

The race memory of such occurrences goes back to the mists of Lemuria and Atlantis and is held today as legend or fairy tale, myth or make-believe by those whose lives would be too turned around to suit their pace or personal self-esteem, were they to take seriously this 'sub-level' of a lifewave, perceived at subconscious levels but denied everywhere except in the play of a midsummer night's dream.

Nevertheless, the serious work of the undines moves on as the oceans and the rivers and the lakes, streams and rivulets and raindrops all play a part in the formation and re-formation of the body of our planet and of man, utterly dependent upon the elementals.

The undines, who also laugh and play in the waves and waterfalls, lovingly follow the example of their hierarchs. Neptune is the king of the deep and his consort, Luara, is mother of tides, governing cycles of fertility and the water element as it affects the emotional body (known as the water, feeling, or desire body) and the communications of mankind's joy, grief, guilt, anger, and love through the astral plane, strongly influencing the collective unconscious of the race.

There is a great difference in the consciousness of the mineral, vegetable, animal, and human kingdoms serviced by the four types of elementals. Just as the body of man is not aware of itself in sleep, so the mineral kingdom does not possess self-awareness but manifests a specific quality of 'mineral density' which elemental life has charged into the substance of matter.

For example, the gnomes, although scarce recognized by the average Westerner—yet made known to the Irish as the "little people," or as mischievous fairies called leprechauns—do exist and impart to the mineral kingdom a wonderful quality of spiritual radiance which passes through the consciousness of the elemental's own being directly from the sun parents of this system—Helios and Vesta. The gnomes are charged with the responsibility of administering the divine pattern for each rock, precious stone, and element of mineral life. By a like token, there are also many ethereal angelic beings (of the devic evolution) responsible for ensouling the God-design in the natural order.

Trees and plants, of course, do not possess the awareness of either the human or the elemental consciousness but have imparted to them, by the advanced devas who watch over them, a greater degree of Life awareness than that retained by the mineral kingdom.

The ensoulment of trees and plants by the devas who direct the specific plant elementals assigned to categories of flora—and exist in such numberless numbers as to tend, literally, everything that grows—accounts for the undeniable fact that people who attune their spiritual centers to the Nature kingdom are able to speak to trees and plants and receive a physically perceptible response to the spark of consciousness communicated to the plant through its "nerve system." The life-force in plants and animals has been isolated in Kirlian photography, revealing an aura of universal energy, an electromagnetic field, also common to man.

Stepping up in the scale of Life-expressions from flora to fauna, we discover by like attunement the group-soul of animal species manifesting qualities of higher intelligence. Many animals possess almost human characteristics and an uncanny sense, almost psychic in its display. This is especially true of certain breeds of dogs and horses, and is marked in the elephant and the lower primates.

Mammals of the sea, fish, seals, and penguins are not excluded from a very wonderful intelligence, and further study by sensitive scientists will reveal a marvelous attunement, through the heart of all Life, everywhere in the Nature kingdom. Entomologists never cease to be amazed at the wonders of the ant; and the goad of the wise man "Go to the ant, thou sluggard . . ."[5] indicates that man has a great deal to learn from the veritable mysteries of Nature.

All this lovely creation imbued with a portion of the Divine Intelligence is deemed the "footstool kingdom" of God and was originally placed under the dominion of man as the manifestation of God. Through contaminating vibrations of cruelty, Nature has absorbed human imperfection. The savage qualities of jungle beasts are considered animalistic, whereas in reality, when the truth of life is known and the record of akasha and the planetary aura is accurately read, it will be learned that animal as well as elemental life originally absorbed their gross and sometimes grotesque outpicturings from mankind.

Savagery, cannibalism, violence, revenge, and killing originated in mankind's lowest evolutionary descent and were transmitted directly by vibration (here proving that the power of example can also be the worst teacher) to the subspecies. Therefore, the animal magnetism in humans—often sub-animal, wreaking a devilish wrath—must be redeemed (i.e., transmuted by the violet flame) in the process of freeing the planet.

This you can begin to effect right now by fervent calls for the action of the circle and sword of blue flame of Astrea, the universal Mother figure functioning at the level of Elohim (personified in the East as Kali) who cuts free her children evolving in every kingdom from the imposed evil matrix of the vengeful fallen angels. The violet fire that flows from your determined, heartfelt decrees literally lifts the pall of human consciousness from all elemental life.[6] It is integral to the reclamation of Nature's beauty.

Beloved Saint Germain and other Ascended Masters have in various associations of their embodiments had contact with elemental life evolving through the animal kingdom. In some cases, this necessitated their later intercession on behalf of certain elementals embodied in animal form. The freeing of these blessed elementals 'imprisoned' in dense bodies has on more than one occasion been the gift of love and violet fire from the ascended one to that elemental part of Life with whom they had prior contact.

Through the radiation of kindness, joy, and gratitude, all Nature will ultimately attain a pristine state of Edenic perfection where "the wolf shall dwell with the lamb, the leopard

with the kid, the calf and the young lion together . . . " [7] The law of the savage jungle will be
abrogated by Christ-power, and those men so
fortunate as to remain upon this planet will be
living Christs. Through their intercession, all
elementals will be set free from confinement to
the temporary animal forms. The radiation of
divine Love rising to a pulsation of great power
will instantaneously sever and dissolve the connection of the evolved elementals with the self-
limiting animal matrix and consciousness.

Some of you will recall reading of my love
for the birds and creatures and that they came to
me without fear. Beloved hearts, in most animals fear is the result of mankind's own feelings
which are, or have been, projected to the animals through the mass mind. Man's survival
instincts retained from prehistoric times sustain
a fierce desire to self-protect. Race memories of
past encounters with savage beasts keep alive a
record and an automatic reflex whereby man
reverts to a defensive posture when sensing the
presence of certain wild animals.

Through Christ-power, men can make an
appeal to the great Law of Life to free them from
this latent fear that engenders alienation from
all elemental life. We do not advocate reckless-
ness in approaching wild animals, for until the
inner action of transmuting all fear and doubt
into love is complete, people would do well not to
expose themselves unduly to dangers from animal life which yet responds to man from the
lowest levels of world consciousness—for the

flame of resurrection is yet to be transferred to them by sons and daughters of a God-mastery regained.

Remember, dear hearts, only when all fear is removed from within yourself, especially the subconscious, by the Great God Presence of Life will the lower-vibrating energy of the cobra, the lion, and all destructive beasts yield to the mighty power of your real attainment in Christ. Thus, we remind those who are beginning to realize that their own self-mastery is the key to the victory of all earth's evolutions: He who keepeth himself (his four lower bodies) and the gateway to his own house (his consciousness, body temple, and chakras) is greater than the ruler of a city.

As Solomon put it—and you would do well to consider his wisdom: "He that is slow to anger [keeping the vigil of God-control in his mental and feeling bodies] is better than the mighty; and he that ruleth his spirit [maintaining the God-control of the sacred fire in a figure-eight flow from the etheric to the physical body] than he that taketh a city."[8]

As you prepare to teach men many of the great laws of Being, you must show them that these laws are interwoven with the realities all around them. How can they extricate themselves from the maya and delusion of the ages unless they are able to see God woven into substance and to recognize the hand of the Infinite in all outer expressions? The day of great golden illumination is at hand!

"Say not ye, There are yet four months and then cometh harvest? Behold, I say unto you, Lift up your eyes and look on the fields, for they are white already to harvest."[9]

Many are called, but few choose to offer themselves to be the Master's vessel.

In love of service to Life, I AM

Kuthumi

Image

"God Created Man in His Own Image"

Beloved Ones of Greater Light Moving toward
 Self-Knowledge of the Kingdom Within—
 Gazing upon the reflected image of Self,
most men do not perceive the reality of Being, but
they are able to comprehend in part its grandiose
meaning through variegated aspects of Truth.
When qualified "mirrors" of spiritual ability
come into being, reflecting the Spirit of Truth to
the same degree of accuracy that a physical
mirror images the physical self, man will have
achieved a greater sense of Reality.

The carnal mind is, and ought to be recognized as, an aspect of the eternal Mind which
has traduced the original intent and become the
channel for the silt which churlishly meanders
along the stream of time but in no way interprets
to man the crystal-clear reality of his Being. To
remove the impure image is the first step, then,
in perceiving man's reality in Truth.

My statements concerning the necessity of regeneration spoken unto Nicodemus, which have been so frequently quoted and misquoted, convey to the elect the truth about man's internal nature: "Except a man be born again, he cannot see the kingdom of God."

"That which is born of the flesh is flesh"[1] refers not alone to the flesh form but to that which is created by and issued forth from the carnal nature of man. That which proceeds from the spiritual nature of man in all of its mighty stream of shining perfection is the reality of each one's Divine Selfhood.

The spiritual nature of man, which is of the Being of God, can be realized only through the Mind of God. Therefore, the carnal mind does not and cannot know the Mind of God: "For to be carnally minded is death, but to be spiritually minded is life and peace. Because the carnal mind is enmity against God: for it is not subject to the law of God, neither indeed can be."[2]

Problems of understanding arise in connection with these teachings which are inherent in the very substance of thy mortality interwoven and overlaid upon thy immortality. Identification with the outer (superficial) layers of consciousness, the mortal mind with its old familiar personality traits—identification with name, family, race, and class—tends to make men oblivious of their divine identity.

The problem of self-identification in God (to this day, some who profess belief in me as their

Saviour vehemently deny that God is their own Real Self!) has to do with the fact that each of the four lower bodies—the very vehicles and faculties necessary to perceive Truth in the physical plane—has a coating of illusion that makes both the problem and the solution to the definition of Being unclear.

Alas, such is the nature of the carnal mind (as it stains the four lower bodies with the dye of nonidentification with the living God), from which the soul must be rescued by the living Christ! O my beloved, do take pity upon the poor souls buried under a heap of carnal illusion spawned by the mass media and the educational systems—saturating the thinking/feeling/memory process of an entire generation!

Now, when I said, "The poor ye have with you always,"[3] I was in no way limiting access to the abundant Life that is available in the universe to every man who will reach out his hand and partake of the waters of Life freely.

I referred to the fact that men and women of the carnal sense are always in the process of shedding that sense—the impoverished sense of material life—for the abundant Life of God. And until they complete the process, they remain poor in both the spiritual and material things of life. (I also referred to the fact that someone always occupies the lowest rung on the karmic ladder; therefore, the poorest of the poor will remain an economic category as well as a spiritual one, just as there is always someone at the top and the bottom of the graduating class.)

The world is no different today—except that there has been a proliferation of both the rich and the poor, increasing the demand for shepherds to feed my sheep and ministering servants to heal both states of consciousness, for the rich as well as the poor have need to be healed of their false belief concerning their true identity.

When I said, "Blessed are the poor in spirit, for theirs is the kingdom of heaven,"[4] I referred to the fact that those who are poor in the 'spirit' of the material sense are usually less encumbered by the things of this world and more ready to accept the spiritual sense. (I also referred to the vacuum created by the spiritually impoverished sense that must be filled with the knowledge of the kingdom of heaven, the state of being not empty but full with the Spirit.)

I should like to call to the attention of my students the statements which I made concerning John the Baptist and those which he made concerning me.

John declared, "I indeed baptize you with water unto repentance, but he that cometh after me is mightier than I, whose shoes I am not worthy to bear. He shall baptize you with the Holy Ghost, and with fire."[5]

Of John, I spake and said, "Verily I say unto you, Among them that are born of women there hath not risen a greater than John the Baptist; notwithstanding he that is least in the kingdom of heaven is greater than he."[6] Obviously, beloved ones, John the Baptist himself was *in* the kingdom of heaven (i.e., caught up in the consciousness of the Spirit) and therefore the great maxim included him also.

To understand my words correctly, it must be seen that they applied only to the outer sense of John the Baptist; although he was the greatest ever born of women and greater, yet this material sense did not yield the spiritual sense of his own immortality. The inner spiritual sense, then, of "the least in the kingdom of heaven" is greater than the outer material sense of anyone on earth.

He said of me, "He must increase, but I must decrease," [7] thus affirming the need for every man to increase his Christ consciousness and decrease his carnal sense.

I make this distinction today for a very urgent reason. Down through the centuries theologians and holy seekers have seldom, if ever, been able to clarify for themselves or the brethren the difference between the immortal, altogether lovely and perfect God Self of man and his human creation.

My statement "The Son of man is come to save that which was lost" [8] denotes that a part of man has strayed from the intended God-design. That part is the soul which by free will chose to try on the various costumes of the carnal logic— and then by enchantment with its glamour, style, and look, did not strip off those garments! Did not prefer the purity of the temple attire! Inasmuch as that which strayed, then, could not, by definition, remain the reflection of the altogether lovely and perfect divine image of God (for it chose not to), it follows that that which has partaken of error is the consciousness of the soul-manifestation (personality) which allowed its energy to flow into patterns of imperfection.

This mere misqualification has become a form of temporal reality to those who believe in the materiality of sense manifestation—and will defend it with their very (material sense of) life. Those who have identified with the human self-misqualification for so long—spanning millions of years of the false belief in mortality, embodiment after mortal embodiment—have for the same time/space stretch persistently ignored the mighty possibility of the great Divine Self.

Why? As you observe the psychology of those to whom you minister, beloved, consider if it is not the defense mechanism of the carnal mind that must preserve the elaborate security system of lies and luring self-delusions in which it has wrapped (and mummified) that lost soul! And, I pray you, have compassion!

The Christ of every man is the Great Mediator between the perfection of God, the Divine Self, and the marred or 'fallen' (i.e., lowered in frequency and vibration) soul image which has become the focal point for the repetition of his human creation, round upon round. It is therefore this image—this self-indoctrinating image allowed by a blinded free will—which must be redeemed and purified so that the soul may once again pattern its works after the perfect image of Christ.

This Christ can be reinstated in the four lower bodies by a cry for help and the act of free will that at last bids welcome to the Real Self. That cry for liberation from the tyranny of the carnal mind is the distress signal that sets in motion the forces of the Great White Brotherhood—the armies of The Faithful and True.[9] It is the call which compels the answer, beloved, of my Christ, your Christ. And you can give it right now.

With the Chart of Your Divine Self before you, face the Supreme Ruler of the Universe, thy God, and affirm with all thy heart in a loud voice: "The Light of God never fails! The Light of God never fails! The Light of God never fails! And the Beloved Mighty I AM Presence is that Light!" Repeat this call four times, expelling the carnal mind from each of your four lower bodies as you do. And accept your freedom and your reality by the authority of the Christ who I AM, who You Are—with you now!

Congratulations! You have begun the redemptive process. The process of redemption is one in which the energies woven into the garment of self in misunderstanding and misqualification are painstakingly undone by the supplicant soul under the direction of the Holy Spirit. The energies of error coalesced around the marred image producing imperfect patterns in the four lower bodies must be released into the pure stream of God's consciousness and transmuted by the fires of trial and purification.[10]

The energies you restore to their original polarity each day by the science of the spoken Word are ready to be invested into a new creation—like the clay which the potter uses over and over again. Thus, the 'repolarized' energy is spun as golden light substance from the Son (Sun) of God into the seamless garment of the living Christ. Thus, dual man, as the son of *man*ifestation and as the Son of God, is reinvested with his Real Image and is become *one* Reality!

To communicate this divine idea, this teaching of his Real Self to the natural man, wedded as he is to his false image, is 'naturally' most difficult. Teleological, theological, and psychological factors relating to his cherished sense of self arise in man's consciousness to speak to him of outer things and to impart to him a false idea of the very dominion with which God has endowed him.

He feels wholly qualified to judge and, rightfully so, does not assign to another the task of choosing this day whom he will serve.[11] His identification with the material sense and self is often so complete that he finds it very difficult— and let every teacher understand this—to accept the science of that Being, that 'Oversoul' which is invisible to his outer senses.

This is why I spake unto Thomas as he thrust his fingers into the nail prints in my hand and his hand into the spear wound in my side, saying: "Because thou hast seen me, thou hast believed; blessed are they who have not seen and yet have believed."[12]

The demands which men make of the Law to perform a cosmic miracle are very great; albeit those who are able to absorb by the power of great faith in God the holy perfection of their own Being—without demanding the expenditure of heaven's energy in creating miraculous (or so-called miraculous) manifestations—are the more advanced disciples. These use the spiritual eye to identify spiritual substance rather than the material eye or empirical evidence to confirm or prove spiritual Truth.

The Great Law of man's Being is "Because Thou art, I AM." Without the identity of God, all Life would cease to be. God is Life and this is the greater Truth encompassing the lesser manifestation. To say that Life is God, while true, is problematical unless the life that is expressed by man be the Life which God created.

The outer form is only Godly, then, when it expresses divine qualities: man himself is only a manifestation of God when he is expressing Godly attributes. His identity is God's only when he self-identifies with God through words and works identical to God's. And this is possible, else I would not have commanded my own, "Be ye therefore perfect, even as [in a like manner as] your Father in heaven is perfect!" [13]

The statements I made to other men which caused some to shudder and do so to the present day—"Ye are of your father the devil, and the lusts of your father ye will do . . . . Ye serpents, ye generation of vipers, how can ye escape the damnation of hell?" [14]—referred to the Great Law in action, the Word who judges every man according to his own word and work and the motives, intents, thoughts, and feelings behind them. These true expressions of self which reveal what a man thinketh in his heart identify in turn his will as it aligns either with the carnal nature of deified evil or with the nature of the Deity Himself and His righteousness in action.

Listen not to the proud talkers boasting about, but observe their doings. Indeed, what do they do to merit eternal Life? And then observe those whose words (except for their perpetual prayer [15]) are few but whose acts of compassion—enlightening, healing, and liberating souls—are many.

Thus, in the end, as in the beginning, man condemns himself to his imperfect image or justifies himself in the image of God—by the quality of his heart—revealed *vibrationally* in his own words and his works. This teach, lest the unwary fall by the wayside and lose the prize.

As the earth shall be full of my knowledge,[16] so the Law of Righteousness shall follow those who pursue it. Men are not here to judge or to criticize one another, but to judge (ascertain) that they themselves do not cast a stumbling block in another's pathway. This they may forestall by recognizing the perfection of their own Being and giving preeminence to its expression while extolling the same possibility for their fellow creatures. By so teaching and imbibing this cup of Life which is God, my disciples shall commune forever with the kingdom of our Father.

Lovingly, I AM your elder brother,

Jesus

Soul

"Unto Thee I Lift Up My Soul"

Beloved Ones in Pursuit
  of the Knowledge of the Higher Self—
Familiarity, with all of its comfort, does not produce spiritual expansion in the heart of Being.

We do not wish to discourage our students' appreciation for the benign aspects of their environment nor to retard their expression of gratitude for material comforts received from the heart of God.

It is our wish to convey to those desiring to progress into the true nature of Being the method and means whereby they may, at will, shatter their own complacency with their surroundings and expand their consciousness into those far-reaching aspects of Being which are verily more a part of Reality than immediate concerns and circumstances.

The contemplation of the Fatherhood of God is an invaluable safeguard when journeying in consciousness from the familiar world of day-to-day routine into the vast and infinite reaches of God's immortal love and loveliness.

When contemplating a landscape, you will note that there is usually a foreground and a background in the painting. The foreground conveys the idea of immediacy and the feeling that one can be a part of the scene. The background, while sometimes within reach, engages the imagination to explore the unknown, and the sky beyond opens the mind to the far reaches of infinity. Through the metaphor of art we shall, by and by, relate the nature of man's being to spiritual Reality.

Beloved hearts, nowhere in the universe is there a lack of beauty, for God is everywhere. Let none, therefore, fear to expand his consciousness. The exploration of earth, the solar systems, and all of cosmos through the expanding soul consciousness offers far more safety and satisfaction in probing the unknown than mankind are presently realizing through scientific exploration by satellite, rocketry, or spacecraft.

Today, when education is held up before the youth as a means to greater economic security, it is not difficult to convince people of its value. Throughout the world many aspire to knowledge—some for career, financial gain, status, and community service, some to self-knowledge through psychology, while others reach for the mysticism of the saints. These represent the near and distant goals approachable in succeeding stages of life, which become legitimate (viable) according to the needs of the soul, the demands of karma, and the impelling of the divine plan.

Yet there are many more who prefer to remain in ignorance rather than exert the effort to rise out of it. This is the lethargy of the sleepfulness of the ages. Left to itself, it becomes a chronic disease of human creation. Hypnotic and loathsome, this malady leaves its victims unable to summon the energy to pursue virtue and honor through lawful occupation (right livelihood).

All admonishments spoken herewith concerning the nature of man's being are given not to condemn but to spur our readers onward and upward into Life and real living by transporting you from the mundane to those immediate areas of Self, just beyond the fringe of present attainment, and thence safely forward on a journey into Being which will expand not only your intellectual capacities but also your awareness of that other self, the inner self, or soul.

While in a very real sense man's true identity is sealed with the Father in heaven (his eternal Shepherd being his Holy Christ Self), often neither his I AM Presence nor his Higher Self is recognized by him. Sometimes this occurs by reason of the very proximity of the Father and the Son, so contrasting man's temporal transfixion with his immediate environment and its manifold problems that heaven seems unreal and beyond reach—as far away as the most distant background and so far into the future as to be totally irrelevant to the now.

In resistance to spiritual prodding from on high, many have desired to express themselves in an entirely physical way, denying the authenticity of spiritual experiences and faculties. Leaning upon the testimony of the senses, they hold to an empirical ideal which must ultimately crumble with the dissolution of the material self upon their own demise.

Quite to the contrary, some souls in their desire to escape from their human creation have espoused the path of sainthood and through asceticism or mysticism have lived differently than their more materialistic counterparts in the world of form.

By striking a balance in the nature of his being, man can experience the spiritual world yet remain tethered to the schoolrooms of earth, mastering the required lessons, enjoying life to the fullest from the inner vantage, not neglecting his duty to family and friends, and ultimately achieve his victory over his outer self and its outer conditionings.

Just as it would be unwise to neglect the care of the physical body, so it is unwise to neglect the care of the spiritual nature. Taking the part of greater wisdom, I admonish you to give compassionate yet unselfish attention to both. When the shell of materiality is outgrown by the victorious spirit, man rises to a dominion of crowning glory greater than that of the angels.

The proper use of free will makes man Godlike by choice. His restoration to the God-estate releases his Adamic nature from the fetters of earth and enables him to righteously regain entrée into that paradise of consciousness from which, through inversion of Principle, he fell.

Energy is impersonal. It flows through man's consciousness to do his bidding either by conscious direction or in a haphazard manner. Consecration and concentration on Ascended Master laws must ultimately yield a higher expression of the nature of Being. Meeting the challenges of life as Christ did in his Palestinian mission, the ministering servant cannot help but be the victor.

Human criteria must not be used in assessing the progress of the soul, yet in the words of the early apostle, "Let none of you suffer as a murderer, or as a thief, or as an evildoer, or as a busybody in other men's matters."[1] Greater Godliness ought to be an expression carried forth with an holy zeal into the whole realm of man's being.

It is not enough merely to rise by the power of prayer to a state where one is able scientifically to wrest the advantage from universal Law. The scriptures have recorded that "the kingdom of heaven suffereth violence, and the violent take it by force."[2] But the kingdom of God, the kingdom of His image and His consciousness called forth through His qualities, is the one true expression that shall win man's permanent victory for him.

Blessed hearts, there are so many aspects to the Law, and yet in practice the Law is quite plain. As it is written: "Love is the fulfilling of the Law"—the whole Law of man's Being.[3] Therefore, we would not complicate man's pathway toward salvation; neither would we oversimplify spiritual matters. This would only mislead our earnest students into byways and pitfalls, wasting precious time and energy and perhaps compromising the possibility of victory.

Men cannot change what they are at a given moment. Indeed, "Can a leopard change his spots?"[4] Well, not on the instant. The cycles necessary for the alchemical precipitation of Christhood must be fulfilled, by law.

Whether a man's status be at the position of zero achievement or a zero plus x, it ought to be acknowledged that the infinite possibilities attainable in the now are won by men and women who, having the power of faith to believe in the justice of universal Christ-love and in the accuracy of divine Law, are willing to implement their belief by right action.

This, coupled with the determination to progress on the path of discipleship and to acquire the necessary spiritual understanding, will push back the shadows of ignorance and light their way to the great throne room—the secret chamber of the heart where the Great Three-in-One is unveiled as the threefold flame of living Life.

Here in the laboratory of Being, the Master Alchemist, the beloved Christ Self, teaches the soul step by step how to wield the sacred sword of the Word to take victorious dominion over every untoward condition in the four planes of

Matter and his corresponding four lower bodies. This necessitates the vanquishing by the all-consuming violet flame of his negative astrology and the ominous forecasts of his descending karma. Both of these he can discern by learning how to chart his personal cycles on the Cosmic Clock.[5]

There are none upon earth bereft of spiritual guidance—except by their own rejection of the Spirit of guidance. The Divine Presence of every man's being is pouring out a Niagara of energy daily for and on behalf of the individual life-stream. The Holy Christ Self is releasing streams of highly qualified God-direction; and the Ascended Masters are adding the momentum of their specialized assistance to all Life upon earth.

It remains for those sensitive, faith-filled individuals to pan for the gold flowing in the stream of their own consciousness and to catch its golden nuggets. Each one must draw wisdom's flame and garment closely about him, bearing in mind the teaching of Jesus that unto the one who ingeniously multiplies his talents more is given, but from the unrighteous steward who has nothing to show for his spiritual/financial endowments shall be taken away even that which he hath.[6]

Be ye therefore unafraid to share in holy wisdom, being careful to select from those nuggets of spiritual Truth, stored for safekeeping in your immortal being, special gifts to bless your brothers and sisters with the illumination that banishes ignorance forever from their spiritual quest.

There is a special act of grace given to all who seek to teach men of lesser comprehension concerning the glories of God's kingdom. Spiritual teachers on earth guided wholly by sincerity are, by reason of their stand, angel ministrants in human form. These are not removed in a corner[7] of obscure or fruitless identity, but stand forth to hold the chaliced Word of God.

"Fear not, little children, for it is your Father's good pleasure to give you the kingdom"[8] is their message. These recognize and should teach that spiritual knowledge is not acquired through merely reading and hearing metaphysical truths but by putting into practice the Presence of Life, of God, and of Charity in all of one's affairs. Only then does knowledge become attainment.

The greatest expansion of Being occurs through sharing. For God is the greatest sharer of all. As Christ brake the loaves on the shores of the sea of Galilee, so the Father breaks the bread of Being and communicates his own Identity—the whole loaf—to every son of God who resolves to return to his Father's house.

I lift my torch before the golden door of your Being.

I AM your brother,

Kuthumi

Corona Class Lesson 47

Heart

". . . In the Integrity of Thy Heart"

Light Emanations from the Father's Heart,
    How I Love Thee!
    The order of Being proceeds in radiant emanation directly from the central heart of God. From the center, or throne, of God-identity, awareness of the total emanation is possible. From a point located upon one of the circles of emanation, either a part or the whole of that particular cycle may be known.
    To reach across or to expand beyond man's present cycle or to reach backward to the central point of origin is sometimes difficult for those geographically and consciously positioned in the outer spheres, afar and apart from the heart center of Identity.
    It has ever been my wish to convey to the children of God the nature of their *total* Being in order to enhance the fulfillment of their hopes, to make possible their union with the allness of God, and to assist them in stretching

their identity into areas of greater happiness
and wholeness. Verily, to heal that which is
lame, to restore crooked limbs, to magnify the
sacred fire of perfection within the crucible of
man's identity is my passion.

Identification of Being with consciousness
is incomplete in man until he becomes wholly
identified with the Center Source of creation.
This enables man to proceed in orderly succes-
sion from that Center through all the concentric
cycles of creation to the periphery of all that is.
There is no limit, no ultimate, no final end in the
wondrous Spirit of God. Indeed, "the wind blow-
eth where it listeth, and thou hearest the sound
thereof, but canst not tell whence it cometh, and
whither it goeth: so is every one that is born of
the Spirit." [1]

The Holy Spirit must needs express qualities of intelligence, qualities of power, and
qualities of great love. It is unthinkable that
even a little child imbued with the holiness of
God should fail to exude the fragrance of a
wistful, searching intelligence and a buoyant
yet balanced outreaching love—a love extending
beyond the borders of persons, places, conditions or things, a love centered in the very heart
of Truth and Identity complete.

As you observe the passing scene and the
fleeting glances on the faces of those around
you, as you interpret the distresses of the
multitudes and see them as sheep gone astray
from the great sheepfold, bear in mind that
many are the self-made victims of a human tide

of transgression against the laws of Being that has occurred throughout history. These tides of aggressive human intent have been willfully and ignorantly expressed in place of (and as counterfeits of) the triune qualities of the Spirit. Mankind's misguided judgment, condemning one another, has brought the curse of Cain upon their own houses. The tyranny, rebellion, and haughty zeal of the carnally-minded and the rich have not brought them an iota of eternal freedom or God-happiness.

Genuine Godliness, the deep, unmovable, abiding love that censures not but seeks to hallow all of Life, transcends all vain theology which attempts to fix men into walled compartments of race and creed. Let none deny the virtue of right use of opportunity and energy. Through wise measurement of the hour at hand and maximum amplification of its potential, men are indeed positioned nearer to the kingdom of God. Yet the most wayward sheep deserve attention and understanding.

It is the stripping of the layers of misqualified energy from the lost sheep to which we must dedicate ourselves; by rightfully vesting them as sons of God we may immaculately behold each emanation of the Godhead as being one, in and from the Father's heart.

To behold in man the completeness of his divinity, identity must be shorn of all elements of human creation with which he has clothed it. His energies must be offered upon the altar of God to be transmuted and consumed by the living flame of Truth and the purified radiance of his true Being. Washed in the Life of the spiritual Lamb of God that taketh away every stain, and wipeth every tear from human eyes,[2] his consciousness is free at last (karmically free) to identify completely with the Being of man who is in truth the Son of God.

Lovingly, I AM

Jesus

Holy Grail

"Are Ye Able to Drink of the Cup?"

To You, Lovers of Truth,
        Who Meditate on the Great Sun Disc—
    Our most gracious elder brother, beloved Jesus, has offered us a wonderful exposition on the nature of Being. As we work in a spirit of co-operative teaching, I am offering to the Presence of Life the consecration of all of God's wholeness that has ever been externalized in my consciousness down through the ages. This I lay at the altar of the Christ-identity of every disciple.

    Little children, think for a moment what the world would be like if the wonderful ideas and hopes of Godliness were not offered to the souls of men. The despairs that tear and sear human hearts, caught in the net of the years, would present such utter hopelessness that few of the spiritually sensitive on the planet, upon whom rests the hope of the multitudes for the healing balm of Life, could endure the rigors of life from day to day.

But the glories that stream from afar and draw so very near—bearing the songs of the angels and the radiant hopes of saintly souls that long ago trod the Earth and the Venus star of the Father's great love—carry energies of renewal, fresh with hope, to each one's being. How miragelike men seem on the desert of life receding before the ever-expanding consciousness of the Son of God, for it cannot be otherwise.

That which is finite is of the temporal, evolving nature which has not yet apprehended infinity. That which is eternal needs no lens through which to gaze upon its own reality, for it is imminently aware of all that it is and ever shall be. It follows, then, that the long night of man's becoming shall break at the dawn of man's Being, softly stealing with the First Ray and expanding unto the sevenfold complement of the individualization of the God flame.

The ancient Egyptians utilized the solar symbol, as did the mystic religions of South America and Atlantis. In the symbol of the solar disc, great truth is enshrined: the Sun of man's Being; the Light of God that never fails; the

Sun-beam, the individualized light ray that may be used by the soul (the 'little Sol') to expand outward from the center or to move as a shuttle backward to the heart of Light.

Man, the monad, man the individual part of the Whole, may slip into the shining sea where only purity can be; but he cannot carry thither his hates and frustrations, his doubts and despairs. These must first be dissolved before complete reunion with God can occur, else the soul which is wedded to the ideational pattern of man's external concepts will itself be dissolved and returned to primal substance by the pressure of the great Light of God and the sacred fires of perfection.

Infinity alone can know the Infinite. It is, then, in the state of becoming Infinite that men truly contact the hem of the garment of their own Being and are made whole.

The issue of blood which troubled the woman for many years ere she touched the hem of Christ's garment[3] symbolizes the issuing forth of man's life-energy in wasted years of fruitless existence. The drying up of the "fountain of blood" through the healing power of the living Christ symbolizes the redirection of Light flowing from the fount of energy, the Mighty I AM Presence, into the chalice of individuality. The Light, skillfully redirected by the Master Physician, restored the 'woman' (symbolizing the feminine nature of the receptive soul) to her original reason for being: evermore to be a Holy Grail of infinite capacity.

Upon feeling the regenerative powers of the Christ, the errant knight of the outer self seeks to drink the cup of true Being and to pursue that Light which has never shone on land or sea,[4] for it is the internal nature of all things which has never been profaned by the grossness of outer expression. It is this Light which maketh all things whole, whose shining gleams forth from the Grail and exhorts the lesser radiance to become the greater.

No loss is ever the portion of that one who, desiring not to abide in the aloneness of outer self-expression, unites with the all-oneness of God. Supreme questing-fulfillment beholds in hope the day-to-day challenge to keep on keeping on—assuredly to find in time and space the priceless, eternal treasure of Being.

All this I AM.

Lovingly,

Kuthumi

Corona Class Lesson 48

Love

"Charity Never Faileth"

To Students of Holy Wisdom
  Who Shall Teach Men the Way—
  The chastisement which, all too often, men feel for themselves in moments of self-censure is easily transferred when disapproval of another registers on the screen of consciousness. This externalization of subjective self-condemnation is known as *projection;* it illustrates the great law that you will never esteem God or his manifestation more than you esteem yourself.
  Thus, to forget the divine origin of all Life, or any part thereof, is to fall short of the Law which always affirms, "Do unto others as you would have them do unto you." Or, in this case, "Do unto yourself as you would do unto others—for you surely shall."[1]
  Between embodiments and awaiting rebirth, hours upon hours pass, according to earth's standards, while teachers at inner levels pronounce and teach this sacred precept of the

Golden Rule—its psychological as well as spiritual ramifications—to novitiate souls studying to show themselves approved[2] in the etheric retreats of the Great White Brotherhood. These students, having failed or fallen short of the mark of the prize of regeneration in their preceding embodiments, are preparing to take upon themselves once again coats of skins[3] (grosser vehicles, i.e., the four lower-vibrating bodies) to meet the challenges of life and karma in the physical octave below.

Is it not well to note again in this dissertation on Being that man stands in a twofold relationship to the Great Law? On the one hand is his relationship to God and the universal Law of Life, Love, and holy Wisdom; on the other is his relationship with man who was created in the selfsame image.

It is difficult for those yet bound in the round of rebirth to see the Whole, for they stand in the manner of one who assembles a jigsaw puzzle and has placed together but a few of the pieces composing the whole picture. This is why faith is needed. We caution that the privilege you retain at all times of rejecting spiritual concepts that seem unclear should not be exercised lightly. Rest assured that in the fullness of time the circle of understanding will be complete.

Is it not peculiar that men are so inclined to express absolute certainty concerning matters about which they know so little, while frequently expressing uncertainty about things of which they ought to know a great deal. The balancing power of Love, when it is directed to all parts of Life, is the greatest lever there is to elevate the character of man to Godhood. It has well been said, ". . . Whether there be tongues, they shall cease; whether there be knowledge, it shall vanish away; but Charity, or divine Love, never faileth."[4]

Think you that in extending the love of the Father to a cynical or scornful one who reviles you and flaunts the love you give, driving it back into your very teeth, you do ill? I tell you nay; for though it be far from him, he will one day remember and perhaps look for the proffered gift. By expressions of hatred and shame, men mar the surface of their own souls; by expressions of virtue and honor, they lay up in heaven a wreath of victory on behalf of all Life.[5]

Consider the billions of lifestreams evolving on the planet. Consider the weight of human despair and discord—the boundless fears generated daily by their uncertainties and struggles. Ask yourself: Would you add one jot or tittle of energy to this world weight (karma), to this distress, and to mankind's unhappiness?

Then mark well the golden moments as opportunities for the dispensation of grace. Let judgment remain the prerogative of the Karmic Board; they render it with good qualifications and compassion. They seal each judgment with the power of opportunity, they are ever mindful that God chastens those whom he loves, and their mercy droppeth as the gentle rain upon the souls of all who suffer the necessity of karmic judgment.

It is no imposition upon the citadel of Being to study holy Wisdom, to generate holy Love, and thus to use the God-given Power to bring forth the kingdom of heaven among men. Were the world and all that it comprises to crumble away, the tower of spiritual glory would remain forever. The annals of God, the true chronology of Being, record every virtue, every noble aspiration, every holy thought. The Angels of Record bear them to an invulnerable fortress locked in regions beyond mortal comprehension.

O Being of Man: With all thy getting, get understanding of the eternal principles![6]

As your precious Kuthumi and I stand before the record of this age and ask ourselves the question, "How can we best relieve human suffering and reestablish mighty principles that will enable man, the instrument, to endure?" we recognize that in the final analysis it is the recognition and self-determination by man himself, as an individual, that sets him apart from his fellows and makes him God's man.

The records of the infamous bear common earmarks: lack of emotional control or self-discipline of one's mental forces, lack of justice toward the weak and the poor, self-centered and manipulative employment of energy, wisdom, and even the quality of love, which is turned, to satisfy the lust of the ego, upon the whim of the self-crowned potentate.

By contrast, we examine the fabric of souls who are the spiritually great in the eyes of God: kings of righteousness such as Melchizedek, king of Salem; holy men such as Elijah the prophet, the Prophet Samuel, and Daniel. We observe, too, the wisdom of those spiritually great men and women contemporary with your precious lifestreams whom we choose not to name at this moment—lest they take their reward before they have run their course.

We note in all of them the very common or uncommon quality (as you may choose to call it) of unswerving faith in the Law of Universal Love, Wisdom, and Power. We see a common reverence for Nature; we see an uncommon sense of assessment whereby self-virtue is recognized only as a reasonable sacrifice and offering.

We see no arrogant demanding for deference or favor that would set them apart from others or exalt them in their person, but only a firm, unyielding devotion to be a vessel in the hands of the Infinite One in order to convey unlimited blessings to others. The patrimony of heaven is given to such souls as these, whether you believe in them or not. Myriad angels stand before them and bow in adoration to the God flame veiled in flesh.

During my Galilean ministry I often said, "Go and sin no more;"[7] I also admonished, "Go and do thou likewise."[8] These Christ commands were intended to evoke a response from the

mighty God-power within souls forgiven or
healed.

Today I say to all: Let all proneness to
human error cease! Go and sin no more! Let all
virtue and wisdom and loveliness; all beauty,
all courage, faith, and determination; all consecration, invocation, and adoration be raised
on high in the citadel of your own Being . . . and
go and do thou likewise! Keep thou the faith,
keep thou the courage, keep thou the determination, keep thou the holy precepts, keep thou the
balance!

Though angels stand ready to bear thee up
lest thou dash thy foot against the stone, yield
not to one subtle temptation of that force which
would tempt thee to turn aside from the path of
the LORD thy God.[9]

Truly the LORD thy God is my God. Truly he
is in me and in thee. Truly in this interchange of
oneness and unity there is hope that the Holy
Spirit of prophecy may fashion in newness a
new generation!

Let the words be spoken of thee, "This man
was in truth the Son of God."[10] So proclaim, so
teach, so let it be shouted from the housetops!

The antennas of the mind receive the waves
of manifold vibrations today. There are vibrations of hatred, fear, and terror. There are
vibrations of violence, distress, and woe. Screen
them out—reject them all! They shall not provide one iota of salvation unto thee.

There are other vibrations far, far above
man's poor power of perception in his present

state which stem from the living fount of God's merciful heart. These speak of infinite mercy, of infinite beauty, of infinite compassion—of the dawn of a mighty civilization when the golden age shall have fully manifested.

In the matrix of the present, let all distinguish in religion those qualities which are Godlike, all-loving, all-knowing, all-perceiving the radiance of heaven. May we together breathe one heart-prayer: "Thy kingdom come, Thy will be done on earth as it is in heaven."

Let there go forth, then, into manifestation, without fear, the courage to live in the consciousness of that Being which I AM, and to die to that transitory folly which in Truth I am not.

O vanity and vexation of spirit, may man forsake thee! O Father, may man find his Being in thy Oneness! That I may say of all:

"Lo, I AM come!"

"Lo, the I AM is come into manifestation on earth in the sons and daughters of God!"

I speak this in Kuthumi's love and name.

Your elder brother,

Jesus

The Magnificat
by Mary, the Mother of Jesus

My soul doth magnify the LORD,

And my spirit hath rejoiced in God my Saviour—the Almighty, the I AM Presence.

For he hath regarded the low estate of his handmaiden: for, behold, from henceforth all generations shall call me blessed.

For he that is mighty hath done to me great things; and holy is his name I AM THAT I AM.

And his mercy is on them that fear him from generation to generation.

He hath shewed strength with his arm; he hath scattered the proud in the imagination of their hearts.

He hath put down the mighty from their seats, and exalted them of low degree.

He hath filled the hungry with good things; and the rich he hath sent empty away.

He hath holpen his servant Israel, in remembrance of his mercy;

As he spake to our fathers, to Abraham, and to his seed for ever.

Luke 1:46–55

May all expectant mothers recite this mantra of the beloved Mother Mary in daily celebration of the universal incarnation of the Christ in Jesus and in the sons and daughters of God.

Notes

"The Alchemy of the Word," a comprehensive glossary of the teachings of the Ascended Masters in *Saint Germain On Alchemy*, is indispensable to your understanding of many of the terms used in the *Corona Class Lessons*. Please confirm the Word of Jesus and Kuthumi by keeping the above at your side as a dictionary of philosophical and hierarchical concepts which will further illumine the lessons you are learning from the Lord and his disciple in order that you might go forth with his gift of knowledge to feed his sheep and "teach men the Way."

CORRESPONDENCE
Corona Class Lesson 1
Brotherhood

1. John 10:1–18.
2. **Each one judged according to works.** Ps. 62:12; Prov. 24:12; Jer. 17:10; 32:19; Matt. 16:27; Rom. 2:5–13; Rev. 2:23; 20:12, 13; 22:12.
3. Gen. 4:7.
4. **"Trees."** "I think that I shall never see / A poem lovely as a tree. / A tree whose hungry mouth is prest / Against the earth's sweet flowing breast; / A tree that looks at God all day / And lifts her leafy arms to pray; / A tree that may in summer wear / A nest of robins in her hair; / Upon whose bosom snow has lain; / Who intimately lives with rain. / Poems are made by fools like me, / But only God can make a tree." Joyce Kilmer (1913)
5. **Touching the hem of the garment.** Matt. 9:20–22; 14:35, 36; Mark 5:25–34; 6:56; Luke 8:43–48.
6. I Kings 8:27; II Chron. 6:18.
7. Gen. 1:26–28.
8. Isa. 55:8, 9.

9. John 12:32.
10. **Weary not in well-doing.** Gal. 6:9; II Thess. 3:13; I Cor. 15:58.
11. Luke 19:41.
12. John 3:19.
13. Heb. 12:23.
14. John 21:15–17.

CORRESPONDENCE
Corona Class Lesson 2
You

1. Acts 28:17–31.
2. Matt. 16:15.
3. Eph. 4:22–24; Col. 3:9, 10.
4. **"Vengeance is mine . . ."** Deut. 32:35; Rom. 12:19; Heb. 10:30.
5. **God's mercy everlasting.** Pss. 103:17; 118:1–4; 136; I Chron. 16:34, 41; II Chron. 5:13; 7:3, 6; Ezra 3:11.
6. II Pet. 1:19; Rev. 2:28; 22:16.
7. I Cor. 3:13–15.
8. **"Ask and ye shall receive."** Matt. 7:7–11; 21:21, 22; Mark 11:23, 24; Luke 11:9–13; John 14:13, 14; 15:7, 16; 16:23, 24; James 1:5; I John 3:22; 5:14, 15.
9. Luke 23:34.
10. Matt. 7:16; Luke 6:44.
11. John 8:12; 9:5.

12. Serapis Bey, Hierarch of the Ascension Temple at Luxor, Egypt, has described how the Master Jesus came to Luxor as a very young man and knelt before the Hierophant "refusing all honors that were offered him" and asked to be initiated into the first grade of spiritual law and mystery. "No sense of pride marred his visage — no sense of preeminence or false expectation, albeit he could have well expected the highest honors." See Serapis Bey, *Dossier on the Ascension* (Livingston, Montana: Summit University Press, 1979), p. 33, $5.95.

13. **"Whosoever will be great..."** Matt. 20:26–28; 23:11; Mark 9:35; 10:43–45; Luke 22:26, 27.

14. Rev. 3:15, 16.

15. Mal. 4:2; Rev. 1:16.

16. Luke 22:19; I Cor. 11:24, 25.

17. Matt. 3:12.

18. John 6:33–35, 48–58; Matt. 26:26.

19. Matt. 20:20–23; 26:27, 28; Mark 10:35–40.

20. **Drink of the water of Life.** John 4:10–14; 7:37, 38; Rev. 21:6; 22:1, 17.

CORRESPONDENCE
Corona Class Lesson 3
Holy Christ Self

1. John 3:16.

2. **The requirement of faith.** Matt. 8:5–13; 9:18–30; 15:22–28; 17:19, 20; 21:21, 22; Mark 5:22–43; 9:17–27; 10:46–52; 11:22–24; Luke 7:2–10, 50; 8:41–56; 17:19; 18:35–43; John 11:21–45; Heb. 11.

3. James 2:14–26.

4. John 16:13.

5. James 4:8.

6. Luke 1:46–52.

7. Isa. 40:4; Luke 3:5.

8. **"Thou shalt not take life!"** Exod. 20:13; 21:12, 14, 20–23; Lev. 24:17, 21; Num. 35:16–24, 30, 31; Deut. 19:11–13; Matt. 5:21; Rev. 13:10.

   In Buddhism, the first of the Ten Precepts is translated as "Refrain from destroying life." According to the doctrine of the Jains, who strictly adhere to the Eastern principle of *ahimsa* (harmlessness, non-injury, non-killing of life), even the unintentional killing of an ant through carelessness may have severe consequences on the soul. The foundation of Hindu law is the Code or Institutes of Manu, an ancient collection of laws based on custom, precedent and the teachings of the Vedas. This highly revered code defined the rules of conduct and their application to all the classes of the community. According to the code, the taking of life warranted the death penalty in order to reduce violence in society by deterring others from committing the same crime and to allow for expiation of sin.

9. Luke 3:22.

10. John 8:58.

11. Phil. 2:5.

12. **The prodigal son.** Read Luke 15:11–32.

13. **Impartiality of the Deity.** Matt. 5:45; Acts 10:34, 35; Rom. 2:11; Eph. 6:8, 9; Col. 3:25.

14. **"An eye for an eye..."** Exod. 21:23–25; Lev. 24:19, 20; Deut. 19:21; Matt. 5:38.

15. Matt. 11:12.

16. **Forty days in the wilderness.**

Matt. 4:1–11; Mark 1:12, 13; Luke 4:1–13.

17. **Jesus in Gethsemane.** Matt. 26:36–46; Mark 14:32–42; Luke 22:39–46.

18. Matt. 7:14.

19. Matt. 22:11, 12; Rev. 19:7, 8.

20. **"I will multiply thy seed..."** Gen. 13:16; 15:5; 22:17, 18; Jer. 33:22; Heb. 11:12.

21. **Trailing clouds of glory.** "Our birth is but a sleep and a forgetting: / The Soul that rises with us, our life's Star, / Hath had elsewhere its setting, / And cometh from afar: / Not in entire forgetfulness, / And not in utter nakedness, / But trailing clouds of glory do we come / From God, who is our home..." William Wordsworth, "Ode: Intimations of Immortality from Recollections of Early Childhood," stanza 5 (1807).

22. Exod. 33:20. For teaching on this verse, see Mark L. Prophet and Elizabeth Clare Prophet, *The Lost Teachings of Jesus II* (Livingston, Montana: Summit University Press, 1986), pp. 121–22, $16.95 paperback, $21.95 hardback.

CORRESPONDENCE
Corona Class Lesson 4
The Father

1. John 11:25.

2. Matt. 11:11; Luke 7:28.

3. Mark 4:39; John 14:27.

4. **The veil.** Exod. 26:31–33; 40:3, 21, 22, 26; Lev. 16:2, 12, 15; 21:23; 24:3; Heb. 6:19; 9:3; 10:20.

5. Gen. 19:26.

6. Gen. 2:16, 17.

7. Ps. 22:27; Dan. 12:1–3; Luke 1:16.

8. **"Love one another..."** John

13:34, 35; 15:9–17; I John 3:11–24.

9. John 8:58.

10. **"Watch with Me."** Matt. 26:36–46. In 1964 the Master Jesus inaugurated the *"Watch with Me" Jesus' Vigil of the Hours*—a one-hour worldwide service of prayer, affirmation, and song for the protection of the Christ consciousness in every son and daughter of God. This service commemorates the vigil Jesus kept alone in the Garden of Gethsemane when he said: "Could ye not watch with me one hour?" The Lord Jesus has called students of the Ascended Masters to give this Watch individually or in group action once a week, at the same time each week, so that at every hour of the day and night someone somewhere is keeping the vigil. Originally, a chart was kept at The Summit Lighthouse headquarters showing who had volunteered and to see to it that at no time would there be a vacancy in this unceasing watch for world peace and freedom. Available in 32-page booklet, $2.95; on single cassette B83143, $6.50; and with healing lecture on 2-cassette album *"Physician, Heal Thyself!"* (A83143), $9.95.

CORRESPONDENCE
Corona Class Lesson 5
Reciprocity

1. Exod. 3:13–15.

2. John 12:23, 28–32.

3. Col. 2:9.

4. John 19:30.

5. Gen. 1:4, 10, 12, 18, 21, 25, 31.

6. Matt. 25:14–30.

7. **Good fruit after its kind.**

Matt. 3:8, 10; 7:16–20; 12:33; Luke 6:43–45; John 15:1–17.

8. Mark 16:20.
9. John 10:10.
10. Matt. 20:1–16.
11. Mark 12:41–44.
12. II Cor. 3:18.
13. **"Be of good cheer..."** Matt. 9:2; 14:27; John 16:33; Acts 23:11.

CORRESPONDENCE
Corona Class Lesson 5
Crown

14. Acts 9:5; 26:14.
15. Luke 7:11–17.
16. Mark 5:22–24, 35–43.
17. John 11:1–44.
18. Rom. 8:7.

CORRESPONDENCE
Corona Class Lesson 6
Constancy

1. Eph. 2:8, 9.
2. James 2:17, 20, 26.
3. John 14:12.
4. Luke 24:27, 32, 45.
5. **"The Lost Chord."** Words by Adelaide A. Procter, music by Arthur Sullivan (1878): "Seated one day at the organ, I was weary and ill at ease, / And my fingers wandered idly over the noisy keys; / I know not what I was playing, or what I was dreaming then, / But I struck one chord of music like the sound of a great Amen, / Like the sound of a great Amen. / It flooded the crimson twilight / Like the close of an angel's Psalm, / And it lay on my fevered spirit / With a touch of infinite calm; / It quieted pain and sorrow like love overcoming strife, / It seemed the harmonious echo from our discordant life. / It linked all perplexed meanings into one perfect peace, / And trembled away into silence as if it were loth to cease. / I have sought, but I seek it vainly, that one lost chord divine, / Which came from the soul of the organ and entered into mine: / It may be that Death's bright angel will speak in that chord again; / It may be that only in Heaven I shall hear that grand Amen."

6. Matt. 6:19–21.
7. Matt. 13:45, 46.
8. "Faint heart never won fair lady." Old English proverb.
9. Luke 1:26–38, 46–55.
10. John 3:30.
11. Isa. 11:6.
12. **"Except ye become as a little child..."** Matt. 18:3; Mark 10:15; Luke 18:17.
13. From the hymn "I'll Be a Sunbeam," words by Nellie Talbot, music by Edwin O. Excell (1900).

PURPOSE
Corona Class Lesson 7
Perfection

1. John 14:1, 27.
2. Matt. 3:10; 7:19.
3. II Pet. 2:18.
4. John 8:32.
5. **The soul versus the ego.** Much of psychology has supported the ego and denied the parallel path of the soul. The distinction accorded the ego has extinguished the path of the soul: the soul yearns to come back into alignment with Reality but psychology has given recognition neither to the soul nor to the God Presence. Its theories are based on "lower mind" concepts and sexual and aggressive drives. The ego seeks recognition

from other egos. The soul seeks recognition from the I AM Presence. Ironically, the root *psyche,* from which this brand of study derives its name, means "soul."

6. Sir Edwin Arnold, trans., *The Song Celestial or Bhagavad-Gita* (London: Routledge & Kegan Paul, 1948), p. 9.

7. I Cor. 3:10.

8. **The Temple of Life's Victory.** On June 3, 1960, the Ascended Master El Morya announced an unprecedented dispensation from the Karmic Board: "A mighty Temple of Victory is to be built in this nation for all mankind, dedicated to the Presence of Almighty God. It shall be called *'I AM' the Temple of Life's Victory*"—the "first temple of the Great White Brotherhood known to the outer world since Atlantean days." The pattern for this magnificent, vast temple was lowered into the etheric realms of earth, but it requires the acceptance of the gift and the full appreciation of its significance by the sons and daughters of God before it can be externalized in the physical plane.

9. John 1:9; 8:12; 9:5; 12:46.

10. Matt. 5:14–16.

Corona Class Lesson 8
Sainthood

1. **That the soul be not puffed up.** I Cor. 4:6, 18, 19; 8:1; 13:4; Col. 2:18.

2. Rom. 3:23; Phil. 3:14.

3. The name **Immanuel** means "God with us." See Isa. 7:14; 8:8, 10; Matt. 1:23.

4. John 1:9.

5. John 8:12; 9:5.

6. John 8:28–32.

7. John 11:25.

8. I John 4:8, 16.

9. **Favor with God and man.** I Sam. 2:26; Prov. 3:1–4; Luke 2:52.

10. Isa. 9:6.

11. John 14:9.

Corona Class Lesson 9
Example

1. Mark 16:15.

2. Luke 23:34.

3. Matt. 18:21, 22.

4. **Jesus accused of being possessed.** Mark 3:22; John 7:20; 8:48, 52; 10:20.

5. **Persecution to be expected.** Matt. 5:10–12; Luke 11:49, 50; 21:12–19; John 15:18–21.

6. **"What must I do to be saved?"** Matt. 19:16, 25; Mark 10:17, 26; Luke 10:25; 13:23; 18:18, 26.

7. Matt. 10:29–31.

8. John 14:9, 10.

9. Luke 2:14.

10. **The two-edged sword.** Ps. 149:6; Heb. 4:12; Rev. 1:16.

Corona Class Lesson 10
Heart

1. The Ascended Masters El Morya, Kuthumi, and Djwal Kul were embodied as the **Three Wise Men** (Matt. 2:1–12). El Morya (Melchior) brought to the Christ Child the gift of gold, Kuthumi (Balthazar) the gift of frankincense, and Djwal Kul (Caspar) the gift of myrrh.

2. John 1:9; Luke 2:10, 11.

3. I Pet. 3:4; Eph. 3:16, 17.

4. **"Thou art my beloved Son . . ."** Ps. 2:7; Acts 13:33; Heb. 1:5; 5:5.

5. Isa. 25:8; I Cor. 15:54.
6. John 4:35.
7. Ps. 46:10.
8. Ps. 121:1, 2.
9. Luke 2:14.
10. Matt. 10:6; 15:24.
11. John 1:14; 3:16, 18; I John 4:9.
12. Matt. 5:16; I Pet. 2:12.

PURPOSE
Corona Class Lesson 11
Innocence

1. Mark 5:25–34.
2. Ps. 1:1; II Thess. 3:11; I Pet. 4:15.
3. Ps. 23:4.
4. Mark 2:19; John 3:29; Rev. 19:7–9.
5. Matt. 25:1–13.
6. **The Fátima message.** See Mark L. Prophet and Elizabeth Clare Prophet, *The Lost Teachings of Jesus II* (Livingston, Montana: Summit University Press, 1986), p. 552, n. 132, $16.95 paperback, $21.95 hardback.
7. Luke 18:11.
8. **Noncondemnation.** See the Ascended Master El Morya's teaching on criticism, condemnation, and judgment in *A Report,* reprinted from his October 26, 1962 *Pearl of Wisdom* (vol. 5, no. 43); 10-page pamphlet (Livingston, Montana: Summit University Press, 1981), $.25.
9. Luke 9:56.
10. John 3:17.
11. Matt. 28:20.
12. Ps. 37:11; Matt. 5:5.
13. **"Whom the LORD loveth he chasteneth..."** Prov. 3:11, 12; Heb. 12:5–11; Rev. 3:19.
14. **"Whosoever will save his life..."** Matt. 10:39; 16:25; Mark 8:35; Luke 9:24; John 12:25.

15. Acts 20:35; Luke 14:12–14.
16. John 14:2.

PURPOSE
Corona Class Lesson 12
Recognition

1. Job 38:7.
2. Luke 2:8–20; Matt. 2:1–12; Rev. 22:16.
3. **"Hosanna!" "Away with him!"** Matt. 21:9, 15; Mark 11:9, 10; 15:13, 14; Luke 23:18–21. See Elizabeth Clare Prophet, March 27, 1983, "The Acceptance and the Rejection of the Living Christ," *Conclave of the Friends of Christ,* 16-cassette album (A83063), The Summit Lighthouse, $85.00 (or single cassette B83063, $6.50); and 1983 *Pearls of Wisdom,* vol. 26, no. 37, pp. 393–418.

PURPOSE
Corona Class Lesson 12
Mission

4. Luke 21:19.
5. **Priesthood of Melchizedek.** Gen. 14:18; Ps. 110:4; Heb. 5:5–10; 6:20; 7.

TRANSFIGURATION
Corona Class Lesson 13
Light

1. **Capitalization of the qualities of God.** When attributes become personifications of the Deity or a member of the Trinity, they are capitalized. Often the distinction is moot as to whether or not a quality of God is, in fact, interchangeable with our conception of God personified in and through and as his attributes. Such words that come under this category are *light, love, truth, mind,* and *being.*

It is up to the reader to discern for himself that God both owns these qualities and professes them. They are always his. He *is* his qualities and endows them with his personhood—e.g., God is Light, God is Love (both with a capital *L*). Contrast: God's light, God's love (lowercased). The Law (capitalized) is God in manifestation.

In some cases, when embodied mankind manifest the attributes of God, they are lowercased. In other instances, a quality of God permeates both heaven and earth, God and man; and wherever it is seen it is clearly through that presence—that omnipresence—as well as that personal God.

The absolute or relative nature of a quality or its infinite or finite nature may also determine whether or not it is capitalized. The choice of deference may vary from individual to individual. Every reader may maintain his own preference. He is welcomed to do so.

If all qualities of God were capitalized, of course, it becomes clear that everything in the book could be capitalized! Thus, for readability, we have lowercased all but the most prominent manifestations of the Deity. The absence of capitalization, however, does not alter the meaning of the word itself—as in *angel*.

2. I John 1:5.
3. Deut. 4:24; 9:3.
4. Eph. 6:16.
5. **The footstool kingdom.** Isa. 66:1; Matt. 5:35; Acts 7:49.
6. John 8:44.

7. For more on the long-hidden history of the **archdeceivers of mankind, creation of mechanization man, genetic experimentation, and laggard evolutions,** see the following Summit University Press publications: the Great Divine Director, "The Mechanization Concept," 1965 *Pearls of Wisdom,* vol. 8, nos. 3–26, pp. 9–142, $16.95; Elizabeth Clare Prophet, *Forbidden Mysteries of Enoch: The Untold Story of Men and Angels,* $12.95; Mark L. Prophet and Elizabeth Clare Prophet, *The Lost Teachings of Jesus II,* pp. 300–332, 340–42, $16.95 paperback, $21.95 hardback; and Elizabeth Clare Prophet, *Life Begets Life,* 16-cassette album (A83034), $85.00.
8. Matt. 17:2; Mark 9:3; Luke 9:29; John 19:23.
9. Rev. 22:1.
10. **The Transfiguration.** Read Matt. 17:1–13; Mark 9:2–13; Luke 9:28–36.

TRANSFIGURATION
Corona Class Lesson 14
Acceleration

1. II Cor. 5:17; Rev. 21:5.
2. Matt. 17:5.
3. Matt. 19:28.

TRANSFIGURATION
Corona Class Lesson 15
Possibility

1. For the Gospel accounts of **Good Friday, the crucifixion, and the resurrection,** read Matt. 27; 28; Mark 15; 16; Luke 22:66–71; 23; 24; and John 18:28–40; 19; 20.
2. Matt. 15:13.
3. John 10:7, 9; 14:6; Matt. 7:7, 8; Luke 11:9, 10.
4. I John 4:18.

TRANSFIGURATION
Corona Class Lesson 16
Obedience

1. I Cor. 15:53, 54; II Cor. 5:4.
2. II Kings 2:1–15.
3. Matt. 25:23.

TRANSFIGURATION
Corona Class Lesson 17
Power

1. See *Saint Germain On Alchemy: For the Adept in the Aquarian Age* (Livingston, Montana: Summit University Press, 1985), p. 171, $5.95.

TRANSFIGURATION
Corona Class Lesson 18
Wisdom

1. Eph. 3:16.
2. I Kings 3:5–15; II Chron. 1:7–12.
3. Mark 9:3.

SIN
Corona Class Lesson 19
Law

1. **Incense and sacrificial offerings.** Exod. 30:1, 7–10; 40:5, 6, 26–29; Lev. 1–7; Num. 15:17, 18, 22–31; 28; 29.
2. John 14:3.
3. John 8:7.
4. Rom. 3:10.
5. Ps. 51:5.
6. Rom. 3:23.
7. John 3:16, 17.
8. **Shekinah** [Hebrew for "dwelling" or "Presence"]: the visible majesty of the presence of God which has descended to dwell among men; God's presence in the world as manifested in natural and supernatural phenomena. Examples of the Shekinah as seen in the Old Testament: the burning bush (Exod. 3:2), the cloud on Mount Sinai (Exod. 24:16,

17), the Divine Presence that rested over the mercy seat of the ark of the covenant (Exod. 25:21, 22; Lev. 16:2), and the glory of the LORD that filled the tabernacle (Exod. 40:34, 35) and later the Temple of Solomon (I Kings 8:10, 11). In the New Testament the Shekinah is seen in "the glory of the Lord" shining round the angel who appeared to the shepherds (Luke 2:9) and in the cloud on the mount of transfiguration (Matt. 17:5). Ultimately, it is seen by Christian theologians to be the glory of God which became incarnate in Jesus—"And the Word was made flesh and dwelt among us, and we beheld his glory, the glory as of the only begotten of the Father, full of grace and truth" (John 1:14).

9. I Cor. 15:56.
10. For further teaching on the **violet flame, dynamic decrees, and the science of the spoken Word,** see the following Summit University Press publications and tape albums:

Mark L. Prophet and Elizabeth Clare Prophet, "The Violet Flame for God-Realization" in *The Lost Teachings of Jesus II*, pp. 395–490, $16.95 paperback, $21.95 hardback.

"Violet Flame: Sacred Fire of Transmutation" in Kuthumi, *Studies of the Human Aura*, special color section following p. 98, $5.95.

Mark L. Prophet and Elizabeth Clare Prophet, *The Science of the Spoken Word*, $7.95.

Jesus and Kuthumi, *Prayer and Meditation*, $9.95.

Mark and Elizabeth Prophet, *The Science of the Spoken Word: Why and How to Decree Effectively*, 4-cassette album (A7736), $26.00.

Elizabeth Clare Prophet, *"I'm Stumping for the Coming Revolution in Higher Consciousness!"* 3-cassette album (A7917), $19.50.

Decrees and Songs by the Messenger Mark L. Prophet (introductory), 2-cassette album (A8202), $12.95.

Rainbow Rays: Out of the Mouth of the Messenger (intermediate), 2-cassette album (A83018), $12.95.

Mantras of the Ascended Masters for the Initiation of the Chakras, 36-page "Stump Booklet" and accompanying 5 cassettes of songs, decrees, and mantras. Booklet $2.00, cassettes $6.50 ea.

Prayers, Meditations, and Dynamic Decrees for the Coming Revolution in Higher Consciousness, Sections I, II, and III (looseleaf), $2.95 ea.

11. **Justice to evildoers.** Jude 4–19; Ps. 37:1, 2, 9; Isa. 31:1, 2; Jer. 21:12; 23:2, 19.
12. **"With what measure ye mete..."** Matt. 7:2; Mark 4:24; Luke 6:38.

SIN
Corona Class Lesson 20
Love

1. Luke 15:11–32.
2. Isa. 25:8; Rom. 6:23; I Cor. 15:54.
3. Matt. 3:1–12; Mark 1:4; Luke 3:3.
4. **Power to remit or retain sin.** Matt. 16:19; 18:18; 19:28; John 20:23.
5. Matt. 9:2, 5; Luke 7:48.

6. John 5:14; 8:11.
7. **God as a consuming fire.** Deut. 4:24; 9:3; Heb. 12:29.
8. Ps. 139:7.
9. John 14:6.

SIN
Corona Class Lesson 21
Conscience

1. Luke 23:34.
2. Prov. 23:7.
3. Exod. 20:3; Deut. 5:7.
4. Matt. 24:24; Mark 13:22.
5. Matt. 5:18; Luke 16:17.
6. **Sin not imputed unto Abraham.** Gen. 15:6; Rom. 4:3, 8, 20–24; James 2:23; Ps. 32:2.
7. I Pet. 1:19; Eph. 5:27.
8. **With God all things are possible.** Matt. 19:26; Mark 10:27; Luke 1:37; 18:27.

SIN
Corona Class Lesson 22
Sacrifice

1. Matt. 5:3.
2. Ps. 23:5.
3. **Atlantean miscreations.** See Mark L. Prophet and Elizabeth Clare Prophet, *The Lost Teachings of Jesus II* (Livingston, Montana: Summit University Press, 1986), pp. 300–304, $16.95 paperback, $21.95 hardback; and Edgar Evans Cayce, *Edgar Cayce on Atlantis*, ed. Hugh Lynn Cayce (New York: Warner Books, 1968), pp. 60–61, 68–72, 99–107, 131–32.
4. **Child sacrifice.** Lev. 18:21; 20:2–5; Deut. 12:31; 18:10; II Kings 16:3; 17:17; 21:6; 23:10; II Chron. 28:3; 33:6; Ps. 106:37, 38.
5. **Nephilim** [Hebrew "those who fell" or "those who were cast down," from the Semitic root *naphal* 'to fall']: A biblical race

of giants or demigods, referred to in Genesis 6:4 ("There were *giants* in the earth in those days..."); the fallen angels who were cast out of heaven into the earth (Rev. 12:7–9). Zecharia Sitchin concludes from his study of ancient Sumerian texts that the Nephilim were an extraterrestrial race who "fell" to earth (landed) in spacecraft 450,000 years ago. See Elizabeth Clare Prophet, *Forbidden Mysteries of Enoch: The Untold Story of Men and Angels* (Livingston, Montana: Summit University Press, 1983), pp. 61–67, $12.95; the Great Divine Director, "The Mechanization Concept," 1965 *Pearls of Wisdom*, vol. 8, no. 15 (Livingston, Montana: Summit University Press, 1980), p. 80, $16.95; Zecharia Sitchin, "The Nefilim: People of the Fiery Rockets" in *The Twelfth Planet* (New York: Avon Books, 1976), pp. 128–72, 410.

6. **Child sacrifice denounced by the prophets.** Jer. 7:31, 32; 19:1–6; 32:35; Ezek. 16:20, 21, 36; 20:26, 31; 23:37–39; Isa. 57:5; Amos 5:25, 26; Mic. 6:7.

7. Matt. 26:28; John 1:29; I Pet. 1:19; Rev. 7:14; 12:11.

8. Heb. 9:22.

9. **Sin blotted out.** Ps. 51:1, 9; Isa. 43:25; 44:22; Jer. 31:34; Acts 3:19; Heb. 8:12; 10:17.

10. "Put off the old man..." Eph. 4:22–24; Col. 3:9, 10; Rom. 6:6.

11. John 7:38.

12. Matt. 11:30.

13. **God is no respecter of persons.** Deut. 10:17; II Sam.

14:14; Acts 10:34; Rom. 2:11; Eph. 6:9; Col. 3:25; I Pet. 1:17.

Sin
Corona Class Lesson 23
Atonement

1. Matt. 15:14; Luke 6:39.

2. Mal. 4:2.

3. Heb. 9:23.

4. John 5:14.

5. Arcturus, January 1959, "Violet Fire—The Divine Memory of Perfection," *The Lighthouse of Freedom*, vol. 1, no. 3 (February 1959), pp. 12–13.

6. Matt. 20:23; Mark 10:39.

7. Matt. 26:39, 42; John 18:11.

8. The eternal **Creator, Preserver, and 'Destroyer'**—Brahma, Vishnu, and Shiva—of the Hindu Trinity parallels the Western concept of the Father, Son, and Holy Spirit. Brahma, as the Father figure and the First Person of the Trinity, is seen as the Immense Being—the Creator, Supreme Ruler, Lawgiver, Sustainer, and Source of All Knowledge. Vishnu, the Second Person of the Trinity, is the immortal Son, the Preserver of the divine design, the Restorer of the universe by Wisdom's light. Shiva, as the Holy Spirit and Third Person of the Trinity, is the Lord of Love outpicturing the dual nature of Destroyer/Deliverer—the fearsome one who drives away sin, disease, and demons of delusion.

According to the law of the conservation of energy, "energy can be neither created nor destroyed." Universal energy goes through successive stages of transformation. Technically speaking, the violet flame purifies, refines, and transmutes. To purify is a part of the process of creation, to refine of preservation, and to transmute of deliverance ('destruction') through the disassociation and repolarization of matter. All three functions change the electronic vibration of matter and consciousness. Hence, the alchemical action of the violet flame is a function of the Trinity: Creator, Preserver, Destroyer in their respective roles as Purifier, Refiner, Transmuter.

9. I Sam. 15:22.
10. Rev. 1:5; 7:14.

Sin
Corona Class Lesson 23
Mercy

11. **The rich man and Lazarus.** Read Luke 16:19–31.
12. Matt. 18:11–14; Luke 15:3–7. See also Jesus' discourse on the Good Shepherd, John 10:1–18.
13. **Vanity and vexation of spirit.** Eccles. 1:14, 17; 2:11, 17, 26; 4:4, 16; 6:9.
14. **The lake of fire.** Rev. 21:8; 19:20; 20:10, 14, 15.
15. Rev. 20:13, 14.
16. Isa. 1:18; Jer. 31:34.
17. **The second death.** Rev. 2:11; 20:6, 14, 15; 21:8; Matt. 25:41.
18. **Angels who fell.** Jude 6; Enoch 7–16; 19; 63; 68:1–18; 85–87; 89:32, 33; 105:12–14; Rev. 12:7–9. See also Isa. 14:12–17; II Pet. 2:4.
19. **The latter days.** Num. 24:14; Deut. 4:30; 31:29; Job 19:25; Jer. 23:20; 30:24; 48:47; 49:39; Ezek. 38:16; Dan. 2:28; 10:14; Hos. 3:5; I Tim. 4:1; I John 2:18.

20. **Mockers in the last days.** Jude 18, 19; II Tim. 3:1–9; II Pet. 3:3.
21. James 4:3.
22. Rev. 21:1.
23. Matt. 7:7, 8; Luke 11:9, 10.
24. Jude 12; II Pet. 2:13.

Sin
Corona Class Lesson 24
Responsibility

1. Henry Wadsworth Longfellow, "Retribution," in *Poetic Aphorisms*, translated from Friedrich von Logau's *Sinngedichte* (1654), taken from the original Greek.
2. Eccles. 3:14–17.
3. Matt. 13:33; I Cor. 5:6–8; Gal. 5:9.
4. Luke 17:21.
5. Rom. 8:7; I Cor. 3:3.
6. Gen. 3:15.
7. Phil. 2:12.

Discipleship
Corona Class Lesson 25
Requirement

1. **Watch and pray.** Matt. 26:41; Mark 13:33; Luke 21:36; I Pet. 4:7.
2. **Bread from heaven.** Exod. 16:4, 14, 15; Neh. 9:15; John 6:31–35, 41, 47–51, 58.
3. Shakespeare, *As You Like It*, act 2, scene 7, lines 138–41. Francis Bacon was the author of the Shakespearean plays.
4. Luke 10:42.
5. Luke 24:13–35.
6. Matt. 4:4.
7. Matt. 7:14.
8. **"Lovest thou me more than these?"** Read John 21:3–17. Here Jesus demonstrates his power as capable of producing money, success, and material affluence. The supreme test of the disciple is to love the

Master for the very presence of the Godhead with him, and to love his power and attainment not for self-gain but as the means to feed his sheep the essence of his Light. Peter, the opportunist, must be reminded one last time that the love transferred to him by his Lord is solely for the comfort, healing, and illumination of the children of God. The temptation will ever be there to build the powerful material church devoid of the Spirit, whose priesthood, themselves empty, fails to impart the true mysteries of the Body of God in the ritual of Holy Communion.

9. **Paul's conversion.** Acts 9:1–22; 22:1–16; 26:9–18.

10. I Cor. 3:13–15.

11. **Paul's teaching on karma.** See Corona Class Lesson 2, pp. 17–18.

12. **Build on the Rock.** Matt. 7:24–27; Luke 6:47–49; I Cor. 10:4.

13. Matt. 16:18.

14. Mark 13:31.

15. **True discipleship.** John 21:15. Christ demanded of Peter a deep love (Greek, *agapas*), a divine love which was and is demanded by the law of discipleship encompassing the initiations of personal Christhood.

16. **The lost sheep.** Matt. 18:12–14; Luke 15:3-7.

17. Isa. 6:8.

DISCIPLESHIP
Corona Class Lesson 26
Consecration

1. I Sam. 3:9, 10.

2. Acts 2:1–4.

3. Prov. 29:18.

4. The origin of the **Peace Prayer**, attributed through the centuries to Saint Francis, is uncertain as it is not among Francis' authenticated writings. According to the research of Fr. James Meyer, O.F.M., the prayer could have come from one of the "Sayings of Brother Giles" in the *Fioretti (The Little Flowers of Saint Francis):* "Blessed is he who loves and does not therefore desire to be loved. Blessed is he who fears and does not therefore desire to be feared. Blessed is he who serves and does not therefore desire to be served..." But it is also possible, Fr. Meyer explains, that Giles drew his inspiration from Francis.

The earliest printed version of the Peace Prayer appeared in a book published in 1917 in France, which attributed its inspiration to the Testament of William the Conqueror. A copy of the prayer was presented to Pope Benedict (1914–1922), who was delighted to have it and requested it to be circulated widely. When it was distributed in Europe during World War I, it was printed on the back of a holy picture of Saint Francis. Francis Cardinal Spellman of New York is credited with popularizing the prayer during World War II by distributing it for the first time in English. Following is the entire prayer translated from the French:

Lord, make me an instrument of your peace: / Where there is hatred, let me sow love; / Where there is discord, harmony; / Where there is injury, pardon; / Where there is error, truth; / Where there is doubt, faith; / Where there is despair, hope; / Where there is darkness, light; / Where there is sadness, joy; / O Divine Master, grant that I may not so much seek / To be consoled, as to console; / To be understood, as to understand; / To be loved, as to love: / For it is in giving that we receive; / It is in forgetting self that we find ourselves; / It is in pardoning that we are pardoned; / And it is in dying that we are born to eternal Life. (See Fr. Marion A. Habig, "Origin of the Peace Prayer," *Franciscan Herald,* May 1974, pp. 151–53.)

5. Matt. 25:40, 45.
6. II Cor. 12:9.
7. **To cleanse the lepers.** Matt. 10:8; 11:5; Mark 1:40–45; Luke 17:12–19.

There is a story told in the *Fioretti* of a leper who was being cared for by the brothers in Saint Francis' order. The leper was so blasphemous and abusive in his speech that none could bear to come near him. When Francis visited him, the leper complained that the brothers had not looked after him as they should, whereupon Francis offered to care for him himself.

The leper asked him what he could do that the others could not. Francis promised that he would do all he wished. The leper said, "I want you to wash me all over because the odor is such that I cannot stand it." Francis then prepared water with many sweet-scented herbs, undressed him and began to wash him with his hands. Miraculously,

wherever Francis touched, the leprosy disappeared and the flesh was healed.

As the leper's body was healed, his soul experienced conversion also. Overcome with remorse for his sins, he began to weep bitterly, accusing himself for all the pain he had caused others. After fifteen days of deep penance, he fell ill and passed on. His soul, brighter than the sun, appeared to Saint Francis while he was praying in a forest. Pouring out gratitude and blessings, he announced to Francis that that day he was going to Paradise.

8. Matt. 10:38; 16:24; Luke 14:27.
9. James 2:14–26.
10. Gen. 37:5–20.
11. Gen. 41:39–44.
12. Gen. 44:2.
13. Matt. 4:18, 19; Mark 1:16, 17.
14. Gen. 41:15–57; 45:6, 11.
15. Acts 17:30.
16. John 10:16.
17. Matt. 5:14.
18. Acts 1:9–11.

DISCIPLESHIP
Corona Class Lesson 27
Vision

1. Suggested reading for those who would truly **"imitate"** the **Master** on the path of discipleship: Thomas à Kempis, *The Imitation of Christ* (New York: Grosset & Dunlap).
2. John 10:38; 14:10, 11; 17:21.
3. **'Evil One'.** The Devil; Lucifer, who first deified *Evil* and then became the personification, or personhood, of that deified energy *veil.* See the Jerusalem Bible, Matt. 13:19, 38; John 17:15; I John 2:13, 14; 3:12; 5:18, 19; and Archangel Gabriel

on **Good and Evil,** *Mysteries of the Holy Grail,* pp. 117–38, 153–62, 195–210, 236–38, $12.95.
4. Phil. 4:8.
5. I Kings 19:12.
6. Rev. 1:15; 14:2; 19:6.
7. **Delight in the Law of the LORD.** Pss. 1:2; 112:1; 119:16, 24, 35, 47, 70, 77, 143, 174; Rom. 7:22.
8. Rev. 8:3, 4.
9. Rom. 6:13, 19; 7:22, 23; I Cor. 6:15; Col. 3:5.
10. I Cor. 13:12.

DISCIPLESHIP
Corona Class Lesson 28
Will

1. **Jesus' control of the elements.** Matt. 17:24–27; 21:18–20; Mark 4:35–41; 6:33–44; 8:1–9; John 2:1–11; 21:3–6.
2. Luke 22:42.
3. John 10:10.
4. John 5:25.
5. John 14:1.
6. Luke 12:32.
7. John 13:16; 15:20; Matt. 10:24.
8. Matt. 26:27.
9. **I think, therefore I am.** "Cogito, ergo sum." René Descartes, *Le Discours de la Méthode,* 1637.
10. **Love thy neighbor as thyself.** Lev. 19:18; Matt. 19:19; 22:39; Mark 12:31; Luke 10:27; Rom. 13:9; Gal. 5:14; James 2:8.
11. James 1:4.

DISCIPLESHIP
Corona Class Lesson 29
The Calling

1. Matt. 4:21, 22; Mark 1:19, 20.
2. **The rich young ruler.** Matt. 19:16–22; Mark 10:17–22; Luke 18:18–23.
3. Matt. 7:13, 14; Luke 13:24.
4. Matt. 7:7; Luke 11:9.
5. Matt. 6:33.
6. I John 2:18.

7. Matt. 20:16; Mark 10:31.
8. Matt. 22:14.
9. Rev. 11:15.
10. II Pet. 1:10.

DISCIPLESHIP
Corona Class Lesson 29
The Opportunity

11. See Corona Class Lesson 28, n. 1.
12. **Meditation of the sacred fire breath.** See Djwal Kul, *Intermediate Studies of the Human Aura,* pp. 67–75, $7.95; and "The Healing of the Etheric Body: Djwal Kul's Breathing Exercise for the Integration of the Four Lower Bodies," on *Emerald Matrix,* 16-cassette album (A82121), $85.00 (or single cassette B82128, $6.50).
13. Isa. 11:9; Hab. 2:14.
14. Heb. 2:3, 4.

DISCIPLESHIP
Corona Class Lesson 30
Mastership

1. John 6:53.
2. I Cor. 9:24; Phil. 3:14.
3. Ps. 61:2.
4. John 12:44, 45, 49, 50; 14:24.
5. Matt. 19:28.
6. Matt. 25:14–30; Luke 12:42–48; 16:1–13; 19:12–26.

HABIT
Corona Class Lesson 31
Illumination

1. I Cor. 13:9, 12.
2. Gen. 11:1–9.
3. Ps. 19:2.
4. For Lord Maitreya's teaching on this subject, see "The Overcoming of Fear through Decrees" in *The Science of the Spoken Word,* pp. 21–23.
5. **The barren fig tree.** Matt. 21:18–22; Mark 11:12–14, 20–26.
6. Jer. 1:10; 18:7, 9; 31:28.

HABIT
Corona Class Lesson 32
Thought

1. II Cor. 6:2; Isa. 49:8.
2. Eph. 2:8.
3. Phil. 2:12.
4. Heb. 13:8.
5. Matt. 5:39.
6. James 4:7.
7. II Tim. 2:15.
8. John 16:2.
9. Matt. 6:23.
10. Matt. 7:3–5; Luke 6:41, 42.
11. **Moneychangers must be cast out.** Matt. 21:12, 13; Mark 11:15–17; Luke 19:45, 46; John 2:13–17.
12. I John 2:18.

HABIT
Corona Class Lesson 33
Character

1. Gal. 4:4.
2. John 5:14.
3. Isa. 61:1.
4. Gen. 4:7.
5. Luke 12:48.
6. Rom. 8:17.

HABIT
Corona Class Lesson 34
Call

1. Matt. 18:19, 20.
2. Matt. 7:9; Luke 11:11.
3. Luke 17:21.
4. II Pet. 3:8.
5. I Cor. 3:16, 17.
6. **The Good Samaritan.** Read Luke 10:30–37.
7. Ps. 139:14.

HABIT
Corona Class Lesson 35
Spirituality

1. Pss. 2:1; 46:6; Acts 4:25.
2. **Saint Francis and the Christ Child.** In 1223 Brother Francis prepared a special Christmas celebration. His heart's desire was to commemorate the birth of Christ in a way which would vividly portray the suffering and discomfort the Saviour had borne. He asked his devout friend Messer John Vellita to set up a real manger filled with hay in a grotto on a steep wooded hill in Greccio. An ox and ass were also brought to the spot, just as at Bethlehem.

At midnight on Christmas Eve, the brothers and neighboring people came bearing candles and lighted torches that brilliantly illumined the night. Together they celebrated a solemn Mass over the crèche; and Francis, with a countenance of supreme compassion and unspeakable joy, delivered a moving sermon on the "Bethlehem Babe." For a moment, his friend John saw a beautiful infant lying in the manger, appearing almost lifeless. Then he saw Francis step forward and lift the Child, who opened his eyes as if waking from a deep sleep and smiled. The vision signified that although Christ had been asleep and forgotten in the hearts of many, he was being brought to life again through the devotion of his servant Francis.

See Thomas of Celano, *The First Life of St. Francis*, and St. Bonaventure, *Major Life of St. Francis*, in Marion A. Habig, ed., *St. Francis of Assisi, Writings and Early Biographies: English Omnibus of the Sources for the Life of St. Francis*, 3rd ed. (Chicago: Franciscan Herald Press, 1973), pp. 299–302, 710–11; Omer Englebert, *Saint Francis of Assisi: A Biography,*

2nd ed., trans. Eve Marie Cooper (Ann Arbor, Mich.: Servant Books, 1979), pp. 232–34; Johannes Jörgensen, *Saint Francis of Assisi*, trans. T. O'Conor Sloane (1912; reprint, Garden City, N.Y.: Image Books, 1955), pp. 216–17; and Felix Timmermans, *The Perfect Joy of St. Francis*, trans. Raphael Brown (1952; reprint, Garden City, N.Y.: Image Books, 1955), pp. 228–31.

HABIT
Corona Class Lesson 36
Seed

1. Rev. 12:5.
2. Ps. 2:9.
3. Rev. 11:15.
4. **"Know Thyself."** One of the ancient maxims of the Seven Wise Men of Greece, inscribed on the walls of the pronaos (vestibule) of the Temple of Apollo at Delphi. Also attributed to Plato, Pythagoras, Socrates.
5. Matt. 24:27.

IMMORTALITY
Corona Class Lesson 37
Perfection

1. Gen. 6:5; 8:21.
2. I Cor. 15:26.
3. Matt. 7:13, 14.
4. **"Lost" Sheep.** Matt. 10:6; 15:24; 18:11–14. The word *lost* is from the Greek *apollumi*, also meaning "marred."
5. Dan. 7:9, 13, 22; Rev. 12:17.

IMMORTALITY
Corona Class Lesson 38
Charity

1. Eph. 2:8, 9.
2. **Karma yoga.** The path of balancing the yoke of karma—of causes and effects set in motion in this and previous lives; the path of good works evidenced in pure thoughts, feelings, words and deeds; the discipline of the four lower bodies with an emphasis on physical action for alchemical change; spiritual/physical exercises including the invoking of the sacred fire (agni yoga) in the giving of violet flame decrees (mantra and japa yoga); nonattachment to the fruit of action or to its reward. The end of the path of karma yoga is freedom from the round of rebirth through the Holy Spirit's all-consuming Love and Grace, and reunion with God, the Mighty I AM Presence, in the ritual of the ascension.

3. **Crotona.** In the sixth century B.C. Kuthumi was embodied as Pythagoras, the Greek philosopher and mathematician who founded a brotherhood of initiates at Crotona, a Greek seaport in southern Italy. The devotees who were accepted into this mystery school pursued a philosophy based on the mathematical expression of universal law, illustrated in music and in the rhythm and harmony of a highly disciplined way of life. About 500 B.C. a rejected candidate of Pythagoras' Academy incited a violent persecution resulting in the Master's death, the dissolution of his community, and the tragic destruction of much of his teaching. Thus do tools of Anti-Christ attempt the destruction of the Community of the Great White Brotherhood in every age.

4. Rom. 1:16.
5. **The Potter and the clay.** Rom.

9:20, 21; Isa. 45:9; 64:8; II Cor. 4:7.
6. Matt. 8:17.
7. Henri Estienne, *Les Prémices*, 1594.
8. Isa. 53:7.
9. Luke 2:49.
10. II Pet. 1:19.
11. Ps. 8:4, 5; Heb. 2:6–9.
12. Heb. 11:35.
13. A joyful noise unto the LORD. Pss. 66:1; 81:1; 95:1, 2; 98:4, 6; 100:1.

IMMORTALITY
Corona Class Lesson 39
Body

1. John 10:10.
2. **Light not to be hidden under a bushel.** Matt. 5:15, 16; Mark 4:21; Luke 8:16; 11:33.
3. Matt. 6:10.
4. Prov. 23:7.
5. Mal. 4:2.
6. Exod. 20:3; Deut. 5:7.
7. **'Kings' of this world.** Nephilim gods called "giants." See Corona Class Lesson 22, n. 5, *Nephilim;* and "Concealed References to the Watchers in Scripture," in *Forbidden Mysteries of Enoch: The Untold Story of Men and Angels* (contains all the Enoch texts, including the Book of Enoch and the Book of the Secrets of Enoch), pp. 263–303.
8. **Wilderness temptations: children of Israel and Jesus.** Exod. 14:10–12; 15:22–26; 16; 17:1–7; 32; 33:1–6; Num. 11; 12; 14; 16; 17; 20; 21:5–9; 25; Deut. 1:26–46; 8; 9; Matt. 4:1–11; Mark 1:12, 13; Luke 4:1–13.
9. Rev. 21:2, 10, 16.
10. John 14:30.
11. Rev. 21:27.

12. Rom. 8:2; I Cor. 15:53, 54; II Cor. 4:11; 5:4.
13. Isa. 60:1.

IMMORTALITY
Corona Class Lesson 40
Threefold Flame

1. **"Light is the alchemical key."** See *Saint Germain On Alchemy,* p. 49.
2. **Tree of Life.** Gen. 2:9; 3:22, 24; Rev. 2:7; 22:2, 14.
3. I Cor. 15:53, 54.
4. **"Balance the Threefold Flame in Me!"** decree 20.03 in *Prayers, Meditations, and Dynamic Decrees for the Coming Revolution in Higher Consciousness,* Section I.
5. **Not of this world.** John 8:23; 15:19; 17:14–18; 18:36.
6. **Saint Germain on the visualization of Light.** In *Unveiled Mysteries,* the Master Saint Germain teaches that "the first step to the control of yourself is the **stilling of all outer activity of both mind and body.**" He explains: "Fifteen to thirty minutes at night before retiring and in the morning before beginning the day's work, using the following exercise, will do wonders for anyone who will make the necessary effort.

    "For the second step: Make certain of being undisturbed, and after becoming very still, picture and *feel* your body enveloped in a dazzling white Light. The first five minutes while holding this picture, **recognize and *feel* intensely the connection between the outer-self and your Mighty God within,** focusing your attention upon the heart center and visualizing it as a golden sun.

"The next step is the **acknowledgment:** 'I now joyously accept the fullness of the Mighty God Presence—the pure Christ.' **Feel the *great brilliancy* of the 'Light' and *intensify* it in every cell of your body** for at least ten minutes longer.

"Then close the meditation by the command: **I AM a child of the Light—I love the Light—I serve the Light—I live in the Light—I AM protected, illumined, supplied, sustained by the Light, and I bless the Light.**

"Remember always: 'One becomes *that* upon which he meditates' and since all things have come forth from the Light, Light is the Supreme Perfection and God-Control of all things.

"*Contemplation* and *adoration* of the 'Light' compels *illumination* to take place in the mind—health, strength, and order to come into the body—and peace, harmony, and success to manifest in the affairs of every individual who will really do it, and seeks to maintain it. . . .

"If you will practice this exercise faithfully and feel it in every atom of your mind and body, with deep, deep *intensity*, you will receive abundant proof of the tremendous activity, power, and perfection that abides and is forever active within the Light. When you have experienced this, for even a short time, you will need no further proof. You become your own proof. The Light is the Kingdom. Enter into it and BE—at peace. Return to

the Father's house. After the first ten days of using this exercise, it is well to do it three times a day—morning, noon, and night." See Godfre Ray King, *Unveiled Mysteries*, 3rd ed. (Chicago: Saint Germain Press, 1939), pp. 11–13.

IMMORTALITY
Corona Class Lesson 41
Alpha/Omega

1. **"To roll up the universe as a curtain."** See Zechariah 5. The prophet envisions the purifying and transmutative process taking place through the action of karmic law symbolized in the "flying roll" (the etheric record of the thoughts, motives, and acts of each individual lifestream). Only the actions of the guilty are punishable; the exactness of judgment is symbolized in the ephah (a standard of measurement) and the talent of lead (the weight of karma) balanced on wings of mercy. Good deeds rest on their own merit; the energy thereof is transported to the storehouse of light, the causal body.
2. Zech. 4:6.
3. Gen. 3:22–24.
4. John 5:39.
5. John 3:34–36; 5:23–27; 12:44–50.
6. John 16:13.
7. Matt. 6:12; Luke 11:4.
8. Matt. 5:8.
9. John 3:3.
10. John 3:5–13.
11. Acts 2:2.
12. **Spiritual interpretation of the menorah.** Seven principles of the seven rays are mastered by the soul through the outpicturing of the threefold

flame in balanced action in the four lower bodies. This is accomplished in seven stages of initiation, or steps of precipitation, under the guidance and tutelage of the Lords, or Chohans, of the Seven Rays. See Zechariah 4: The angel shows the prophet a "candlestick all of gold, with a bowl upon the top of it, and seven lamps thereon, and seven pipes to the seven lamps, which are upon the top thereof: and two olive trees by it, one upon the right side of the bowl, and the other upon the left side thereof."

This vision depicts in the golden candlestick the silver cord which extends from the heart of God in the Great Central Sun to the individualized Mighty I AM Presence, passing through the Holy Christ Self and anchoring in the heart of man the illumination to carry out the will of God in love.

The bowl represents the consciousness of man, which is fed by the self-luminous, intelligent light energy which flows over the silver cord. The seven lamps represent the seven receptacles of man (spiritual centers called in the Hindu *chakras*, i.e., wheel of the Law), sustained by the sacred fire from the one Source, flowing through the seven pipes. The seven pipes typify the seven rays, or facets, of the creation which must manifest the light of God through the seven lamps.

The three central candles of the menorah blaze forth the threefold flame of power, wisdom, and love (blue, yellow, and pink) embracing the threefold nature of the Divinity—the Father, the Son, and the Holy Spirit. The two candles to the left of the blue flame of power represent the etheric and mental bodies of man, which are designed to outpicture the Fourth Ray of purity (white) and the Fifth Ray of science (green) respectively. To the right of the pink flame of love are the candles representing the emotional and physical bodies, which are designed to outpicture the Sixth Ray of devotion (purple and gold, and the ruby ray) and the Seventh Ray of ordered service (violet) respectively.

The two olive trees on either side of the candles are "the two anointed ones that stand by the Lord of the whole earth"—i.e., they represent the authority of God invested in his representatives on earth in every age who hold the scepter of power in Church and State. The tree to the left is the blue plume of power directing all levels of government, and the tree to the right is the pink plume of love which presides over the religious life of the people.

The entire symbol of the candelabra (specifically the menorah in Hebrew terminology) is enfolded in the yellow plume of illumination, the key to man's fulfillment of his sevenfold identity. Thus the complete thoughtform of the two olive trees (power and love) at either side of the candlestick (wisdom) represents the action of the threefold flame in human society, while the candles in the center interpret man's inner and outer unfoldment in the fulfillment of the divine plan.

13. **Alpha and Omega.** Rev. 1:8, 11; 21:6; 22:13.

14. **"Thy Christ, my Christ."** The consciousness of your Holy Christ Self and my Holy Christ Self, which are one as the manifestation of the only begotten Son of God, the universal Christ. See John 20:17.

IMMORTALITY
Corona Class Lesson 42
Alchemy

1. Gen. 1:4, 10, 12, 18, 21, 25, 31.
2. Ezek. 18:4, 9, 20.
3. **Come apart.** Lev. 20:24, 26; Deut. 7; Ezra 9; 10; Neh. 9:2; 10:28–30; 13:23–30; II Cor. 6:14–18.
4. **The wedding garment.** Matt. 22:11–14. See also Serapis Bey, "The Great Deathless Solar Body," in *Dossier on the Ascension*, pp. 151–59.

BEING
Corona Class Lesson 43
Man

1. Ps. 8:4; Heb. 2:6.
2. Prov. 16:18.
3. Isa. 40:31.
4. Matt. 18:14.
5. I Cor. 13:12.
6. I John 3:2.
7. Rom. 8:7; James 4:4.
8. Phil. 2:5.
9. Gen. 5:24; II Kings 2:1, 11; Mark 16:19; II Cor. 12:2–4; Heb. 11:5; Rev. 11:12.
10. Mark 9:24.
11. John 14:20.
12. John 1:5, 9.

BEING
Corona Class Lesson 44
Life

1. Mark 13:31.
2. Mark 16:20.
3. I Cor. 15:35, 40.
4. **The elements.** In the study of alchemy, the primordial substance, *materia prima*, is described as being without form, like the world before the creation ("And the earth was without form and void..." Gen. 1:2)—before all things were separated into distinct elements. In his book, *Alchemy*, Titus Burckhardt explains that the four elements—fire, air, water, and earth—"do not proceed directly from *materia prima* but from its first determination, ether, which fills all space equally." Stanislas K. De Rola in *Alchemy: The Secret Art* writes: "From the interplay of the Four Elements, and their metamorphosis one into the other, all is evolved, and the fifth element, the Quintessence, distilled."

There has been debate through the centuries as to whether ether should be considered as a fifth element. Aristotle defined it as such and the Hindus and Theosophists also speak of five elements. When discussing the transmutation of elements from one form to another, however, the alchemist is referring to the four qualities of fire, air, water, and earth, as the fifth, ether (or quintessence), is considered eternal and unchangeable.

5. Prov. 6:6.
6. See "Cosmic Cooperation between the Children of the Sun

and Elemental Life," a four-part series dictated by the Hierarchs of the Elements, in *A Prophecy of Karma to Earth and Her Evolutions* (1980 *Pearls of Wisdom*, vol. 23, nos. 14–17), pp. 75–104; and *Saint Germain On Prophecy*, pocketbook, $5.95.

7. Isa. 11:6.
8. Prov. 16:32.
9. John 4:35.

BEING
Corona Class Lesson 45
Image

1. John 3:3, 6.
2. Rom. 8:6, 7.
3. Matt. 26:11; Mark 14:7; John 12:8.
4. Matt. 5:3.
5. Matt. 3:11.
6. Matt. 11:11.
7. John 3:30.
8. Matt. 18:11; Luke 19:10.
9. Rev. 19:11–16, 19.
10. I Cor. 3:13–15; I Pet. 1:7; 4:12.
11. Josh. 24:15.
12. John 20:29.
13. Matt. 5:48.
14. John 8:44; Matt. 23:33.
15. Luke 2:37; Acts 6:4; I Thess. 5:17.
16. Isa. 11:9; Hab. 2:14.

BEING
Corona Class Lesson 46
Soul

1. I Pet. 4:15.
2. Matt. 11:12.
3. Rom. 13:10.
4. Jer. 13:23.
5. The science of the **Cosmic Clock,** taught by Mother Mary to the Messenger Elizabeth Clare Prophet, is a new-age astrology that provides the scientific means of under-standing and charting the cycles of personal and planetary karma that return to us daily as the tests and trials of the path of initiation. For further study on the Cosmic Clock, see "The Cosmic Clock: Psychology for the Aquarian Man and Woman," in *The Great White Brotherhood in the Culture, History, and Religion of America*, pp. 173–206, $10.95 (also on 8-cassette album *Shasta 1975*, cassettes B7528, B7529, $6.50 ea.); *The ABC's of Your Psychology on the Cosmic Clock: Charting the Cycles of Karma and Initiation*, 8-cassette album (A85056), 12 lectures, $50.00; "Charting the Cycles of Your Family According to the Cosmic Clock," on 8-cassette album *Family Designs for the Golden Age* (A7440), $50.00, single cassette MTG7421, $6.50; and "Childhood Stages of Development: Karma, Christhood, and the Cosmic Clock," on 4-cassette album *The Freedom of the Child* (A83131), $33.00.

6. Matt. 25:28, 29; Luke 19:24, 26.
7. Isa. 30:20.
8. Luke 12:32.

BEING
Corona Class Lesson 47
Heart

1. John 3:8.
2. John 1:29; Isa. 25:8; Rev. 1:5; 7:14, 17; 21:4.

BEING
Corona Class Lesson 47
Holy Grail

3. Mark 5:25–34.
4. "Ah! then, if mine had been

436   Notes to Pages 407-412

the Painter's hand, / To express what then I saw; and add the gleam, / The light that never was, on sea or land, / The consecration, and the Poet's dream." William Wordsworth, "Elegiac Stanzas Suggested by a Picture of Peele Castle in a Storm," stanza 4 (1807).   Rev. 21:23; 22:5.

BEING
Corona Class Lesson 48
Love

1. **Do not condemn yourself** and you will not condemn others. If you sincerely want to stop condemning others, then stop condemning yourself and, further, find out why,

psychologically or otherwise, you do condemn yourself when you, as a son of God, have the infinite capacity bestowed by your Father to become Godlike. Then invoke the violet flame with great zeal and love to consume the cause and core of all self-condemnation.
2. II Tim. 2:15.
3. Gen. 3:21.
4. I Cor. 13:8.
5. II Tim. 4:8; James 1:12; I Pet. 5:4; Rev. 2:10.
6. Prov. 4:7.
7. John 5:14; 8:11.
8. Luke 10:37.
9. Matt. 4:6.
10. Matt. 27:54; Mark 15:39.

Dictionary definitions for each section page are taken from *Webster's Third New International Dictionary* and the *Oxford English Dictionary*.

Unless otherwise noted, all publications and audiocassettes are Summit University Press (Box A, Livingston, MT 59047), released under the messengership of Mark L. Prophet and Elizabeth Clare Prophet.

Postage Rates for Books. For books $5.95 and under, please add $.50 for the first book, $.25 each additional book; for books $7.95 through $15.95, add $1.00 for the first, $.50 each additional; for books $16.95 through $25.00, add $1.50 for the first, $.75 each additional.

Postage Rates for Audiocassettes. For single audiocassettes, please add $.50 for the first cassette and $.30 for up to 4 additional cassettes; for 2- or 3-cassette albums, add $.90 for the first, $.30 for each additional album; for 4-cassette albums, add $1.15 for the first, $.25 for each additional album; for 8-cassette albums, add $1.30 for the first, $1.15 for each additional album; for 16-cassette albums, add $1.70 for the first, $.95 for each additional album.

Pearls of Wisdom. Since 1958, the Ascended Masters have released their teachings through the Messengers Mark and Elizabeth Prophet as Pearls of Wisdom. These weekly letters dictated for their students throughout the world are the intimate contact, heart to heart, between the Ascended Masters and their disciples. Delivered as a Holy Spirit prophecy, they contain both fundamental and advanced instruction with a practical application of Cosmic Law to personal and planetary problems from the immortal saints and spiritual revolutionaries of East and West who comprise the spiritual hierarchy known as the Great White Brotherhood. The Corona Class Lessons were originally dictated as Pearls of Wisdom by Jesus and Kuthumi. The Pearls are sent free weekly to those who support the publishing of the Ascended Masters' teachings with a minimum yearly love offering of $40 to cover printing and postage costs. If you would like to receive the eleven-week introductory series, please send a love offering of $5. Bound volumes are also available.

Index of Scripture

*References to the Book of Enoch are from *Forbidden Mysteries of Enoch: The Untold Story of Men and Angels* by Elizabeth Clare Prophet, pp. 89–228 (translation by Richard Laurence).

Corona Class Lessons

Sermon or Study Topics

with Related Scriptural References
". . . for those who would teach men the Way"

<small>CORRESPONDENCE</small>

1	**Brotherhood**	"Lovest Thou Me?" John 21:4–17
2	**You**	"Flesh and Blood Hath Not Revealed It" Matt. 16:13–20
3	**Holy Christ Self**	Deeds Wrought in God John 3:14–21
4	**The Father**	"If a Man Keep My Saying..." John 8:51–59
5	**Reciprocity**	"Where I AM, There Shall My Servant Be" John 12:23–32
	Crown	"They Crucify to Themselves the Son of God Afresh" Heb. 6:4–12
6	**Constancy**	The Works of the Friends of God James 2:14–26

<small>PURPOSE</small>

7	**Perfection**	"I Go to Prepare a Place for You" John 14:1–6, 12–15
8	**Sainthood**	"I Speak Not of Myself" John 14:7–11
9	**Example**	"Love One Another" John 13:13–20, 34, 35
10	**Heart**	"The Spirit of the LORD Is upon Me" Isa. 9:2; 42:6–8; Luke 4:16–22; Matt. 4:17
11	**Innocence**	The Son of Man Is Come to Save Luke 9:46–56

12	**Recognition**	"That I Should Bear Witness unto the Truth" John 18:29–38
	Mission	"Be Strong and of Good Courage: For the LORD Thy God Is with Thee" Josh. 1:1–18; 6:13–15

TRANSFIGURATION

13	**Light**	"My Spirit Shall Not Always Strive with Man" Gen. 6:1–8
14	**Acceleration**	Jesus Was Transfigured before Them Matt. 17:1–13
15	**Possibility**	The Father's Care for You Matt. 6:25–34
16	**Obedience**	The Light of Father and Son Abide in the Obedient Heart John 14:16–26
17	**Power**	"They Preached Everywhere, the Lord Working with Them" "If I Go Not, the Comforter Will Not Come" John 14:27–31; 16:7; Matt. 28:16–18; Mark 16:15–18; Matt. 28:19, 20; Mark 16:19, 20
18	**Wisdom**	"Let a Double Portion of Thy Spirit Be upon Me" Gen. 5:24; II Kings 2:9–14; Acts 1:7–11

SIN

19	**Law**	"Neither Do I Condemn Thee" John 8:1–11
20	**Love**	"Thy Sins Be Forgiven Thee" Mark 2:1–12
21	**Conscience**	"She Loved Much" Luke 7:36–50
22	**Sacrifice**	"Forgive Us Our Debts as We Forgive Our Debtors" Matt. 18:21–35

46	Soul	"He That Acknowledgeth the Son Hath the Father Also" I John 2:15–29
47	Heart	"That We Should Be Called the Sons of God" I John 3:1–10
	Holy Grail	"That We Should Love One Another" I John 3:11–24
48	Love	"Herein Is Our Love Made Perfect" I John 4:1–21

For thirty years Mark and Elizabeth Prophet have been writing down the teachings of the immortal saints and gurus of East and West, setting the highest standard of metaphysical writing and pioneering the new-age movement. They have produced more than fifty books, including such classics of esoteric literature as *Climb the Highest Mountain, Studies of the Human Aura, Saint Germain On Alchemy, The Science of the Spoken Word* and annual volumes of *Pearls of Wisdom* published weekly since 1958. Their works are widely read and used as the authoritative source on the Ascended Masters. Mark L. Prophet passed on in 1973. An international lecturer, Elizabeth Clare Prophet is based at the Royal Teton Ranch in southwestern Montana, a 33,000-acre self-sufficient spiritual community. Here she conducts workshops and retreats on the practical application of Jesus' life and teachings. For further information write Summit University, Box A, Livingston, Montana 59047.

SUMMIT UNIVERSITY

I n every age there have been some, the few, who have pursued an understanding of God and of selfhood that transcends the current traditions of doctrine and dogma. Compelled by a faith that knows the freedom To Be, they have sought to expand their awareness of God by probing and proving the infinite expressions of his Law. Through the true science of religion, they have penetrated the mysteries of both Spirit and Matter and come to experience God as the All-in-all.

Having discovered the key to Reality, these sons and daughters of God have gathered disciples who desired to pursue the disciplines of universal Law and the inner teachings of the mystery schools. Thus Jesus chose his apostles, Bodhidharma his monks, and Pythagoras his initiates at Crotona. Gautama Buddha called his disciples to form the *sangha* (community) and King Arthur summoned his knights of the Round Table to the quest for the Holy Grail.

Summit University is Maitreya's Mystery School for men and women of the twentieth century who are searching for the great synthesis—the gnosis of Truth which the teachings of the Ascended Masters afford. These adepts are counted among the few who have overcome in every age to join the immortals as our elder brothers and sisters on the Path.

Gautama Buddha and Lord Maitreya sponsor Summit University with the World Teachers Jesus and Kuthumi, the Lords of the Seven Rays, the Divine Mother, the beloved Archangels and the "numberless numbers" of "saints robed in white" who have graduated from earth's schoolroom and are known collectively as the Great White Brotherhood. To this university of the Spirit they lend their flame, their counsel and the momentum of their attainment, even as they fully give the living Teaching to us who would follow in their footsteps to the Source of that reality which they have become.

Founded in 1971 under the direction of the Messengers Mark L. Prophet and Elizabeth Clare Prophet, Summit University holds three twelve-week retreats each year—fall, winter, and spring quarters—as well as two-week summer and weekend seminars, and five-day quarterly conferences. Each course is based on the development of the threefold flame and the unfoldment of the inner potential of the Christ, the Buddha, and the Mother flame. Through the teachings of the Ascended Masters dictated to the Messengers, students at Summit University pursue the disciplines on the path of the ascension for the soul's ultimate reunion with the Spirit of the living God.

This includes the study of the sacred scriptures of East and West taught by Jesus and Gautama, John the Beloved and other adepts of the Sacred Heart; exercises in the self-mastery of the chakras and the aura under Kuthumi and Djwal Kul; beginning and intermediate studies in alchemy under the Ascended Master Saint Germain; the Cosmic Clock—a new-age astrology for charting the cycles of personal psychology, karma, and initiation diagramed by Mother Mary; the science of the spoken Word combining prayer, meditation, dynamic decrees and visualization—all vital keys to the soul's liberation in the Aquarian age.

In addition to weekend services including lectures and dictations from the Masters delivered through the Messengers (in person or on videotape), a midweek healing service—"Be Thou Made Whole!"—is held in the Chapel of the Holy Grail at which the Messenger or ministers offer invocations for the infirm and the healing of the nations. "Watch with Me" Jesus' Vigil of the Hours is also kept with violet-flame decrees for world transmutation.

Students are taught by professionals in the medical and health fields to put into practice some of the lost arts of healing, including prayer and scientific fasting, realignment through balanced nutrition, and natural alternatives to achieve wholeness on a path whose goal is the return to the Law of the One through the soul's reintegration with the inner blueprint. The psychology of the family, marriage, and meditations for the conception of new-age children are discussed and counseling for service in the world community is available.

Teachings and meditations of the Buddha taught by Lord Gautama, Lord Maitreya, Lanello, and the bodhisattvas of East and West are a highlight of Summit University experience. The violet-flame and bija mantras with those of Buddha and Kuan Yin enhance the raising of the Kundalini under the sponsorship of Saint Germain. Classes in Hatha Yoga convene daily, while spiritual initiations as a transfer of Light from the Ascended Masters through the Messengers are given to each student at healing services and at the conclusion of the quarter.

Summit University is a twelve-week spiral that begins with you as self-awareness and ends with you as God Self-awareness. As you traverse the spiral, light intensifies, darkness is transmuted. Energies are aligned, chakras are cleared, and the soul is poised for the victorious fulfillment of the individual divine plan. And you are experiencing the rebirth day by day as, in the words of the apostle Paul, you "put off the old man" being "renewed in the spirit of your mind" and "put on the new man which after God is created in righteousness and true holiness." (Eph. 4:22–24)

In addition to preparing the student to enter into the Guru / chela relationship with the Ascended Masters and the path of initiation outlined in their retreats, the academic standards of Summit University, with emphasis on the basic skills of both oral and written communication, prepare students to enroll in undergraduate and graduate programs in accredited schools and to pursue careers as constructive members of the international community. A high school diploma (or its equivalent) is required, a working knowledge of the English language, and a willingness to become the disciplined one—the disciple of the Great God Self of all.

Summit University is a college of religion, science and culture, qualifying students of any religious affiliation to deliver the Lost Teachings of Jesus and his prophecy for these troubled times. Advanced levels prepare students for ordination as ministers (ministering servants) in Church Universal and Triumphant. Taking its sponsorship and authority from the Holy Spirit, the saints and God's calling upon the Messengers, Summit University has neither sought nor received regional or national accreditation.

Summit University is a way of life that is an integral part of Camelot—an Aquarian-age community located in the Paradise Valley on the 33,000-acre Royal Teton Ranch in southwest Montana adjacent to Yellowstone Park. Here ancient truths become the joy of everyday living in a circle of fellowship of kindred souls drawn together for the fulfillment of their mission in the Universal Christ through the oneness of the Holy Spirit. The Summit University Service/Study Program offers apprenticeship training in all phases of organic farming and ranching, construction, and related community services as well as publishing—from the spoken to the written Word.

Montessori International is the place prepared at the Royal Teton Ranch for the tutoring of the souls of younger seekers on the Path. A private school for infants through twelfth grade, Montessori International was founded in 1970 by Mark and Elizabeth Prophet. Dedicated to the educational principles set forth by Dr. Maria Montessori, its faculty strives to maintain standards of academic excellence and the true education of the heart for the child's unfoldment of his Inner Self.

For those aspiring to become teachers of children through age seven, Summit University Level II in conjunction with the Pan-American Montessori Society offers, under the capable direction of Dr. Elisabeth Caspari or her personally trained Master Teachers, an in-depth study of the Montessori method and its application at home and in the classroom. This six-month program includes an examination of one's personal psychology, tracing behavioral characteristics from birth through childhood and adolescence to the present, taking into consideration the sequences of karma and reincarnation as well as hereditary and environmental influences in child development. Following their successful completion of this information course, students may apply for acceptance into the one- or two-year internship programs, which upon graduation lead to teacher certification from the Pan-American Montessori Society.

For information on Summit University and related programs or how to contact the center nearest you for group meetings and study materials, including a library of publications and audio- and videocassettes of the teachings of the Ascended Masters, call or write Camelot at the Royal Teton Ranch, Box A, Livingston, MT 59047 (406) 222-8300.

What has Christianity been missing for centuries?

THE LOST YEARS OF JESUS

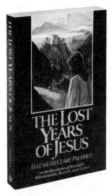

In a masterpiece of investigative reporting Elizabeth Clare Prophet takes you behind the scenes of one of the most intriguing literary and historical controversies of our time and provides overwhelming evidence that Jesus was in India for the 17 years unaccounted for in scripture.

The Gospels record Jesus at age 12 in the temple. Then age 30 at the River Jordan. Where was he in the interim? Ancient Buddhist manuscripts discovered in a remote monastery in the Himalayas say Jesus went to India where he prepared for his Palestinian mission.

"Elizabeth Clare Prophet puts together the missing pieces in the life of the Master that have baffled biblical scholars for centuries."
—Jess Stearn

Now, under one cover, Mrs. Prophet brings together the testimony of four eyewitnesses to these remarkable documents with variant translations of the controversial texts!

Magnificently illustrated in full color. Maps and drawings, 17 selected paintings by Nicholas Roerich, and 40 pages of photos of Ladakh. Softbound, 416 pp., #1593, $14.95; hardbound, #2080, $19.95.

The sacred mysteries unfold . . .

THE LOST TEACHINGS OF JESUS

In this two-volume sequel Mark L. Prophet and Elizabeth Clare Prophet first demonstrate that much of Jesus' teaching has been lost—either removed from the Gospels, suppressed, kept secret for those being initiated into the deeper mysteries, or never written down at all. Then, in a modern vernacular, they present the lost teachings Jesus gave his disciples 2,000 years ago—and the very personal instruction he is imparting today to those whose hearts are receptive to Truth.

As the pages unfold you will find yourself discovering the key to the sacred mysteries and being quickened to your inner reality—a path and a self-knowledge essential to the fulfillment of your destiny on earth and beyond.

Together the two volumes present 32 finest-quality Roerich art reproductions and full-color illustrations of the chakras in the body of man. *The Lost Teachings of Jesus I*, softbound, 520 pp., #2040, $14.95; hardbound, #2075, $19.95. *The Lost Teachings of Jesus II*, softbound, 650 pp., #2076, $16.95; hardbound, #2077, $21.95. Hardbounds in beautiful gold-stamped blue leatherette.

Vital keys to your spiritual, and physical, survival in this age

SUMMIT UNIVERSITY 🕊 PRESS®

Available wherever fine books are sold or directly from the publisher, Summit University Press, Dept. 259, Box A, Malibu, CA 90265. After Feb. 15, 1987, Box A, Livingston, MT 59047. For books $14.95, please add $1.00 postage and handling for the first book, $.50 each additional book; for books $16.95 through $21.95, add $1.50 for the first, $.75 each additional.

FOR MORE INFORMATION

For information about the Keepers of the Flame fraternity and monthly lessons; Pearls of Wisdom, dictations of the Ascended Masters sent to you weekly; Summit University three-month and weekend retreats; two-week summer seminars and quarterly conferences which convene at the Royal Teton Ranch, a 33,000-acre self-sufficient spiritual community-in-the-making, as well as the Summit University Service/Study Program with apprenticeship in all phases of organic farming, ranching, construction, publishing and related community services; Montessori International private school, preschool through twelfth grade for children of Keepers of the Flame; and the Ascended Masters' library and study center nearest you, call or write Summit University Press, Box A, Livingston, Montana 59047 (406) 222-8300.

Paperback books, audiocassettes and videotapes on the teachings of the Ascended Masters dictated to their Messengers, Mark L. Prophet and Elizabeth Clare Prophet—including a video series of Ascended Master dictations on "Prophecy in the New Age" and a Summit University Forum TV series with Mrs. Prophet interviewing outstanding experts in the field of health and Nature's alternatives for healing—are available through Summit University Press. Write for free catalogue and information packet.

Upon your request we are also happy to send you particulars on this summer's Summit University Retreat at the Royal Teton Ranch—survival seminars, wilderness treks, teachings of Saint Germain, dictations from the Ascended Masters, prophecy on political and social issues, initiation through the Messenger of the Great White Brotherhood, meditation, yoga, the science of the spoken Word, children's program, summer camping and RV accommodations, and homesteading at Glastonbury.

All at the ranch send you our hearts' love and a joyful welcome to the Inner Retreat!